Higher Education Strategy and Planning

Higher Education Strategy and Planning draws together a team of expert contributors from across the sector to offer contemporary descriptions of practice in higher education and critical reflections on that practice. Many of the tools and techniques transcend the particular national system within which they are situated and therefore have global relevance for all those interested in strategy and planning in higher education.

Containing chapters on each of the major functions or capabilities of strategic planners, critiques of global policy trends, framework examples and explanations of the main league tables both in the UK and globally, the book is divided into five main parts:

- Context and positioning;
- Integrated planning;
- Centrality, co-ordination and connection;
- Analytical capacity and capability;
- Insight and information.

This text offers a contemporary representation of strategic planning and will be an indispensable guide for all those who work in or study higher education, particularly aimed at those who work in strategy, planning and leadership roles.

Tony Strike is University Secretary and Director of Strategy, Planning and Governance at the University of Sheffield, UK. He is currently chair of UK Russell Group Directors of Strategy and Planning and a member of the Higher Education Strategic Planners Association (HESPA) National Executive Board. Tony has a PhD (2009) in higher education management and policy from the University of Southampton and is a member of the Society for Research into Higher Education (SRHE) and of the European Association for Institutional Research (EAIR).

"With chapters from some of the superstars of university planning across the globe, sometimes in partnership with colleagues from other parts of the institution, [this book] provides a delightful tour through all the key areas of university planning. There are, among others, chapters which provide international context, advice on building developing and (in my opinion critically) monitoring a strategic plan, the opportunities presented by data analytics, research planning and benchmarking – the latter often underdeveloped in some institutions. In sum, they represent a brilliant resource for higher education professionals both inside and outside planning departments."

Professor Sir Ian Diamond, Principal and
Vice-Chancellor, University of Aberdeen, UK

"HESPA is proud to be associated with this publication and endorses its use within the sector. Most of the chapter authors are HESPA members, each thought leaders in their field, and the editor, Dr Tony Strike, is a member of the HESPA national executive. HESPA offers its membership a wide variety of resources and training to help them perform their roles and share their applied practical knowledge. I hope you will see this book as a must-have definitive guide to strategy and planning in higher education."

Alison Jones, Chair of HESPA, Director of Planning,
Legal and Governance, University Secretary,
University of Bradford, UK

Higher Education Strategy and Planning

A Professional Guide

Edited by Tony Strike

Routledge
Taylor & Francis Group

LONDON AND NEW YORK

HIGHER EDUCATION STRATEGIC PLANNERS ASSOCIATION

First published 2018
by Routledge
2 Park Square, Milton Park, Abingdon, Oxon OX14 4RN

and by Routledge
711 Third Avenue, New York, NY 10017

Routledge is an imprint of the Taylor & Francis Group, an Informa business

British Library Cataloguing-in-Publication Data
A catalogue record for this book is available from the British Library

Library of Congress Cataloging-in-Publication Data
A catalog record for this book has been requested

ISBN: 978-1-138-63521-0 (hbk)
ISBN: 978-1-138-63526-5 (pbk)
ISBN: 978-1-315-20645-5 (ebk)

Typeset in Galliard
by Apex CoVantage, LLC

MIX
Paper from
responsible sources
FSC   FSC® C013056
www.fsc.org

Printed and bound in Great Britain by
TJ International Ltd, Padstow, Cornwall

Contents

Foreword

When the University of Aberdeen first opened in 1495, there were 36 students and staff and the budget was no more than a couple of hundred Scots pounds. I might suggest that hiring a director of planning was not high on the first principal's to do list. Move forward a little over 500 years and universities are very different – large, complex institutions with multiple goals and a wide range of funding streams but still fundamentally dedicated to scaling the twin peaks of excellence in teaching and research. And for all serious universities, a strategy and planning team is central to the effective prosecution of those university's goals.

Strategic planners are central to the higher education endeavour because the best systems of higher education are characterised by institutions that are autonomous and agile; and because higher education does not operate in a vacuum, but rather is impacted by government policies both direct and indirect, international and national competition, and by societal change. Some of these impact in an incremental way, but others are much more disruptive.

Thus as I write this in Scotland in December 2016, considering for our university and those across Scotland, the potential impacts of the UK government's Higher Education and Research Bill and their immigration policy; the Scottish government's Higher Education Governance Bill; a spending review; a review of enterprise agencies; and the UK vote to leave the European Union, the need to have coherent, timely and evidence-based advice becomes ever more critical.

Evidence, to drive that advice, is needed more than ever and needs to be, very often, data led. Being in the era of big data and analytics gives enormous opportunities for higher education institutions if they can utilise their data effectively. Rather than poring over pages of data in an annual review, as I used to, planners can now access important data in real time and through exciting analytics influence critical decisions, enabling then to be made quickly and agilely.

So far, so good; but to intending planners, understanding the opportunities can be challenging, as the planner's role has evolved quickly in recent years and, if one is not careful, wheels would be reinvented across the world with a resulting duplication of effort and lack of efficiency. And that is where this wonderful book comes in. With chapters from some of the superstars of university planning across the globe, sometimes in partnership with colleagues from other parts of the institution, it provides a delightful tour through all the key areas of university planning.

There are, among others, chapters which provide international context, advice on building, developing and (in my opinion critically) monitoring a strategic plan, the opportunities presented by data analytics, research planning and benchmarking – the latter often underdeveloped in some institutions. In sum, they represent a brilliant resource for higher education professionals both inside and outside planning departments.

While I am clear that the context facing university leaders will change in the future, the importance and relevance of this book will not. Congratulations to all those involved in its production.

Professor Sir Ian Diamond

Preface

The Higher Education Strategic Planners Association (HESPA) is a membership organisation representing strategic planners working in higher education across the UK. We particularly encourage planners at all stages in their career to engage with HESPA and hope that we have something to offer everyone.

HESPA's objectives are:

- To provide an active forum for strategic planners in the higher education sector to network, discuss, improve and influence;
- To be the primary organisation for the professional and career development of those working in strategy and planning in UK higher education;
- To represent a compelling and unified voice for members, while recognising their contrasting needs and ideas;
- To shape the future of higher education by pushing boundaries, challenging external pressures and conducting advocacy work to influence policy makers;
- To promote awareness and understanding of strategy and planning issues;
- To share professional best practice amongst our members.

We have a website (www.hespa.ac.uk/) where readers can find out more about our professional association.

HESPA is proud to be associated with and endorse this publication. Most of the chapter authors are HESPA members, each thought leaders in the area in which they have written, and the editor is a member of the HESPA national executive.

HESPA offers its membership a wide variety of resources and training to help them perform their roles and share their applied practical knowledge. I hope you will see this book as a must-have definitive guide to strategy and planning in higher education. In addition, I hope you will continue your professional development through active involvement in HESPA as your professional network.

Alison Jones
Chair of HESPA
Director of Planning, Legal and Governance
University Secretary
University of Bradford

Acknowledgements

I would like to thank Bruce Roberts at Taylor & Francis for inviting the proposal that led to this book. Also Lucy Hodson and subsequently Alison Jones, who as chairs of the HESPA National Executive Board each gave their endorsement to and encouragement for this project. Thanks go to Giles Carden, Craig Hutchison-Howorth and Anna Grey for their advice and support. Thanks also to Jen Summerton at HESPA, who did so much to assist with content on the HESPA website and at conference.

The contributing authors agreed to share their expertise and in doing so have suffered chasing and nudging as well as having to respond to proposed edits and comments through the drafting, copyediting and proofs. I thank each of them for so generously being part of this project and for being so careful and patient in sharing their work.

I am indebted to Professor Sir Keith Burnett, Vice-Chancellor at the University of Sheffield and to Professors Sir William Wakeham and Sir Howard Newby, both former Vice-Chancellors at the University of Southampton, who were kind enough each in their part to invite my advice and service. In doing so they each in their turn shaped me and my practice.

Professor John Taylor was Director of Planning at the University of Southampton before I held that post and was subsequently my PhD supervisor and friend. I was fortunate that John led weekly meetings of his students, recruited from around the world, and I learnt so much from those postgraduate research coffee morning debates on global higher education issues.

My own team at the University of Sheffield I hope already know they are an exceptional and talented group of people. Working with them on our shared goals and challenges makes each day a pleasure, and that is a great gift for which I owe them thanks. I owe a particular debt to Angela Davison, my Executive Assistant, who has daily pointed me off in the right direction with diary and papers in hand and who supported the production of this book.

I have for some years belonged to a peer group of Russell Group University Directors of Strategy and Planning, a group I am presently privileged to chair. The four meetings of that group each year, always preceded by a dinner, meant I enjoyed the company of friends and colleagues who understood each other's professional trials and tribulations as a community of practice.

Caroline, my wife of 25 years, knows I am never happier than when I have a project. Each requires a sacrifice of her time, and she is always generous in giving support and encouragement that is never taken for granted. Our children, Jessica, Peter and Joseph, are grown up now, and the earlier answer to them that I played on computers, made calls, drank coffee and talked to people for a living has long since failed to satisfy. This book could be considered a late but fuller answer to the question 'What is it you do again?'

Abbreviations

ANUP	Australian Network of University Planners
ARWU	Academic Ranking of World Universities
ASHE	American Association for the Study of Higher Education
BI	Business Intelligence
BICC	Business Intelligence Competency Centre
BIS	Business Innovation and Skills
CPD	Continuous Professional Development
CUC	Committee of University Chairmen
DBEIS	Department for Business, Energy & Industrial Strategy
DLHE	Destination of Leavers from Higher Education survey
DTC	Doctoral Training Centre
EAIR	European Association for Institutional Research
ETER	European Tertiary Education Register
ETL	Extract, Transform, Load
EU	European Union
EUMIDA	European University Data Collection
FRS	Financial Reporting Standard
FT	Full-Time
FTE	Full-Time Equivalent
HE	Higher Education
HE-BCI	Higher Education – Business and Community Interaction
HEDIIP	HE Data & Information Improvement Programme
HEDW	Higher Education Data Warehousing Forum
HEFCE	Higher Education Funding Council for England
HEFCW	Higher Education Funding Council for Wales
HEI	Higher Education Institution
HEIDI	Higher Education Information Database for Institutions
HEP	Higher Education Provider
HESA	Higher Education Statistics Agency
HESPA	Higher Education Strategic Planners Association
HR	Human Resources
IAG	Information, Advice and Guidance

IAU	International Association of Universities
IR	Institutional Research
ISO	International Organization for Standardization
IT	Information Technology
KIS	Key Information Set
KPI	Key Performance Indicators
KPT	Key Performance Target
LEP	Local Enterprise Partnership
MDM	Master Data Management
MI	Management Information
MSP	Managing Successful Programmes
NGO	Non-Governmental Organisation
NSS	National Student Survey
OECD	Organisation for Economic Co-operation and Development
OfS	Office for Students
OR	Operational Reporting
PESTLE	Political, Economic, Social and Technological, Legal and Environmental
PGT	Postgraduate Taught
PGR	Postgraduate Research
PhD	Doctor of Philosophy
PDCA	Plan, Do, Check, Act
PRES	Postgraduate Research Experience Survey
PT	Part-Time
PTES	Postgraduate Taught Experience Survey
QAA	Quality Assurance Agency
RAE	Research Assessment Exercise
RAG	Red Amber Green
RAM	Resource Allocation Model
REF	Research Excellence Framework
RG	Russell Group
SFC	Scottish Funding Council
SNC	Student Number Control
SORP	Statement of Recommended Practice
SP	Strategic Planning
SQL	Structured Query Language
SRHE	Society for Research into Higher Education
SSR	Staff-Student Ratio or Student-Staff Ratio
STEM	Science, Technology, Engineering and Mathematics
SWOT	Strengths, Weaknesses, Opportunities and Threats
TEF	Teaching Excellence Framework
TRAC	Transparent Approach to Costing
UCAS	Universities and Colleges Admissions Service
UG	Undergraduate

UK	United Kingdom
UKVI	United Kingdom Visas and Immigration
US	United States
UUK	Universities UK
WHED	World Higher Education Database

Contributors

John Baker, Corporate and Business Planning Manager, London South Bank University

Rhiannon Birch, Deputy Director of Strategy, Planning and Governance, University of Sheffield

Jane Boggan, Deputy Director of Planning, Cardiff University

Giles Carden, Director of Strategic Planning and Analytics, University of Warwick

Steve Chadwick, Director of Strategy, Planning & Change, University of Bristol

Dominic Foster, Planning Manager, University of the West of England

Martin Hanlon, Director, Planning and Quality Unit, University of Technology Sydney

Lucy Hodson, Director of Planning, Aberystwyth University

Nicki Horseman, Lead Higher Education Analyst, Times Higher Education

Alison Jones, Director of Planning, Legal and Governance, University of Bradford

Andrew Keeble, Director of Finance, University of Essex

Mike Kennerley, Head of Strategy, Planning and Performance, University of Leeds

Olivia Kew-Fickus, Director of Strategic Planning, University of Birmingham

Dan Kidd, Head of Training and Consultancy, HESA

Rebecca Lambert, Deputy Director, Strategic Planning, University of Birmingham

Thomas Loya, Director, Strategy, Planning and Performance, University of Nottingham

Claire McDonald, Risk and Strategy Manager, Durham University

Kris Olds, Professor, Department of Geography, University of Wisconsin-Madison

John Pritchard, Director of Strategic Planning, Durham University

Rachel Pye, Senior Planning Analyst (Risk and Business Continuity), Sheffield Hallam University

Susan L. Robertson, Professor, University of Cambridge

Tony Strike, University Secretary and Director of Strategy, Planning and Governance, University of Sheffield

David Swinn, Senior Governance and Policy Officer, University of Sheffield

Sonia Virdee, Director of Strategic Planning and Change/Deputy Secretary, University of Essex

Elizabeth Westlake, Deputy Director, Research Planning, University of Birmingham

James Wilsdon, Professor of Research Policy, University of Sheffield

Michael Wykes, Director of Policy, Planning and Business Intelligence, University of Exeter

Andy Youell, Director of Data Policy and Governance, HESA

Figures

Tables

Introduction

This book was born of the discovery I could not purchase for two colleagues a textbook that described the work of the team they were anticipating joining. I shared this frustration with someone standing behind a conference bookstand who turned out to be the commissioning editor; who of course challenged me to fix the problem I had described. My nomination to the Higher Education Strategic Planners Association (HESPA) National Executive Board led to my offering to edit a book on strategy and planning, which they as a professional association might endorse. The aim was to create a book that would be a showcase of the professional talent and techniques in strategic planning in higher education and provide a reflective critical evaluation of practice. This meant, rather than writing the book, I wanted to draw on and give voice to the well of talent and expertise in the higher education sector for the benefit of a wider audience.

Critical positioning

This is where as editor, rather than author, I explain the book; how it was created and the editorial choices made. In this introduction it is not my job to be neutral. Each contributor has a point of view and the selection of contributors and my guidance to them has shaped what you are about to read.

This book offers scholars, practitioners and postgraduate students a contemporary representation of strategic planning in higher education. Those new to strategy and planning or those hoping to work in the area will I hope find this book a useful introductory text. More experienced strategic planners will want to read what leading colleagues have written. Academic leaders who need to plan the future of their academic units and to work with professional planners will find what can and is being done to support them in those leadership roles. Those teaching or studying higher education management and policy will I hope find their scholarship informed by contemporary practice.

Reading this book will leave an impression for which responsibility must be borne. The chapters cover topics which I conceive as being within the scope of work of strategic planners, and others may have made alternative choices. The contributors were primarily approached and selected as leading practitioners on their topic and not because of any ideological stance. The content chapters are contemporary descriptions of practice and contain critical reflections on that practice. The chapters often contain examples, but they are not case studies. The content is admittedly UK-centric but situates that practice globally in relation to other national systems as an essential part of the comparative criticality. Many of the tools and techniques described transcend the particular national system within which they are situated and so have wider relevance to an international readership.

The power of naming

Recognising a range of job titles exist in different higher education institutions and in different countries for the work done which is being described, I suggested contributing authors use 'strategic planner' as a consistent identifying label for those whose role it is to plan. I hope this naming device has a cohering effect through the book in identifying and providing coherency to an activity and to a profession. I could have done more to recognise separate roles such as student number planners, data analysts, policy officers, risk managers and other such titles, but these are subsets within the larger category. To avoid use of university, college, university college, higher education provision in further education, community colleges and so on I have suggested use of either university or higher education institution (HEI) as the consistent means of identifying the employing or awarding institution. These two identifiers were selected in preference to the now more common usage of higher education provider (HEP), which in my view has connotations of instrumentalism and marketisation. I have also preferred the term 'academic leader' over 'manager' as senior academic leaders will not normally self-define as managers and those in the administrative estate professionally serve rather than manage the academy.

Attributes of strategic planners

One of our defining attributes as humans is our common ability to imagine the future or various possible futures. We can assess our lives and so the likelihood of our imagined futures becoming our future reality. We can take actions now that are aimed at affecting our future, based on our view of the opportunities and threats that lie ahead of us. We can assess the risks we face and we can seek to avoid or mitigate those risks. We have this ability to turn our future visions into our new realities not only as individuals, in managing our own lives, but we can and do plan our futures as families, as clubs and societies and in our work-based organisations. While this is something we all do, to different extents based on our personalities, when looking back through time, different societies and cultures reference individuals to help them see or influence the future.

On the wall of my study at home, I have hung a large print of the Delphian Sybil painted by Michelangelo in the Sistine Chapel. Whether prophets, sybils, sages, oracles or seers, the role of these individuals was to bring tidings of the future to guide rulers in their decisions each in their own day. If these are defined as a person considered as providing wise and insightful counsel or predictions of the future, then strategic planners perhaps fit the job description. Strategic planners, however, do not rely on religious prophecy or seeing stones or mysticism. The tools used in today's age of rationalism are scenario planning, analysis, forecasting and expert opinions based in reason and knowledge.

Strategic planners engage in policy, planning, analysis and change. To work in strategy and planning in my view requires six attributes which taken together are hard to find. First, an understanding of and belief in the public good that higher education does. This can be borne of personal or family experience of the power of education to change the direction of lives or perhaps how a research breakthrough can do the same. Second, an ability to deconstruct and critically appraise policy narratives and evaluate their impact. Third, comfort with statistics and quantitative analysis. Fourth, planners need the ability to communicate to audiences insights from their policy and numerical analysis. Most people access and understand information and data often through its visual representation and when used to evoke a feeling or emotion rather than an analytical response. Fifth, enough confidence to stand in a room of academics (any one of which could be an international leader in any aspect of what you are about to say) and hold your own in that conversation. Sixth, the planning and project skills to see through the changes or actions proposed if the argument is won and the direction sought is given or agreed. This means that strategic planners often come to these roles from elsewhere in higher education and sometimes from planning roles in other sectors. Those who join the higher education planning community from new sectors are often graduates holding degrees which have a substantial quantitative element, frequently from the social sciences. Master's and doctoral programmes in higher education management and policy are now readily available and make ideal preparation. I have been lucky to work with some exceptional strategic planners.

A service to the academy

All that said, some academics can fear or disdain the work of strategic planners and planning more generally, taking what we do as evidence of managerialism (or new public management) or proof of the unwelcome metrification of the craft of academe. This would be true if strategic planners were primary decision makers on academic strategy or if improving metrics were an end in itself. One emotional response to metrics is a tendency to reject one analysis by asking for more, different or further analysis. The playing out of this contradiction can keep strategic planners busy in ever more complex crunching which is no longer answering a clear question. Curiously, this means it is often the planners who find they are resisting more data analysis.

One pro vice-chancellor for research said to me only half-jokingly that I could be perceived to be 'dangerous'. I had numerically profiled a faculty, its performance on various measures and how it compared to peer institution benchmarks and then modelled forecasts which re-profiled the staffing, activity, space usage and income based on the inter-quartile ranges of those same disciplines elsewhere, with the object of demonstrating alternative and more sustainable possible futures than the path they were presently on. As informative as these theoretical faculty models were, however, only the faculty members could determine which, if any, of those scenarios made sense given their research and education strategies. I have nothing to say about the academic direction of the discipline as against those who work in it. This truth puts strategic planners at the service of the academy, whether to brief, inform, challenge or change.

Chasing third-party league table rankings has become a 'rabbit hole' for some planners. It is not in my view the mission or purpose of HEIs to seek to be more highly ranked one over another vertically as if the institution and its ranking were of itself an end goal. Third-party tables perhaps have some utility in informing prospective students about some measurable elements of the place they may choose to apply to study and so help them cut through any marketing blurb. This same aim of information provision is not well served by putting HEIs into a single rank order as if the student experience at each place was going to be the same, only better or worse, by some standard measures. HEIs have wide social, economic and cultural purposes which are pursued through research, education, enterprise and public engagement. Each HEI will have governance structures, strategies, plans and success criteria. Each will compete for students, for research funding and for industrial partnerships. These activities are directed to societal goals, solving global challenges, improving lives, discovering and understanding. It only takes a day on any campus in one place compared to another to see and feel they are different and will offer different experiences and will have unique ways of measuring what they define as success each in their own terms. This horizontal differentiation is under attended to in an age of university league tables. As the truism goes in many American high schools, 'College is a match to be made, not a prize to be won'.

Uncomfortable truths

The strategic planner can often feel he or she is the person in the room who has to speak truth to power when rhetoric and hyperbole separate from the facts. This is as much true when influencing or responding to national policy as at the disciplinary, departmental, school, faculty or institution levels. Evidence can be relegated when ideology or personality drives policy or decision making, but the ideologues and personalities should still be constructively and positively challenged with pertinent truths, even (and perhaps especially) when it punctures arguments. Liberal intellectual campus cultures can cause an intellectual bubble where some views cannot be spoken. This can mean the strategic planner has to speak to unpopular or unlikely potential scenarios. In the UK the campus pre-referendum debates on Brexit were not truly debates as no one could be found to speak up for leaving the EU. Those dissenting voices either did not exist or were silenced by fear of vilification. UK strategic planners were working on Brexit scenarios and risks in a context where no one thought this was useful until after the vote. Strategic planners' ability to challenge orthodoxy, to marshal an argument with facts, to consider the unlikely, is part of what draws senior academic decision makers to seek their advice. HEIs, though, are thankfully led by people and not algorithms, and the instincts of leaders and the politics of the board room are part of that humanity – so planners do need the humility to accept they will not always be heard, however apparently rational their voice.

Two tribes

In some countries the work of strategic planners includes what can be called institutional research. Many strategic planners have postgraduate qualifications and write, publish and think critically about their practice. This book is evidence, I hope, of that fact. Planners' work can sometimes appear as research and have research outputs, such as, Why do black and minority ethnic students with similar entry grades to their peers find themselves statistically less likely to gain a good honours degree from the educational system? We are, as strategic planners, not driven only by our own curiosity but also by the goals of the institution for which we work. The objectives of strategic planners' work are applied, practical and not governed by academic freedom or curiosity. In the absence in the UK of a tradition of institutional research, strategic planners can be aligned academically with departments of education or management. It is a sadness to me that in the UK strategic planners do not typically attend the academic conferences of those who study higher education, for example SRHE (Society for Research into Higher Education) seminars and conferences, and academics who study higher education do not attend practitioner fora, for example HESPA (Higher Education Strategic Planners Association) events and conferences. Sad because, even if the two communities of academe and praxis were to meet and exchange ideas, they do not (yet) share a common frame of reference, understanding or lexicon. On the mainland of Europe and in the US this seems different. For example, at EAIR (European Association for Institutional Research) and ASHE (the American Association for the Study of Higher Education) events, academic leaders, strategic planners and academic researchers mix as research and practice communities under an institutional research umbrella. What distinguishes strategic planners from institutional researchers is the required planning and action to implement strategy. Strategic planners are less interested in findings for their own sake but in actions with measurable or evidential outcomes based on those findings. Strategic planners are, I hope, interventionists, who research practice in order to engage, activate and create change with consent and driven by institutional strategy. It would be a help to both communities to find some common ground on which to exchange ideas.

Nobody's stooges

The social contract between the public and higher education is changing as the funding models change. The role of strategic planners is affected by this political and societal change but is not dependent on it. In the commercial sectors much of the strategic planning literature assumes a market, competition and profit-related goals. Higher education does not naturally behave as a market but instead as a social endeavour producing public goods. Universities are more akin to charities than businesses and they have societal not profit-orientated goals. The benefits of higher education and research, as seen by the HEIs, are collective and benefit everyone including those who do not directly participate. The whole of society benefits from the skills of graduates and the outcomes of research. The new politics of consumerism suggest HEIs should be rivalrous when more commonly they collaborate at individual, disciplinary and institutional levels to pursue global societal challenges as a public service. Increasingly, governments want to see higher education as a competitive market and to see private individuals asserting their rights as paying consumers rather than seeing themselves as members of a scholarly community who earned that place through hard work. HEIs and the strategic planners who work for them have to respond to this new orthodoxy while holding true to their institutions' missions, values and identities. This requires that strategic planners locate themselves intellectually and critically within the new orthodoxy, as for planners to behave unthinkingly (as if the market does rule) helps to make that social construct a reality. As noted above, in the point about league tables, the higher education system is vertically and horizontally stratified, but stratification is not evidence of market competition. The diversity in higher education is instead evidence that the homogeneity of provision normally caused by market forces has not yet had a significant effect.

As the public loses sight of the public good of higher education (and public funding for higher education reduces), so the demand for public accountability and regulation perversely at the same time increases, as governments struggle to reconcile market rhetoric with the public benefits they also want. Society needs doctors, engineers, teachers, architects and so on as much as individuals seek those skills and credentials for themselves. It is not the role of strategic planners to help state regulators hold to account the system they work within. It may be the role of strategic planners to aid the HEIs they work for to best meet the accountability burdens placed on them. These two things are not the same. Strategic planners in my view need to consciously situate themselves in their HEIs and signal their service role to their colleagues. It is in my view a mistake for strategic planners to allow themselves to become sole agents for any particular orthodoxy or politics. When student numbers were allocated formulaically and income came through block grants in a more centrally planned but less highly regulated system, HEIs still employed strategic planners to help administer that system.

Care and critical reflexivity

I have attempted in the choice of chapters and authors to find voice for different types of institutions, for practitioners who vary in seniority and to ensure the book is not gendered. I have sought academic and practitioner voices. I did not find voices from consciously ethnic or religious perspectives, and I hope the invisibility of both can be forgiven, as I would have preferred a text which was not blind to these important owned identities. I, for example, care about what I do and how my work impacts on others, and I am an activist; care and activism both come from my faith background and are public manifestations of my Catholic religion. I do not subscribe to Weber's impersonal bureaucracy theory. National and ethnic norms have similar effects, which are insufficiently attended to here as elsewhere.

I was in a student presentation about visible and invisible identities, and the presenter rhetorically asked, 'Who is doing the counting, and what markers are they using to mark or denote us?' Of course, strategic planners often manage the coding system and the counting, and it powerfully reminded me that not only do we choose how and what to report as findings, but prior to that even data structuring is not a neutral act. Strategic planners need to tread carefully and thoughtfully through their world, as what we do creates realities, interpretations and understandings. After the UK EU referendum, for example, I had to consider a change from reporting 'Home/EU' and 'International' students to reporting 'Home', 'EU' and 'International' students. It was a heartbreaking switch in identity and representation. The many hundreds of data denoting decisions strategic planners make change how we represent reality in our figures and so define the data subjects. It would be a mistake to read this as a book written by and for technocrats.

Structure of the book

Context and positioning

The book opens with a contextual section, which seeks to describe global trends in higher education and then to map the development of the planning function and to describe the role of contemporary strategy and planning departments. This first section is intended to locate the reader within the world of the strategic planner. In Chapter 1 Robertson and Olds locate universities in a globalising world. They argue universities and higher education sectors around the globe have faced significant challenges and undergone major transformations in their missions, governance structures, funding streams, institutional footprints, student populations and relationships to the wider economy and societies they serve. Their chapter sets out a global perspective on how higher education is being reshaped because of responses to local and global dynamics. Their purpose is to step back and understand the nature, scope and scale of such responses and especially the organising logics at work. In Chapter 2 Strike, Hanlon and Foster describe the functions of strategy and planning. This chapter uses survey data from recent Russell Group, Australian National Planners Group and HESPA questionnaires about the strategy and planning functions in universities to describe the role, purpose and scope of the contemporary strategy and planning function. Pritchard in Chapter 3 provides a practical guide to the process of developing an effective institutional strategy. It focusses on defining institutional priorities and provides guidance on supporting the development of a new vision and strategic aims and on the various elements of a strategy framework while emphasising the importance of organisational and behavioural dynamics.

Integrated planning

Although the focus of the book then switches from the wider context to operational planning, Chadwick and Kew-Fickus remind us in Chapter 4 this is nevertheless a strategic conversation linked to the institutional strategy and to the environmental context. Chadwick and Kew-Fickus explore the challenge facing universities in using a planning process to help implement strategy. Their chapter covers the facilitation of an ongoing strategic conversation between academic leaders, academic units, professional services and students and approaches to doing this in a systematic, orchestrated and logical sequence. In Chapter 5 Hodson continues the planning conversation by focussing on student number planning, tracing the development of student number planning capability and describing how the sector has moved from a controlled to an open marketised environment, including reference to the tools being used. Her chapter draws out the importance of contextual information, the degree to which local departmental ownership of student number planning is helpful, the link between forecast student numbers and a university's financial planning, and the reliance that is placed on the numbers by an institution. Boggan, Lambert, Westlake and Wykes in Chapter 6 switch our attention again from student to research planning. Informed by interviews with strategic planners based at a range of HE institutions, their chapter explores the ways in which planners can develop institutions' research strengths. They examine the data which is available to understand research performance, geopolitical considerations and the importance of networks. They address the research funding landscape, strategies to support collaborative and interdisciplinary research, and how collaborations extend internationally with non-academic partners. This chapter concludes with a consideration of the balance between teaching and research and a call for strategies to present clear priorities.

Centrality, co-ordination and connection

We then move from annual planning processes to the centrality of strategy and planning to leadership, governance and decision-making, to risk management and to resource allocation. These various connecting factors are necessary to drive strategy, planning and implementation. In Chapter 7 Strike and Swinn describe the role governing bodies have in being collectively concerned with determining the strategic direction of the institution, and they link strategy and planning as a function to institutional-level steering and governance. They argue the overall performance of a university, particularly its standards of educational provision, long-term plans and the achievement of short-, medium- and long-term objectives, standards of educational provision and risk management are core both to good governance and to strategy and planning. Their chapter explores how the governing body ensures institutional sustainability by working with the executive body to set and support the delivery of the institutional mission and strategy. Birch, Pye, McDonald and Baker in Chapter 8 pick up the subject of risk management in more detail and provide a guide to implementing and embedding risk management in universities. Their chapter deals with the processes which characterise good risk management, including the practical tools. The chapter concludes by considering the role of internal audit and how good audit practice can help to support the development of a strong risk culture. Virdee and Keeble in Chapter 9 look at the link between strategy and planning and finance, resource allocation and income forecasting. Their chapter sets out principles through which higher education institutions might link institutional strategy, the planning process and financial planning and forecasting. Different approaches taken to resource allocation and financial forecasting are described, with the aim of showing how value and insight can be gained from a strategic approach to financial modelling and resource allocation.

Analytical capacity and capability

The book then shifts its focus again to the analytical role of strategy and planning functions. Youell and Kidd open up this theme in Chapter 10 looking at data capabilities across the information landscape. Their chapter sets out an analysis of current and desired future states of the information landscape and considers some of the opportunities and challenges associated with delivering this level of change and the impact on the roles and skills of strategic planners. Loya and Carden follow up on this opener in Chapter 11 by looking in detail at the uses and potentials of business intelligence and analytics. Their chapter explores the use of business intelligence as a means of exploiting data assets – whether internal or external – for operational excellence and decision support. They argue that effective business intelligence aids decision makers through data visualisations by providing genuine insights, whether that be about past, current or future student numbers and experiences, dynamics in research or philanthropy, or in other areas of university activity.

Insight and information

In Chapter 12 Kennerley gives specificity to the use of business intelligence by looking at indicators for measuring and managing performance. Kennerley considers the use of performance indicators to support the measurement and management of the organisation's performance. Kennerley recognises people don't necessarily take a rational approach to making decisions and that there is a need to understand how individuals make decisions and what role data and information play in that process. Horseman in Chapter 13 provides a critique of the appropriate use of benchmarking and rankings. Her chapter covers potential data sources and an explanation of the main league tables both in the UK and globally (Guardian, Times, Complete, ARWU, QS, THE, Leiden, U-Multirank) with a factual review of their methodologies and their data sources. Horseman discusses the potential uses and abuses of these tables, and how they can be used by institutions in monitoring their performance and in benchmarking. The book closes with Wilsdon in Chapter 14 reflecting on the uses and abuses of metrics, the impact on the academy and how with ever-more-commonplace data it can and should be used responsibly. Wilsdon asks us to consider how we can develop measurement and management systems that are both effective and supportive of responsibility, diversity and integrity.

Conclusion

There is a wide range of topics and contributors in this book. The professionalism and passion of the contributors as leading experts in their field gives the narrative a driving purpose. I hope the reader also observes that strategic planners in higher education maintain a thoughtful criticality in relation to their work, internalise the values of the institution in which they work, are aware of the limitations of any measuring instruments they seek to employ and seek to pursue shared goals with and for the academy.

While there is not a chapter dedicated specifically to higher education policy, to policymaking, trends and analysis, as a subject it recurs as a golden thread through the chapters described above. The reader will I hope leave the text provided here feeling that institutional strategic development, integrated annual planning and data analysis form a single coherent cycle. This cycle of activity is informed by, has to take account of and seeks to influence the higher education policy environment. Strategy and planning functions in institutions are often responsible for providing regular political and policy briefings to senior colleagues, for co-ordinating and drafting responses to governmental policy consultations and for scenario planning or action planning the consequences of different political or policy proposals.

I hope you enjoy reading the chapters that follow. More than that, I hope this book gives you additional insights and tools to further your practice, whether as a strategic planner, as an academic leader in planning the future of your department, faculty or university, working with professional strategic planners, or in your study or teaching of contemporary higher education.

Part I

Context and positioning

Chapter 1

Locating universities in a globalising world

Susan L. Robertson and Kris Olds

Global dynamics/local spaces

Few will disagree that since the 1980s universities and higher education sectors around the globe have faced significant challenges to and undergone major transformations in their missions, governance structures, funding streams, institutional footprints, student populations and relationships to the wider economy and societies they serve (Barnett, 2009; King, 2009). No longer is it a truism that changes in the sector happen at glacial pace. Far from it! Almost overnight, new university infrastructures mushroom; a visible outcome of strategies deployed by respective governments and institutions aimed at creating talented, highly skilled labour through 21st-century knowledge innovations. From Singapore's Global Schoolhouse project (Olds, 2007) to Malaysia's EduCity, Qatar's Education City, Melbourne's Knowledge Index, to more recently, Stanford University's 'Stanford Ignite' offering entrepreneurship courses, Silicon Valley-style, to high-fee-paying students in London (Coughlan, 2015: 1), all suggest institutional ambition, innovation, place and pace are qualities to be harnessed and nurtured.

Cities, too, appear to change overnight, their colour and character an outcome of institutional entrepreneurship, national export strategies promoting education as a profitable services sector, and the investment decisions of aspiring middle-class families around their child's and their own futures. Cities like London, Prague, Sydney, New York, Los Angeles, Auckland and Vancouver have all been transformed by large numbers of largely international students attending education institutions – from language classes and foundation courses to graduate and undergraduate programmes.

Check the websites of the respective institutions, and one is immediately struck by the creative application of a series of reputational devices used in the marketing of the university. One or more of the proliferation of world university rankings is used to promote some quality of the institution, the city as a place to study, the historical significance of the institution or the articulation of the degree to other opportunities around the world (see Chapter 13). For example, Lingnan University in Hong Kong markets itself as 'A Top 10 Liberal Arts College in Asia' citing the Forbes, 2015 ranking index. By way of contrast, its neighbour – the University of Hong Kong – illustrates its shift up the reputation ladder by referring to its better performance on the Times Higher's world university ranking. New Zealand's universities draw on the government's Brand New Zealand stamp of approval, which aims to boost confidence in its quality. Shift geography and we can see that the University of Bologna, in recently setting up an institutional presence in Buenos Aires, Argentina, cited its history – as one of the oldest universities in Europe (founded in 1088) as its unique selling point (University of Bologna, 2015). In doing so, it also joins a rapidly growing number of universities with branch-campus portfolios around the world. Macquarie University in Australia markets its programmes as Bologna compliant; a gesture in the direction of its undergraduate and graduate students wanting to ensure that they can parse their qualifications in the global marketplace.

In England, UK, government policy in higher education is being reshaped as a result of responses to local and global dynamics. These include dramatic reductions in funding to drive down the fiscal deficit, the governing of the sector through introducing a more explicit set of policies and mechanisms aimed at unleashing market forces, opening up the sector to for-profit providers, and a shift in the relationship between government and the Higher Education Funding Council for England (HEFCE) (Browne, 2010; BIS, 2011a, 2011b; Robertson, 2013). With the maximum undergraduate fee permissible at a state-funded university set at around £9,250 with any increases likely to be linked to the new Teaching Excellence Framework, and the block grant for many subjects receiving funding from the sector's regulator removed (except for science and research budgets), university leaders and managers within the sector are unclear what the long-term future might look like and how best to manage in this very different governance environment (see Chapter 7).

Adding extra pressure in this already unstable environment are immigration policies that have placed new restrictions on those arriving in the UK to study; the UK has now experienced an ongoing decline in the numbers of international students enrolled in UK universities (BIS, 2013). It is also unclear what the longer-term ramifications will be – both to government and to student aspirations – as a result of significant graduate unemployment, the introduction of student fees and the spiralling costs of the student loan book. These root and branch changes in the governing of English higher education have created new uncertainties about the future of higher education, and what this might mean for the very idea of the university, as well as for questions of quality, access, social mobility and longer-term sustainability (Reay, 2011; McGettigan, 2013; Robertson, 2013).

One could cite many more examples of the manifestations of changes in the sector, both global and local. However, the purpose here is not to provide an exhaustive catalogue of changes, interesting though that is. Rather, it is to step back a bit and look at their dynamics so as to understand their nature, scope, scale and organising logics at work. And if, as Boaventura de Sousa Santos argues, these transformations are part of a wider 'paradigmatic transition' facing all societies and universities around the world (Santos, 2010: 1), it is important to understand what this means so as to guide them in ways that are useful for the institutions and for the sector, as well as how best to manage their intended and unintended outcomes. This opening chapter will also explore some of the key issues and challenges facing the contemporary university, including issues of access, student mobility, the positional good nature of higher education, new pedagogical innovations, expanding institutional geographies of universities, the rise of new players in the sector including for-profits, and the commercialisation of ideas, knowledge and education.

Competition and higher education in the new world order

The challenge facing many higher education sectors and their academic leaders and managers, to broadly realise a new knowledge-based development model, is driven by three logics anchored in what Streeck calls 'capitalism's animal spirit' – *competition* (Streeck, 2009). Streeck describes competition as:

> the institutionally-protected possibility for enterprising individuals to pursue even higher profit from an innovative manner at the expense of other producers. The reason why competition is so effective as a mechanism of economic change is that where it is legitimate in principle, as it must be almost by definition in a capitalist economy, what is needed to mobilise the energy of innovative entrepreneurship is not collective deliberation or a majority vote but, ideally, just one player who, by deviating from the established way of 'doing things' can force all others to follow, at the ultimate penalty of extinction.
>
> (Streeck, 2009: 242–243)

The rise of recruiters of international students to feed institutional numbers, Australia's rapid development as a highly sophisticated, intelligence-driven, export machinery in higher education, and the emergence and expansion of Europe's Bologna Process to create a European Higher Education Area, are all cases in point. As Sassen (2006) observes, such innovative entrepreneurship (almost unknowingly) sets in train a new way of doing things – or a new logic – so that it is impossible not to respond. In other words, new logics signal a change in the rules of the game. As we know, *competition* (wrapped in the rhetoric of access, efficiency, effectiveness and quality) has been on the agenda of a number of governments, as well as influential international organisations, from the Organisation for Economic Co-operation and Development (OECD) to the World Bank. Competition, however, takes numerous forms – each with its own logic. For the purposes set out here in analysing the higher education sector, three logics are analysed that are central to how many universities function today.

A tale of three logics powering higher education in a global world

Logic 1: corporatisation

The first logic, corporatisation, is anchored in the idea of New Public Management (Hood, 1991) and popularised by highly influential writers such as Osborne and Gaebler (1991) in the 1990s. New Public Management asks: *How can the values of business (competition, frugality, risk, choice, value for money, entrepreneurship) be used in the re/organisation of public services so as to enable those services to be delivered more efficiently and effectively?*

Corporatisation was the outcome of the New Public Management (NPM) which emerged in the 1980s and 1990s as a way of describing a family of changes in public administration (Hood, 1991; Osborne and Gaebler, 1991) which were globalised. These changes were designed to slow down, or reverse, growth in government spending and staffing. Driven by the 'crowding out' thesis, the view was that by removing government from key areas of activity this would enable the private sector to thrive and stimulate growth and greater efficiencies. In its earlier days, this included the privatisation of a range of university activities, from catering services to cleaning, technology contracts, and publishing. More recently it has included services by firms such as INTO, Study Group and Navitas, sometimes in the form of joint ventures, aimed at both recruiting international students into foundation programmes and at helping them prepare for university studies, then setting them on their way through undergraduate programmes in the respective universities. Another example is the growth of private providers, many backed by real estate investment trusts (REITs), of student housing on or near university campuses (ICEF Monitor, 2015).

NPM had a major impact on the way in which universities delivered their core mission of teaching and research through the deployment of indicators and targets, the use of explicit standards and measures of performance, and parsimony in the use of resources. As Deem put it in the late 1990s:

> Those who run universities are expected to ensure that such value is provided and their role as academic leaders is being subsumed by a greater concern with the overt management of sites, finance, staff, students, teaching and research. Universities are also being exhorted to raise both the standards of educational provision, and the quality of their teaching, learning and research outcomes, whilst prevailing government and funding council policies also require annual so-called 'efficiency gains' to be made, resulting in a declining unit of resource per student taught, less money for equipment and a decrease in research resourcing. At the same time, the emphasis on competition between universities for students, research income and academic research 'stars', has also served to stress the extent to which higher education can be described as operating under quasi-market conditions.

> (1998: 48)

A key cultural shift for universities was therefore the emulation of the core values and practices of business, both in the ways in which the university was governed and the ways in which the university itself governed its academic and non-academic faculty (Deem, 1998; Olssen and Peters, 2005). NPM has dramatically altered the vision and mission of the university, away from Newman's 'Idea of a University' that had stood as a fundamental anchor for more than a century (Newman, 1910), towards one which is necessarily mindful of the bottom line, and of its competitors – locally, nationally and internationally.

Logic 2: comparative competitivism

A second logic – 'comparative competitivism' – arises from the influential work of Michael Porter (1985) and was mobilised by the developed economies as a response to the global crisis for the developed West in the early 1970s, processes of deindustrialisation, and the rise of the Asian newly industrialising countries (sometimes deemed the 'Asian Tigers') (Robertson, 2013). Comparative competitivism asks: *What is it that we can do or produce (trade, or gain a greater market share in), where we have an existing or potential advantage in relation to our competitors?* For countries like the United Kingdom, Australia and New Zealand, one answer was that once public sectors, like higher education, could open up private places to international students and charge full fees. Over time, these 'service sectors' would become a major revenue generator for institutions and for governments, and begin to form a major role as part of a new diversified and more globalised services-based economy (Marginson and Considine, 2000; King et al., 2009).

Whilst not exhaustive, the *key* forms that comparative competitivism has taken in higher education institutions around the globe include: (i) widening access to help boost the amount and quality of human capital; (ii) exporting education services (recruitment of international students, branch campuses); (iii) teaching in English; (iv) the recruitment of talented students for research and development; (v) the recruitment of world-class staff (especially researchers and faculty); and (vi) innovations on curricula and governance. These initiatives have generated a raft of monitoring tools that provide the nation, the institution, the student, the industry and allied associations with key information about the sector. At the same time, this increasingly diverse set of actors and activities is constitutive of the sector itself. It alters who does what, and how they see and assess what they do.

Whilst often parsed as the widening participation agenda anchored in social equity arguments, it is also the case that widening access refers to discourses around building competitive knowledge economies measured through the stock of high-skill human capital (Marginson and Considine, 2000). A university-level education was thus regarded as a critical investment in the kind of human capital that would stimulate a knowledge economy. Over the course of three decades, many countries have now moved from educating a small elite (4%–6%) to educating up to 50% or more of their eligible population in universities or some form of higher education. UNESCO Institute for Statistics figures are drawn upon by the British Council to chart this huge expansion in numbers globally: from around 13 million in 1960 to 170 million in 2009. Four countries alone have a combined share of 45% of total global tertiary enrolments (UIS, 2012: 4); these are China, India, the USA and Russia (British Council, 2012: 4–5).

In countries like the United Kingdom, this expansion has a definite economic tone, not least because of the growing costs to families, and the need to legitimate families shouldering a growing amount of the burden of this once state-funded investment. The idea of the 'graduate premium' refers to the fact that students undertaking university-level studies will, it is argued, over their lifetime significantly improve their earnings (Goastellec, 2010) and therefore their route to social mobility, though evidence shows that this has slowed in countries like the UK and the USA (Brown et al., 2011).

For individuals, their competitive comparative advantage is enhanced by university-level education in ways that can be invested in as a 'positional good'. Fred Hirsch coined the concept of positional good in his book *Social Limits to Growth* (1977) where he argued a positional economy is composed of

> all aspects of goods, services, work positions and other social relationships that are either (i) scarce in some absolute or socially imposed sense, or (ii) subject to congestion and crowding through more extensive use.
>
> (Hirsch, 1977: 27)

Having a university qualification when others don't enables the valorisation of that qualification to secure advantages in the labour market that would otherwise be unavailable. The greater the number of others who also hold a similar qualification, then either an even higher level is required (from master's to doctoral level), or some other means of distinguishing reputational value is necessary. Here either personal reputation (prizes and other awards) or institutional reputation (in the form of what position in a ranking system) is also used by employers, scholarship allocators and high skills recruiters to make decisions about individuals and their qualifications, employability and financial returns.

Perhaps the most significant of the changes that have been set in train as a result of comparative competitivism is in international student mobility. For countries like the United Kingdom, Australia and New Zealand, sectors like higher education were reimagined in the late 1980s/early 1990s in government policy as potential exports as part of a services sector. These countries had the advantage of having a mature higher education sector, capacity to expand, they taught in the global *lingua franca* – English, and could use old colonial ties for new purposes. Before long, these early entry entrepreneurs, encouraged by key international organisations (Organisation for Economic Co-operation and Development, the World Bank and the World Trade Organization), came to view higher education institutions as producers of education services which could be given an economic value (Kelsey, 2008).

By the late 1980s, aid programmes which had enabled scholars from low-income countries to study abroad had been replaced with *trade* programmes, mostly targeted at the aspiring middle classes in emerging economies like China, Malaysia, Singapore and Nigeria, and more recently Eastern Europe, India and Latin America. A new set of firms also emerged in the higher education sector around these kinds of activity, from those who 'test' the health of the system by gathering the views of graduates and selling the data back to universities (i-graduate), to professional recruiters of international students such as ICEF (Robertson and Komljenovic, 2016).

The most remarkable of the changes since the early 1990s in the global higher education landscape is the sheer scale of numbers of students studying for either undergraduate or graduate degrees in a country of which they are not a citizen (OECD, 2014). The OECD, in its annual *Education at a Glance*, shows that in the 1990s, around 1.3 million students were enrolled outside of their country of citizenship. By 2015, the figure is now more than three times that number – with around 4.5 million students now studying in another country (OECD, 2014: 342). According to some pundits, this figure is set to reach the 5 million mark in the next couple of years (UNESCO, 2014). By anyone's reckoning, this is a very large population on the move, and all the more remarkable because by 2008, 24.4% of this population of international students came from just three countries – China, India and South Korea – with the largest population by far being from China (14.9%).

Taking all these phenomena together, it is clear that a complex combination of dynamics is at work, giving momentum to these flows. It is also important to take notice of the newer players in the sector – such as China, Malaysia and Singapore – not as the major sending countries as they once were, but as increasingly important destinations. The rise of China as a global power and its comparative economic strength (despite recent falterings) in relation to the USA has resulted in a healthy 'study-abroad' programme, particularly for American students now seeking to acquire some understanding of China and engagement with Mandarin as a potential contender to English (UNESCO, 2014).

Though the US continues to have the largest share of international students, this has, in fact, decreased with time as newer players have entered. Whereas the US accounted for 40% of all international students in the early 1990s, by the late 1990s this proportion had shrunk to 32% (OECD, 2014). The attraction of the United States, of course, is not only its prestigious universities, but it has been a preferred destination for graduate students because of its world-class research facilities and its generous scholarship programmes, particularly in the sciences, mathematics and engineering. It also teaches in English and is home to the top science and engineering journals, a litmus test of dominance in global knowledge production (Marginson, 2014). Only more recently has the US begun to consider increasing its recruitment of international students into its undergraduate programmes to help manage the financial pressures many of its institutions are now facing – and recent data released by the Institute of International Education

(2016) highlights a renewed growth in US international student enrolment levels. In contrast with the US, which has around 4% of international students in its overall student body, Australia has, over the past three decades, built up huge intakes into its undergraduate programs, with around 1 in 5 students being an international student, and of this number, 8 in every 10 come from the Asian region (OECD, 2014: 349).

Yet such dependencies also create their own problems. In 1997, the Asian financial crisis had a major impact on the flow of Asian students to New Zealand and Australia, creating major institutional instabilities. Similarly, in the UK, increasing government intransigence regarding immigration numbers – and students are also included in these figures – has caused a drop in the numbers of international students and an increasing number to feel unwelcome. And despite reports, such as the one by Deloitte's (2015) on *The Value of International Education to Australia* on the contribution of graduates likely to migrate after their studies and who are estimated would improve gross domestic product or GDP per capita by 0.5% per capita or A$8.7 billion (US$6.6 billion) in GDP, there is little sign that the UK higher education representatives have had much success in advancing an industry perspective. Add to this picture a volatile political landscape, with the election of Donald Trump in the United States and the United Kingdom set to leave the European Union, and it is evident that the more higher education globalises, the more challenges it faces in terms of national state rather than self-control over its flows of students and the wider policy terrain in which it operates.

Many universities have also begun to establish branch campuses in other parts of the world as a means of ensuring their international futures. Branch campuses are 'off-shore' operations where the unit is operated by the source institution (though can be in a joint venture with a host institution), and the student is awarded the degree of the source institution. In a major report for the Observatory on Borderless Higher Education released in September 2009, Becker noted that since 2006 there has been a 43% increase in international branch campuses, with more host and source countries involved. The number of host countries increased from 36 in 2006, to 51 in 2009 and 217 in 2014 (Olds and Robertson, 2014). Setting up in distant spaces is not for the naïve; it demands considerable local knowledge and an awareness of the complexities of place, culture and politics.

Amongst the host countries, the Arab Emirates has been the leader (Becker, 2009: 7); these initiatives are part of the Arab region's strategy to develop a knowledge-based economy, and to be a provider of education services within the Arab region. However, a new pattern is emerging worth noting. Where higher education capability is built through the establishment of branch campuses, in select cases, these initiatives are then incorporated into, or organised around, a new set of metaphors which are driving these developments, such as hubs and hotspots (cf. Singapore, Malaysia, Hong Kong). Once established and embedded, these hubs act as regional suppliers of education services, generating new regional capacity in higher education. These developments challenge existing patterns of geo-strategic interest as the new regional players seek to gain a competitive comparative advantage in the global distribution of education markets. Recent data on branch campuses has flagged a geographic rebalancing, with China now the leading host country (O'Malley, 2016).

The growth in trans-border mobility has been paralleled by governments' trade department efforts to represent the value of higher education as an export sector. Different countries use different means to calculate these figures, but even so, that education is the fourth largest generator of GDP behind iron ore, or that the New Zealand government returns more value from education than the wine industry, also creates it own momentum, and it is difficult to see how this might be turned back.

The English language, as a medium of instruction and a dominant form of dissemination of research, has been a key lever for advancing a comparative advantage. In more recent years a range of countries, including continental Europe, the Scandinavian countries and Japan, have responded by promoting English as an acceptable medium of instruction so as to develop their higher education systems into more attractive destinations. English has also gained particular prominence as the language of the research community because of its role in scientific dissemination and as the largest shared language of the research community. However, the use of English continues to generate huge debates about the loss of local knowledges and cultures, and what this means long term for the arts and humanities.

The global competition for (fee-paying) international students is nuanced by the global competition for 'talented' students. It is this dimension, too, which has differentiated the USA's approach to international students in comparison to the Australian approach, though this is changing, in both directions (US institutions are now looking for full foreign fee-paying undergraduates *and* talented graduates). After being stagnant for several years, the figures for international graduate students have begun to increase again. The USA has a particular advantage in this area – with large research and development (R&D) budgets able to attract science, technology, engineering and mathematics (STEM) students, and sufficiently flexible immigration packages that enable very large numbers to stay on. Indeed, as Douglass and Edelstein (2009) note, these students have been instrumental in enabling the US to build a highly skilled workforce in this area. More recently, Canada, Europe and Australia have also sought to secure a share of the talented graduate market, with lures like immigration points and residence permits, and organised scholarship programmes like the Erasmus Mundus scheme in Europe, to make the offer more attractive. Europe, however, is particularly nervous of its long-term capacity to secure a competitive advantage in R&D because of its changing demographic. Whilst this is not the case in the US, there would need to be a change in levels of participation in US higher education, particularly the sciences, for the US to secure its future from within its own nationals as opposed to those who come from Asia.

There are also interesting innovations in curricula and governance across the higher education sector. Perhaps the most remarkable of these is the Bologna Process which has been rolled out across Europe now includes 47 countries, involving well over 16 million students (Robertson et al., 2016). The creation of a European Higher Education Area, on the one hand, and a European Research Area, on the other, has been under way since 1999 and 2000 respectively so as to make Europe a more competitive region through the development of a common degree architecture, and through joint research projects. However, recent developments in the United Kingdom around leaving the European Union might well generate major changes to the overall shape of the area if other countries also follow suit. That it will be business as usual according to UK universities might well be wishful thinking by a sector that has been a major beneficiary of research funding and from the presence of European students on UK campuses.

The rapid growth in online learning by new for-profit providers (though this has recently slowed because of government regulation of the sector) (see Kinser, 2006; Henschke et al., 2010), and most recently the potentials offered by Massive Open Online Courses (MOOCs) being pioneered by elite US universities (such as Harvard, MIT, Stanford, Yale) are also causing ripples in the governance and curricula of universities. Analysts argue MOOCs could lead to the 'unbundling' of the relationship between teaching/learning credits and credentials, with students potentially being able to engage with a range of different HE providers and turn these credits into credentials using newer kinds of services. Only time will tell as to whether these initiatives cause more than temporary turbulence in the sector.

Logic 3: 'competitive comparison'

A third logic – 'competitive comparison' – asks: *How well does this unit (institution/ city/nation/region) do in relation to another?* This third logic uses hierarchical orderings (with their implied superior/inferior registers of difference) to generate a social identity (world class, 5*, enterprising). Comparison acts as a moral spur and de facto form of governance, giving direction to competitivism through its insistence that if we *aspire* to improve (despite very different resources and positions in the global hierarchy), that we will make it. These three competitiveness logics give direction, form, content and disciplinary power to neoliberalism as a political and hegemonic project, as it is mediated through higher education.

Logic 3's competitiveness works in a rather different way. In asking: *How well is one unit doing in relation to another?* it assumes a continuum can be developed with labels at each end registering a location on a 'telos' of development – placing units into a hierarchical ordering along this axis, so that comparison can take place between units, allocating social identities (world class, 5*). This move gives rise to registers of difference, such as developed/underdeveloped, superior/inferior. Those doing the assessing, or offering their services to determine our progress, have the power to set and reset the rules of the game sufficiently to ensure a spur to action. This is a moral and status economy, whose symbolic power is the elevation to a space close to a god, or in the opposite direction the humiliation of the 'shadow lands'.

A rather different example of the way in which indexes, generated out of a myriad of indicators and other indexes, are used to allocate an identity as a result of comparison, which in turn stimulates activity in the direction of an imagined future, is the KAM. The World Bank's KAM (Knowledge Assessment Methodology) is an instrument developed to help realise a knowledge-based economy. The KAM is an interactive, diagnostic and benchmarking tool that provides a preliminary assessment of countries' and regions' 'readiness for the knowledge economy' (World Bank, 2007). The World Bank's programme of indicators is based on four pillars:

- An economic and institutional regime that provides incentives for the efficient use of existing and new knowledge and the flourishing of entrepreneurship.
- An educated and skilled population that can create, share, and use knowledge well.
- An efficient innovation system of firms, research centres, universities, think tanks, consultants and other organisations who can tap into the growing stock of global knowledge, assimilate and adapt it to local needs and create new technology.
- Information and communication technologies (ICT) that can facilitate the effective communication, dissemination, and processing of information.

The KAM enables countries from around the world to benchmark themselves with neighbours, competitors, or other countries they wish to learn from on the four pillars of the knowledge economy. It is therefore a tool aimed at promoting 'learning' amongst both developing and developed countries about the elements that constitute the World Bank's version of a knowledge economy.

Education at a Glance is a statistical representation of higher education around the globe by the OECD. First produced in 2000, over time the OECD has collected more and more material on the sector, and it uses these representations and implicit comparisons to enable countries to 'learn' about their system and their performance in relation to other systems. The problem with this kind of representation is set out by Cliff Adelman (2009) in his paper on *The Spaces Between Numbers: Getting International Data on Higher Education Straight*. Using graduation rates in the US to make his point, he shows how the OECD report assumes that universities in the US are the only institutions producing higher education graduates. As a result, the numbers are represented as small in comparison to other OECD countries. This of course feeds a crisis mentality in the US. As he further notes:

> Indicators are the means for fulfilling the challenges of variability in any comparison of multinational inputs: out of complexity, they seek to tell a common

story. They find ways to reconcile vastly different systems of accounting, cultural definitions, traditional national reference points, idiosyncrasies of institutions, and nuances of behaviour through common templates.

(Adelman, 2009: 36)

A proliferation of quality assurance mechanisms variously directed at teaching, research and institutional management also works with competitive comparison. In relation to research, governments have become increasingly interested in research output and the development of measures of quality. The UK is an instructive example. Serving multiple purposes, from stimulating research outputs (as one measure amongst others of a competitive knowledge economy) to controlling academic work, the research assessment tools in the United Kingdom have been copied in a range of countries. Leaving aside the 'not unimportant' fact that the research assessment exercise (RAE) has consumed vast quantities of staff energy and finance, and shaped the recruitment of staff and their academic labour in very significant ways, it has also privileged the idea of 'international' in what counts as quality research, and more recently in the impact that research is to have. In the UK the research assessment exercises have deepened the divisions within and between the different kinds of higher education providers (HEP) around teaching and research through the establishment of league tables. And the impending rollout of the Teaching Excellence Framework, with its blunt 'Gold', 'Silver' and 'Bronze' rankings, will be sure to generate even more divisions, in part by enabling new revenue flow pathways.

Since 2003, global league tables such as the Shanghai Jiao Tong, QS, and the recently revamped Times Higher have also provided policymakers and universities with a new language and set of tools to advance the idea of a 'global' university (Hazelkorn, 2016). The Shanghai Jiao Tong privileges a particular form of knowledge and how it is circulated; this includes disciplines such as science, mathematics and technology, Nobel Prize holders, the presence of international students, and citations. There is considerable concern over the use of the Shanghai Jiao Tong, for it significantly privileges US universities, along with the UK's Oxford and Cambridge. Nevertheless, governments and individual institutions have used and so help to legitimate these ranking 'technologies' to advance their own projects and interests, such as leveraging funding, branding their institutions, departments and star performers, as a means of marketing, recruiting staff and students, disciplining staff and so on.

By way of conclusion: strong questions in need of strong answers

One thing academic researchers, policymakers, industry analysts and popular commentators agree upon concerning the higher education sector is that universities and institutions of higher education around the world are at a crossroads, as they 'stand on the cusp of profound change' (Ernst and Young, 2012: 4). From new

technologies which are transforming where and how we learn, to highly innovative multi-institutional developments aimed at altering the interface between
graduate education and the new economy, to players in the sector whose business
partners and models are very different from those that have characterised the sector to date, these are challenging our traditional conceptions of what a university
is, who it is for and what it looks like. In the words of Harvard professor Clayton
Christensen (in Christensen and Eyring, 2011), these developments are changing the DNA of higher education, and thus demand challenging conversations.

This chapter has detailed some of contours of these changes, arguing that they
are being driven by three distinct logics that are having a mutually reinforcing
role in creating competitive economies, institutions and individuals. This is a
three-pronged epistemology, of creating an organisational infrastructure and
orientation that emulates the private sector; of securing an advantage through
innovatively using territorial intelligence, material capabilities and new forms of
institutionalisation; and of using comparison as the tool for generating momentum towards the realisation of this goal, which in turn gives these tools considerable power.

These logics are changing higher education institutions and changing the
nature of strategic planning, away from administering national state mechanisms
as a public service and towards competitive and market-based models based on
the interests of each institution and its participants. Universities are not only a
site of human capital formation but increasingly also a business endeavour best
organised using the disciplinary values and principles of competitivism and economic rather than human progress. Together, these two planes offer a limited
range of social identities for institutions. Its moral economy is punitive in that
while difference becomes the basis on which social identities are allocated, there
is little scope for diversity.

Its development trajectory, of progress away from a relatively autonomous
institution whose social relations are decommodified, towards one where value is
in the form of commodities within a knowledge economy, highlights not only a
narrowing of what knowledge counts, but the potential to close down space for
diversity and responsiveness regarding what forms of knowledge are produced,
with whom, and for whom. In the face of global issues of sustainability, and the
sustainability of the model based on enrolling more and more international students, it is important academic leaders and planners take the time to assess the
development of the sector as a whole and to think more strategically about the
short, medium and long term regarding their responsibilities to curate universities in ways that secure a less competitive and more open-minded future for the
population as a whole.

Santos (2010) recently argued that what confronts the modern university, and
indeed places the modern university at this crossroad, is that it has tended to
answer strong questions with weak answers. Weak answers are technical answers
devised of the moment. They are answers that focus on the problem as if it were
disconnected from wider social, economic and political phenomena. Answers to

strong questions must not only have a strong awareness of the context, but have a strong theory about that context as well. Strong answers not only see the importance and the enormity of the strategic planning task at hand, but take seriously the responsibility to map, make sense of and advance an agenda and set of strategies, institutionally and sectorally, that seeks to challenge and if necessary change the current state of affairs.

To some extent this also means posing questions that might offer new ways of thinking about the role of the university in the 21st century. Can we, and if so how can we, reconstruct the missions of our universities (in the current environment) to include social, political and not just (narrow) economic ends? Can we also work to ensure universities address challenging questions that go against the grain of political thought? One year after the 2007–8 global economic crisis, for example, Harvard's President Drew Faust (2009, p. BR19) had this to say:

> Universities are meant to be producers not just of knowledge but also of (often inconvenient) doubt. They are creative and unruly places, homes to a polyphony of voices. But at this moment in our history, universities might well ask if they have in fact done enough to raise the deep and unsettling questions necessary to any society.
>
> As the world indulged in a bubble of false prosperity and excessive materialism, should universities – in their research, teaching and writing – have made greater efforts to expose the patterns of risk and denial? Should universities have presented a firmer counterweight to economic irresponsibility? Have universities become too captive to the immediate and worldly purposes they serve? Has the market model become the fundamental and defining identity of higher education?

Or is it possible to have a progressive form of competition, one that takes as its compass the creation of teaching and learning opportunities that give rise to a critical cosmopolitan mind? What might it look like if translated into the kinds of tools which also assesses our activities? What can we learn from others (comparison) that might enable us to reject the narrowness of current models on offer? These are difficult questions for complex times, but if not now, when can and should they be grappled with?

Bibliography

Adelman, C. (2009) *The Spaces between Numbers: Getting International Data on Higher Education Straight*, Washington: Institute for Higher Education Policy.

Barnett, R. (2009) Knowledge interests and knowledge policies: Rethinking the University in the twenty first century, in R. Barnett, J.-C. Guedon, J. Masschelein, M. Simons, S. Robertson, and N. Standaert (eds.) *Rethinking the University after Bologna*, Antwerp: UCSIA, pp. 6–14.

Becker, R. (2009) *International Branch Campuses: Markets and Strategies*, London: OBHE.

British Council (2012) *The Shape of Things to Come: Higher Education Global Trends and Emerging Opportunities to 2020*, London: British Council.

Browne, J. (2010) *Securing a Sustainable Future for Higher Education: An Independent Review of Higher Education Funding and Student Finance*, London: BIS.

Brown, P., Lauder, H., and Ashton, D. (2011) *The Global Auction*, Oxford: Oxford University Press.

Business, Innovation and Skills (2011a) *Students at the Heart of the System*, London: HMSO.

Business, Innovation and Skills (2011b) *A New Fit-for-Purpose Regulatory Framework for the Higher Education Sector – 'Technical Consultation'*, London: HMSO.

Business, Innovation and Skills (2013) *International Education: Global Growth and Prosperity*, London: HM Government.

Christensen, C. and Eyring, H. (2011) *The Innovative University: Changing the DNA of Higher Education*, San Francisco: Forum Futures.

Coughlan, S. (2015) Silicon Valley entrepreneur course comes to London, *BBC News*, 18th March, www.bbc.co.uk/news/business-31840175 last accessed 21st June, 2015.

Deem, R. (1998) New managerialism and higher education: The management of performances and cultures in universities in the United Kingdom, *International Studies in the Sociology of Education*, 8 (1), pp. 47–70.

Deloitte (2015) *The Value of International Education to Australia*, London: Deloitte.

Douglass, J. and Edelstein, R. (2009) The Global Competition for Talent: The Rapidly Changing Market for International Students and the Need for a Strategic Approach in the US, UC Berkeley Center for Studies in Higher Education (CSHE), Research and Occasional Paper Series, 8.

Ernst and Young (2012) University of the Future, Ernst and Young: Australia, http://www.ey.com/Publication/vwLUAssets/University_of_the_future/$FILE/University_of_the_future_2012.pdf accessed 14th November, 2016.

Faust, D. (2009) The university's crisis of purpose, *New York Times*, 1 September, p. BR19.

Goastellec, G. (2010) Merit and equality: International trends and local responses, in H. Eggin (ed.) *Access and Equity: Comparative Perspectives*, Rotterdam: Sense Publishers, pp. 35–54.

Hazelkorn, E. (ed.) (2016) *Global Rankings and the Geopolitics of Higher Education*, London and New York: Routledge.

Henschke, G. Lechuga, V., and Tierney, W. (2010) *For-Profit Colleges and Universities*, Stirling Virginia: Stylus.

Hirsch, F. (1977) *Social Limits to Growth*, London: Routledge and Kegan Paul.

Holmwood, J. (ed.) (2011) *A Manifesto for the Public University*, London: Bloomsbury.

Hood, C. (1991) A public management for all seasons? *Public Administration*, 69, pp. 3–19.

ICEF Monitor (2015) Homeward Bound: The Growing Global Investment in Student Housing, ICEF Monitor, http://monitor.icef.com/2015/10/homeward-bound-the-growing-global-investment-in-student-housing/

Institute of International Education (2016) IIE Releases Open Doors 2016 Data, www.iie.org/Who-We-Are/News-and-Events/Press-Center/Press-Releases/2016/2016-11-14-Open-Doors-Data#.WCngwdxW3go last accessed 14th November, 2016.

International Universities Association (2010) Internationalisation of Higher Education, Regional Perspectives, Paris: IAU.

Kelsey, J. (2008) *Serving Whose Interests?*, New York: Routledge Cavendish.

King, R. (2009) *Governing Universities Globally: Organizations, Regulation and Rankings*. Cheltenham: Edward Elgar.

King, R., Marginson, S., Naidoo, R., (2009) *Handbook on Globalization and Higher Education*, Cheltenham: Edward Elgar.

Kinser, K. (2006) *From Main Street to Wall Street: The Transformation of for-Profit Higher Education*, New York: ASHE with Wiley.

McGettigan, A. (2013) *The Great University Gamble: Money, Markets and the Future of Higher Education*, London: Pluto Press.

Mandelson, P. (2009) Higher Education and Modern Life, a Speech Given by the Minister for the Department for Business, Innovation and Skills, Birkbeck University, London, July.

Marginson, S. (2014) University rankings and social science, *European Journal of Education*, 49 (1), pp. 45–59.

Marginson, S. and Considine, M. (2000) *The Enterprise University: Power, Governance and Reinvention*, Cambridge: Cambridge University Press.

Newman, J.-H. (1910) *The Idea of a University, in Essays, English and American, with Introduction and Notes and Illustrations*, New York: P. F. Collier and Son.

OECD (2014) *Education at a Glance, 2014*, Paris: OECD.

Olds, K. (2005) Articulating agendas and traveling principles in the layering of new strands of academic freedom in contemporary Singapore, in B. Czarniawska and G. Sevón (eds.) *Where Translation Is a Vehicle, Imitation Its Motor, and Fashion Sits at the Wheel: How Ideas, Objects and Practices Travel in the Global Economy*, Malmö: Liber AB, pp. 167–189.

Olds, K. (2007) Global assemblage: Singapore, Western universities, and the construction of a global education hub, *World Development*, 35 (6), pp. 959–975.

Olds, K. and Robertson, S. (2014) Globalizing Higher Education and Research for the Knowledge Economy, MOOC offered by University of Wisconsin-Madison, Coursera.

Olssen, M. and Peters, M. A. (2005) Neoliberalism, higher education and the knowledge economy: From the free market to knowledge capitalism, *Journal of Education Policy*, 20 (3), pp. 313–345.

O'Malley, B. (2016) China overtakes UAE as top host of branch campuses, *University World News*, www.universityworldnews.com/article.php?story=20161110144407523 accessed 14th November, 2016.

Osborne, D. and Gaebler, T. (1991) *Reinventing Government: How the Entrepreneurial Spirit Is Transforming the Public Sector*, New York: Plume.

Porter, M. (1985) *The Competitive Advantage*, New York: Free Press.

Reay, D. (2011) Universities and the reproduction of inequalities, in J. Holmwood (ed.) *A Manifesto for the Public University*, London: Bloomsbury, pp. 112–126.

Robertson, S. (2009) 'Producing' the global knowledge economy: the World Bank, the knowledge assessment methodology and education, in M. Simons, M. Olssen and M. Peters (eds.) *Re-Reading Education Policies*, Rotterdam: Sense Publishers, pp. 235–256.

Robertson, S. (2013) Hullabaloo in the groves of academe, the politics of instituting a market in English higher education, in P. Zgaga, U. Teichler, and J. Brenner (eds.) *The Globalisation Challenge for European Higher Education: Convergence and Diversity, Centres and Peripheries*, Bern: Peter Lang, pp. 161–184.

Robertson, S., de Azevedo, M., and Dale, R. (2016) A cultural political economy of higher education regionalism in Europe, in S. Robertson, K. Olds, R. Dale, and Q.-A. Dang (eds.) *Global Regionalisms and Higher Education*, Cheltenham: Edward Elgar, pp. 24–48.

Robertson, S. and Komljenovic, J. (2016) Unbundling the university and making higher education markets, in T. Verger, C. Lubienski and G. Steiner Khamsi (eds.) *The Global Education Industry, World Yearbook 2016*, London and New York: Routledge, pp. 211–227.

Santos, B. (2010) The European University at the Crossroads, Keynote Address to the XXII Anniversary of the Magna Charta Universitatum, Bologna: University of Bologna.

Sassen, S. (2006) *Territory, Authority, Rights*, Princeton: Princeton University Press.

Streeck, W. (2009) *Reforming Capitalism*, Oxford: Oxford University Press.

UIS Institute of Statistics (2012), Global Education Digest, UNESCO, http://www.uis.unesco.org/Education/Documents/ged-2012-en.pdf last accessed 14th April 2017.

UNESCO (2014) *The International Mobility of Students in Asia and the Pacific*, Bangkok: UNESCO.

University of Bologna (2015) University of Bologna: Campuses and Structures, www.unibo.it/en/university/campuses-and-structures/buenos-aires-campus last accessed 22nd June, 2015.

World Bank (2007) *Knowledge for Development*, Washington: World Bank Group.

Chapter 2

The functions of strategic planning

Tony Strike, Martin Hanlon and Dominic Foster

Introduction

This chapter seeks to describe the strategic planning function. It does not look at activities related to strategic planning to see if and where they are performed, but starts with the roles, teams or departments whose titles suggests they are responsible for strategic planning and examines what functions they perform. An answer is sought to a question: What is it that strategic planning offices do? This is intended as useful to those who wish to engage with such an office for support, for those responsible for designing professional services and for those who work in or intend to work in a strategic planning unit or role.

With a body of practice, academic research and writing about strategic planning, it is possible and even reasonable to start out by thinking it was a well-defined, recognisable and bounded set of activities that belong together in a single function. Strategic planning has its academic gurus – for example Ansoff (1979), Drucker (1999), Porter (2002) and Mintzberg, Ahlstrand and Lampel (2005). Strategic planning, like other management disciplines, has its theories, its tools and its trends. Organisations have job roles in strategy and planning, and consultancies operate profitably in the field. Describing and defining the role and purpose of strategy and planning as a function in higher education might have therefore been simple.

Problems began in attempting that definition and in scoping the function almost immediately. First, there is no unified naming convention. The term institutional research (IR) was more commonly used within higher education (HE) in Europe and in the United States than in the United Kingdom or Australia, which preferred strategic planning (SP). IR suggested responsibility for investigating data and the conduct of internal studies and analysis, related to issues of strategic importance to the university. Strategic planning was more commonly used in the UK and Australia in HE and by those with similar strategic roles to those held outside of the HE sector. SP suggested provision of information and analysis, in support of informed decision-making, for academic leaders. In practice, these terms of art were increasingly linked (e.g. Office of Planning and Institutional Research) or were becoming interchangeable (like personnel management and human resources management). Even in UK HE the titles of the departments and of their leaders differed.

Early attempts to define IR in HE in the US can be found in the literature. At a high level of description, these definitions seemed perfectly functional. For example, (Dressel, 1981 pp. 237) wrote:

> Institutional research has to do with what decision makers need to know about an institution, its educational objectives, goals and purposes, environmental factors, processes, and structures to more wisely use its resources, more successfully attain its objectives and goals, and to demonstrate integrity and accountability in so doing.

Saupe (1990) later similarly defined IR in the US context as 'research conducted within an institution of higher education to provide information which supports institutional planning, policy formation and decision making'. These are good but they are not snappy definitions. Definitions of this type might be summarised as 'organisational intelligence' or as 'decision support'. Terenzini (1993) took this view of the US IR function further by describing the three types of intelligence required by institutional researchers:

- technical/analytical intelligence (factual knowledge or information, and analytical and methodological skills and competencies),
- issues intelligence (knowledge of the major issues or decision areas that face institutions and the people who manage them) and
- contextual intelligence (informal as well as formal campus political structures and codes, governance, decision-making processes, and customs).

Terenzini's typography seemed to lack two types of intelligence that contemporary strategic planners in HE may want to add to Terenzini's original IR portfolio:

- political intelligence (knowledge of the national, regional and sectoral political and policy context in which the university is operating) and
- competitor intelligence (how other universities are performing, what they are doing to achieve those results and how to benchmark them).

Volkwein (1999), unlike Terenzini (1993), took a functional rather than a skills/knowledge-based approach to defining IR and described five roles: information authority, policy analyst, spin doctor, knowledge manager and researcher.

By expanding Terenzini's list of intelligence types and mapping them against the functional roles described by Volkwein, it is possible to see an activity map emerge which begins to capture the wide domain of functions performed by strategic planners, which they might themselves recognise. This activity map is shown in Table 2.1.

It could be argued that SP is less passive than IR, and looks for actionable insights and action plans in a way IR need not. The main problem with Terenzini when considering IR is that SP arguably has an action orientation, to plan

Table 2.1 Strategic planning activity map

Strategy Activity Map		Role configuration				
		Information authority	Policy analyst	Spin doctor	Knowledge manager	Researcher
Intelligence type	**Analytical**	Data analysis	Narrative analysis	Evidence-based marketing	Corporate data modelling	Institutional research
	Issues	Secretariat	Policy-driven proposals	Promoting action	Capturing and logging issues	Issue-based analysis
	Context	Governance advice	Decision-making processes	Promoting a culture	Tracking issue resolution	Cultural analysis
	Political	Political advice	Political briefing	Promoting values	Environmental scanning	Social research
	Competitor	Comparative analysis	Policy bench marking	Promoting unique selling points	Survey and data capture	Market analysis

the implementation of strategy as well as to support its development through research. Strategic planners manage or co-ordinate change, help deliver sought outcomes and capture or measure resultant benefits. However, generalised arche-typal definitions of this or any sort, however attractive, offered false hope.

Charting the functional scope of SP turned out to be complex, and a unifying distinctiveness proved elusive. This chapter offers a schema for strategy and planning in HE (based on functional surveys in the UK and Australia), but it does not duck the diversity and differences found in the practice of strategic planning in one university compared to the next. Strategy and planning functions in the UK and Australia are not standardised; they are differentiated and possibly (appropriately) contingent on the history, culture, politics and priorities of the particular place.

This chapter utilises survey data from three sources:

- a 2015 UK Russell Group Strategy and Planning Director's survey,
- a subsequent 2016 HESPA (Higher Education Strategic Planners Association) member's questionnaire about the strategy and planning functions in UK universities and
- a similar survey conducted in Australia amongst directors of planning in Australian universities (i.e. members of the Australian Network of University Planners or 'ANUP') administered in April–May 2015.

The results and findings are used to attempt a description of the role, purpose and scope of the contemporary HE strategy and planning function. This chapter will describe the functions and activities undertaken by staff in strategic planning offices, or by staff with planning responsibilities in HE in the UK and Australia, and how they vary in range and focus. The UK HESPA website (www.hespa. ac.uk/) explained its members were likely to undertake work including responsibility for some or many of the following:

- Strategic planning;
- Annual planning and resource allocation;
- Performance measurement, including key performance indicators (KPIs), benchmarking, league tables and UK performance indicators;
- Management information and business intelligence: data, trends, scenario analysis, and forecasting;
- Statistical returns to the Higher Education Statistics Agency (HESA) and funding councils, now including the Key Information Set (KIS);
- Data governance and quality;
- Research management including the Research Excellence Framework (REF) submission preparation;
- Surveys, including the National Student Survey (NSS), Destination of Leavers from Higher Education (DLHE), Postgraduate Taught and Research Experience Surveys (PTES and PRES);
- Interactions with representative bodies and agencies including Universities UK (UUK), Universities Scotland, funding councils, HESA, Universities and Colleges Admissions Service (UCAS);
- Governance support, including risk management;
- Environmental scanning and public policy work, including preparation of responses to government and other consultations and external enquiries, and the analysis of impact; and
- Access agreements (England), outcome agreements (Scotland), fee plan (Wales).

What follows below explores the role and function of higher education strategic planners in more detail, to support any such taxonomy with evidence. It looks at the strategy and planning function in higher education; the work that planners are engaged in and the range of functions usually undertaken by strategy and planning departments. Part of the purpose of this study is to capture a snapshot of the scope of work of strategy and planning as an administrative function, to define it.

The UK RG survey was undertaken collaboratively across 24 research-intensive HE institutions, with UK Russell Group Directors of Planning as the primary participants. This initial survey provided the design for a second open HESPA member's survey (advertised through the HESPA website) to collect data from a wider range of contributors and HE institutions. In Australian universities (i.e. members of the Australian Network of University Planners or 'ANUP') the survey was administered by the planning unit of the Australian National University (ANU) and, like the RG survey, only one response per university was permitted.

It was initially hypothesised that the SP (or IR) function had adapted and the emphasis had moved from external regulatory or statutory reporting and statistical returns (information authority with technical/analytical intelligence) to a more strategic and consultative role within universities which were themselves operating in a more marketised competitive environment. In the US a 2015 survey showed that data reporting of various kinds (federal and state mandatory reporting, for data books or for data sharing) was the primary responsibility held by institutional research offices (Swing, Jones and Ross, 2016). This was not believed to be true in the UK or Australia in SP.

The UK and Australian results reported here showed the strategic planning function was more likely to be involved in strategy development, internal performance monitoring, developing and monitoring key performance indicators and providing external competitor analysis than in producing and sending external statutory returns (although this is also done by some or many SP functions with a corporate information role). However, in neither jurisdiction was there was one activity for which every strategy and planning director held the primary responsibility that could be used to identify and define them or their department's role. The diversity found meant that there was either:

- no 'right' way to devise and deliver the strategic planning function, or
- the function was still evolving to some future normative state, or
- that it was highly contingent on the local organisational strategy and on the wider context in which it was found, or
- the very strength of the function lay in its being unbounded, rather than bounded to a particular set of functional activities.

Context

How the SP function should be best established needs thought if it is to be successful. While responsibility for effective strategy, planning and performance is often shared between senior academics, the challenges facing today's university leaders has led to the creation of professional SP (or IR) functions. Research into the practice of university management remains a significant theme in higher education research (Tight, 2012). This research has included the role of professional support services (Whitchurch and Gordon, 2011). University corporate planning, at least in the UK, gained prominence following the Jarratt Report (1985) which required the bringing of 'planning, resource allocation and accountability together into one corporate process linking academic, financial and physical aspects'. The Higher Education Funding Council for England (HEFCE) produced a detailed guide recommending higher education institutions have systematic planning processes (HEFCE, 2000). The IR function, so titled, in mainland Europe was originally conceived for facilitating the compilation and analysis of data for reporting to other agencies, much as the planning function in the UK provided external reporting in its national setting. This European IR function had equally evolved to provide a more diverse set of activities designed to enhance university decision-making, inform institutional policy development and provide the insight required to underpin institutional planning (Middaugh, 1990).

Some observed this new public management with trepidation (Deem, Hillyard and Reed, 2007). Others encouraged wider use of the information resources which strategic planners and institutional researchers provided. For example, Presley (1990, p. 106) stated:

> When institutional research is perceived simply as a number crunching activity, not only does the professional lose, but so does each and every institution where this attitude prevails.

The genesis of SP or IR in HE may have been to satisfy statutory, regulatory or reporting requirements imposed from outside the institution. Today an increasingly marketised and competitive higher education environment demands institutional leaders understand the policy environment, competitor and collaborator behaviour and the institution's strengths and weaknesses, and that they are served with analysis and insight to support their intentions, decisions and choices. Watson (2000) put it thus: 'Members of the senior management team have to marry a volatile and unpredictable external environment with the internal dynamics and trajectory of their own institution.' While some management functions such as human resources have well-developed literature around their adding value as a business partner (Ulrich, 1997), similar theoretical underpinning is not yet pervasive in the SP and IR functions in higher education.

The UK Russell Group survey results

The first survey undertaken was a collaboration between the UK Russell Group (RG) universities aimed at better understanding the strategy and planning function through benchmarking across universities in a similar mission group, focussing on what being an HE planner meant in practice. The aim was to help senior managers analyse their current approach and identify where improvements could be made and to inform the development of these value-adding specialist roles.

This was a qualitative interpretivist fieldwork project undertaken across 24 case-study institutions with the RG Directors of Strategy and Planning as the primary participants. The research data underlying the findings came from a workshop, from a questionnaire designed by the participant directors and a meeting with planners from each institution. The RG Planning Directors met in June 2015 to agree to the project, and some attended a workshop in September 2015 to share different working models, with the aim of bringing back to the wider peer group some benchmark role profiles and to develop case studies of the range of practice found within this planning community. This emergent exploratory phase led to the design of a forced-choice benchmarking questionnaire administered with consent from the group in December 2015. The survey examined the planning functions and processes at the institutional and faculty level and the relationship between the two. Results from the questionnaire were shared with the participant group in February 2016 to gain critical responses from those data subjects.

The first empirical outcome to note was even within a group of 22 institutions in the same nation-state (the UK) and mission group (the Russell Group) the SP function varied substantially, with no core functions held in common. They were located within the organisation differently, used planning processes that differed in nature and scope and the functions undertaken by SP in each university differed both by type and by depth of involvement.

All the UK Russell Group universities had a director or head of planning leading a department, which was similarly named. A range of titles was found in use, which included the following:

- Director of Strategy, Planning and Assurance;
- Director of Strategic Planning;
- Director of Planning;
- Head of Planning;
- Director of Planning and Resource Allocation;
- Director of Policy, Planning and Business Intelligence;
- Director of Strategy, Planning and Performance; and
- Director of Strategy, Planning and Governance.

In the preliminary workshop, the directors listed 20 activities in which at least one of them was primarily involved. In the survey questionnaire the group were then asked to score each activity saying whether this was for them a primary activity (Prime), one they shared with others (Shared), one to which they contributed (Contributory), one with which they were only remotely involved (Remote) or one in which they were not involved (NA). There were 22 responses to the questionnaire and 2 non-respondents. The initially listed 20 activities in which at least one of the group was involved was as follows:

- strategy formulation,
- business planning/planning round,
- student intake target setting,
- student fee policy/setting,
- planning or forecasting research income,
- planning or forecasting human resources,
- planning or forecasting capital or space requirements,
- making statutory returns,
- resource allocation model,
- performance monitoring/performance indicators,
- external competitor analysis/benchmarking,
- environmental scanning and assessing impact of HE policy,
- risk management,
- governance support/secretariat,

- internal audit,
- research management/research excellence,
- market research/surveys,
- data for decision support,
- project management and
- business cases or bids for new activity.

While this list represents a potential functional taxonomy, there was no single activity in the list of 20 for which every respondent planning director replied saying they held the prime responsibility that could then be used to distinguish or define them as a group (see Table 2.1). Nineteen of the 22 respondents said they had a primary role in internal performance monitoring through key performance indicators (however, 3 did not) and 16 had the primary responsibility to undertake external competitor analysis (but 6 did not.) Twelve had the primary responsibility for external statutory returns (eight did not). Such was the variation seen in the group that some directors had primary responsibility for activities in one university for which some of their peers had no involvement (for example market research surveys, governance support services and research management). Strategic planners in the UK Russell Group had no defining core function for which they all shared the primary responsibility. The diversity found within the group meant that there was no normative or 'right' way (HEFCE, 2000) to deliver strategy and planning, and that many variations existed on how SP was devised and delivered. This high level of variation had already been found in the writing of institutional strategic plans (Strike and Labbe, 2016).

Possibly the SP function in the UK was still evolving to a recognisable legitimised scope. All 20 functions described were done in every one of the 22 respondent universities, but they were not necessarily located together within the strategy and planning administrative unit or department. Table 2.2 below shows the RG SP survey results by activity and function.

University strategy

Supplementary questions were asked about the role of the RG planning director in producing the university strategy. Twenty-one of the 22 RG planning directors reported their university had an externally published university strategy. In one the planning director was the primary author, in another 13 the planning director co-ordinated or facilitated the development of strategy and the process of writing, in 6 cases the director contributed to the university strategy without a co-ordinating role and notably in 2 cases the planning director had little or no involvement in producing the university strategy.

The annual planning cycle

When it came to the annual planning cycle, 20 of the participant RG universities had an internal annual planning process (2 RG universities did not). Eighteen

Table 2.2 Responsibilities held by planning departments in UK Russell Group universities

Activity	Primary function	Shared function	Contributory function	Remote function	NA
Strategy formulation	7	7	8		
Business planning/planning round	15	5	1	1	
Student intake target setting	13	7	1	1	
Student fee policy/setting	5	10	3	3	1
Planning or forecasting research income	1	4	8	7	2
Planning or forecasting human resources		2	8	8	4
Planning or forecasting capital or space requirements	1	3	9	8	1
Statutory statistical returns	12	6	2	2	
Resource Allocation model	8	2	5	5	2
Performance monitoring/indicators	19	1	2		
External competitor analysis/benchmarking	16	5	1		
Horizon scanning/assessing impact of HE policy	12	8	2		
Risk management	10		7	4	1
Governance support/secretariat	5	2	5	4	6
Internal audit	1		4	6	11
Research management/REF	4	2	2	8	6
Market research/surveys	4	5	4	4	5
Data for decision support	8	10	3		1
Project management	6	3	4	5	4
Business cases or bids for new activity	2	4	11	4	1

directors co-ordinated their university's annual planning process (in one case as the primary decision maker), but notably two planning directors were contributors to the planning process without a co-ordinating role. With these two exceptions noted, the normative position was to have an annual planning process. This was in the majority of cases led by the vice-chancellor or deputy vice-chancellor or by a pro vice-chancellor with a planning brief. The director of planning in most cases both co-ordinated and contributed to the annual planning process.

The primary purposes of the annual planning process in 20 of these RG universities (see Table 2.3) were to set student number targets (in 17 cases but not in 3), to set budgets (in 14 cases but not in 6), to plan staffing (in 10 cases but not in 10) and to evaluate performance (in 10 cases but not in the other 10).

In relation to institutional performance indicators, the modal position was for the UK RG universities to have performance indicators (PIs), for performance to

Table 2.3 Different outputs from the annual planning cycle in UK Russell Group universities

Purpose of the planning process	Primary function	Shared function	Contributory function	Remote function	NA
Objective setting	6	5	4	2	3
Student intake targets	17	2	1		
Budget setting	14	4	2		
Staff planning	10	4	4	2	
Space planning	1	5	11	2	1
Initiating strategic projects	1	12	6	1	
Evaluation of strategy/performance review	10	4	3		3

be reported in relation to other institution's performance, for the indicators to be disaggregated to department/school level, for this activity to be co-ordinated through the planning director and for these PIs to be treated as complementary to (but separate from) financial monitoring. Three respondents of twenty-two said their university did not have performance indicators (PIs), two did have PIs but not to compare their own university's results with others and eight of the nineteen who had performance indicators said they were not co-ordinated through the planning function.

The findings from the UK RG survey may suggest either:

• The connections between university performance and SP functional practice are based on best-fit (contingency) and not best-practice (universal) approaches. The most effective SP policies and practices may depend on their match to the local university strategy, organisational structure and culture rather than to some more normative 'gold-standard' design benchmark for SP functions, or
• What was observed is an evolving function with different universities' SP functions performing at different levels of maturity in their functional scope, where it is possible to present the normative position to those who have not yet reached it as being an ideal type to which each should then aspire.

HESPA members' survey results

The same list of 20 activities as were used in the RG survey described above were then included in a questionnaire delivered through the website of the UK Higher Education Strategic Planners Association (HESPA). Again, respondents were asked to say whether their contribution was Prime, Contributory, Shared or Remote. HESPA has members working in strategy and planning roles who are not necessarily located in specialist strategy or planning teams.

After the data was cleaned, 90 individual responses were received to the HESPA member's survey from 74 individual institutions. Fifty responses came from individuals affirming their equivalence to the director of planning role.

A further 40 responses came from individuals representing a team which undertook some planning activities, but who were not the head of function. This provided a larger data set than provided by the RG survey.

This second survey sought to gain an initial indication of whether planning done by planning or strategy offices could be said to be distinctive across the sector from planning which is done by other teams. If it was, we might have expected to see planning teams and their directors making a consistently significant contribution to a distinctive set of the planning functions. Again, no respondent gave an identical response to another in rating their contribution to the 20 planning activities described. To try and assess the data, looking first at only the 16 institutions returning multiple responses to the survey, two rules were applied:

- The respondent's team title needed to include either 'Planning' or 'Strategy'.
- The planning director or team needed to have responded with Prime, Shared or Contributory (not Remote or NA) to the activity described.

Looking first at the 16 institutions returning multiple responses to the survey, the six activities all 'Planning' or 'Strategy' teams returned as Prime, Shared or Contributory were:

- strategy formulation,
- business planning/planning round,
- student intake target setting/modelling,
- external competitor analysis/benchmarking,
- decision support through reporting and
- to prepare business cases or bids for new activity.

Just one returned a 'Remote' response for the 'internal performance monitoring/indicators', its Student Records team returning a 'Contributory' response, so it typically sat with 'Planning' or 'Strategy' teams with this one exception and so arguably 'internal performance monitoring/indicators' could or should be added to the core functional list given above.

Similarly, just one returned a 'Remote' response for the 'horizon scanning/interpreting the impact of HE policy' activity, while its External Returns team also returned a 'Remote' response, so again it could be added to the list above (given only one exception).

Amongst the remaining 45 institutions that only made one institutional response and had 'Planning' or 'Strategy' in the team title, four activities were consistently returned as either Prime, Shared or Contributory:

- business planning/planning round,
- internal performance monitoring/indicators,
- external competitor analysis/benchmarking and
- decision support through reporting.

So they showed similar results to the institutions with multiple responses with three activities in common (or all four if we allow the two exceptions). Two teams returned a 'Remote' response for 'strategy formulation' and a different team returned a 'Remote' response for 'student intake target setting/modelling'. Four teams returned a 'Remote' response and four an 'NA' response for 'To prepare business cases or bids for new activity'.

In analysing only the directors' Prime responses, the most common grouping of remits combined together by the directors across the sector were:

- business planning/planning round,
- internal performance monitoring/indicators,
- external competitor analysis/benchmarking and
- student target setting/modelling.

Again, these show some overlap with the lists above if we permit the two exceptions.

Between 64%–74% of all responding directors claimed more than one of these remits as a Prime responsibility, and 54% claimed Prime responsibility for all four. If Shared responsibility were included, the figure increases to 86%. This begins to suggest a core set of functions, which are typically but not always present (which in some cases are reinforced by the RG survey). It is possible to infer from these commonalities that those SP teams which do not have these functions in their core list are outliers from an identifiable normative position.

Across the total 90 responses from planning directors and all responding teams, we might have expected minimal gaps in the responsibilities across these remits. One hundred per cent of directors and 80% of teams identified themselves as having Prime or Shared responsibility for internal performance monitoring/ indicators. But gaps begin to appear after that, with 98% of directors claiming Prime or Shared responsibility for the business planning round, and 96% claiming responsibility for student target setting. Eighteen per cent aren't responsible for horizon scanning and 28% aren't responsible for strategy formulation. Thirty per cent aren't responsible for market research and surveys, only 50% are responsible for preparing business cases for new activities and only 26% are responsible for internal audits. So gaps quickly appear.

It is clear that activities defined in some institutions as planning in some other institutions fell under the responsibility of other roles, which the HESPA survey did not reach. We can say things are located differently in different organisations, but we are not yet at the stage of having comprehensively mapped the full spread of locations for the 'Prime' and 'Shared' responsibility for these activities across the UK sector.

A derivative of 'Planning' was included in the team title of 66 respondents, and 25 included a derivative of 'Strategy'. Twenty-one teams responding included no reference to either 'Planning' or 'Strategy' in their team title. The next most common derivative team title, with 17 incidences, was 'Business Intelligence/Data

Analysis'. All other multiple derivatives were in single figures, with 9 incidences of 'Policy' the most common, and a further 10 derivatives including: 'Change' (3), 'Compliance' (3), 'Corporate' (3), 'Faculty' (2), 'Finance' (5), 'Governance' (5), 'Performance' (7), 'Projects' (4), 'Returns' (2) and 'Student Records' (2).

Directors and teams without 'Planning' or 'Strategy' derivatives in their team titles were still significantly involved across the planning activities. Between the 17 teams without 'Planning' or 'Strategy' in the title, only 'Fee Setting' and 'Project Management' failed to register a Prime, Shared or Contributory response. 'Fee Setting' was amongst the least common activities across those without 'Planning' or 'Strategy'.

Australian Network of University Planners' survey results

An international comparison point for both the UK Russell Group and UK HESPA member surveys is a similar survey conducted in Australia amongst directors of planning in Australian universities (i.e. members of the Australian Network of University Planners or 'ANUP'). The planning unit of the Australian National University (ANU) administered the survey. Similar to the UK surveys, the Australian survey aimed at benchmarking the functions, location and size of central planning units across all of the universities attracting funding from the Australian government. The survey was conducted through a short forced-choice questionnaire administered in April–May 2015. Twenty-four functions were included in the questionnaire. (Unlike the UK surveys, the choice was dichotomous – i.e. 'yes' or 'no'.) There were 29 respondents to the survey, with around a 75% response rate amongst ANUP members. Only one response per university was allowed.

While again all respondents had a central planning unit, as in the UK the name of the unit varied considerably. Most (21) had the term 'planning' in the title and a third had 'strategy' or 'strategic'. Other common terms were 'quality', 'performance', 'information' and 'intelligence'. There was also great variability in where the planning unit was situated within the university, with the three most common reporting arrangements being to the chief operating officer (COO) or equivalent, the deputy vice-chancellor (DVC) or equivalent or directly to the vice-chancellor. Resourcing of units in terms of full-time equivalent staff varied considerably, but with a modal position of a third reporting 16–20 staff and almost another third reporting 11–15 staff.

Looking at the results for functions undertaken by each planning unit in Australia, only one function was noted as being undertaken by almost all units (97%): key performance indicator management (HESPA survey cross reference: performance measurement/KPIs). Five functions were noted as being undertaken by a high majority of units (79%–86%):

- business intelligence (HESPA cross ref: management information),
- university strategic planning (HESPA cross ref: strategy formulation),
- student load planning (HESPA cross ref: student intake target setting/ modelling),

- support for local planning at faculty and unit levels (HESPA cross ref: business planning/planning round) and
- National Survey Administration (QILT Surveys) (HESPA cross ref: surveys including NSS etc.).

Following this grouping were another four functions undertaken by a slightly smaller majority of Australian planning units (69%):

- government student submissions (HESPA cross ref: statistical returns to HESA etc.),
- data warehousing,
- other student surveys (e.g. internal surveys) and
- university rankings (HESPA cross ref: league tables).

Three other functions were undertaken by around 60% of respondents (advanced analytics – 66%; subject/unit/teaching evaluations – 62%; and statutory annual reports – 59%).

These results established that most but not all strategy and planning teams in Australian universities undertake a common core of functions around internal performance monitoring/KPIs, business planning/planning round, business intelligence, student load planning (i.e. student target setting/modelling) and (student and graduate) survey administration. Most units undertake a range of additional functions; however, the combination of these functions varies. All but four of the units participating in the Australian survey undertook at least 9 of the 24 functions listed in the ANUP questionnaire, with the median scope of activity across all participating units being 15 functions.

Findings

In summary, the results collected from the surveys suggested there was a small core of activities that consistently commonly sat firmly within the remit of the typical strategy or planning director or their team. These might most commonly include business planning/planning round, external competitor analysis/benchmarking and internal performance monitoring/indicators. So it would appear to be the case that if the SP function was born of a need to satisfy external statutory, regulatory or reporting requirements, it had as hypothesised moved beyond or expanded on those external statistical reporting functions. A core set of functions exists which commonly sat with SP functions, and those SP units without them were outliers. The location of the rest of the activities listed in the SP taxonomy were more unpredictable, and even for the core, other teams regularly made significant contributions. The obvious conclusion was that strategic planners were not neatly confined to functional teams or roles with 'Planning' or 'Strategy' in the title and nor did they consistently own a set of functions that neatly bound or identified them.

Direct comparisons between the results of the Russell Group and HESPA surveys and the Australian ANUP survey have to be made cautiously given the different functional listings used and the different jurisdictional contexts. Comparing the UK Russell Group results with the Australian results is more problematic because the Australian survey included all Australian universities, not just the research-intensive universities (which are more directly comparable to Russell Group members). However, some meaningful comparisons can be made between the two jurisdictions. First, it is clear there is almost a universal focus on internal performance monitoring for the planning units in both countries. Second, the functions of student intake target setting and the business planning/planning round are also core to the planning units in both countries. Third, most planning units in both countries also undertake strategy formulation and co-ordinate participation in (national student) surveys. Finally, while the independent design of each benchmarking survey precludes a conclusive finding, there are indications that the variation in functional responsibility across planning units in the UK is higher than that in Australia. Whether this is simply a function of the greater number of universities in the UK or due to other factors is unclear at this point. There is potential to explore this further through future independent and collaborative benchmarking activities.

The findings set out above are consistent with those from a national survey of institutional research offices conducted in the US for the Association for Institutional Research (Swing, Jones and Ross, 2016). That survey 'confirmed much of what was already believed about institutional research; there are vast differences in IR capacity and organisational arrangements that are idiosyncratic to individual colleges and universities.' Given these differences, in that study an attempt was made to produce three archetypes or 'personalities' for institutional research offices, which were classified as 'Broad', 'Focussed' and 'Limited Responsibility'. Volkwein (2008) had earlier suggested a different taxonomy involving 'craft structures', 'small adhocracies', 'professional bureaucracies' and 'elaborate profusion'. It is certainly clear that the functional array differs, which means the staff count also differs. The size of the strategic planning team can vary from one to three individuals through to departments with greater than thirty staff. When looking at the data, one has to decide whether one is observing contingent diversity, chaos or seeking to impose order; whether the function being observed is still maturing or is highly adaptive to changing conditions.

A smaller planning department in the UK sector (with < 10 staff) may have an internal structure which reflects the shorter list of functions which are found commonly in the functional scope of most planning offices. For example, where the planning function deals with the business planning/planning round and related to that with student target setting/modelling and is also responsible for internal performance monitoring/indicators and external competitor analysis/benchmarking. In this more limited activity list, it may have a structure as shown in Figure 2.1.

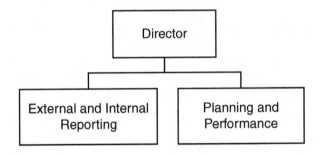

Figure 2.1 Craft structure of a smaller planning office

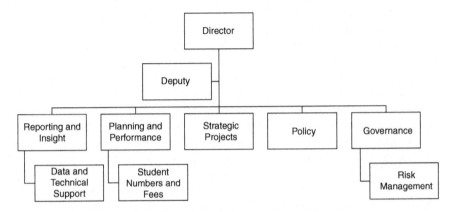

Figure 2.2 Professional structure of a larger strategy and planning office

A larger strategy and planning function in the UK sector (with > 20 staff) may have an internal structure which reflects the wider range of functions found in most but not all planning offices. This larger professional bureaucracy may have a structure as shown in Figure 2.2.

Concluding remarks

It is argued here that strategic planning as a function is adapting to the changing demands from academic leaders, as they shape and discover what strategic planners can offer them, so the function itself is changing and adapting.

This would mean the strategic planning function must regularly seek feedback from stakeholders about its scope of work and its effectiveness and be willing to flex, change and adapt in scope and function. The diversity found around a common core of activities may be evidence of exactly that shaping and flexibility to local and changing demands. Strategic planning as a function should do all it can within the constraints imposed on it to deliver clarity and transparency about institutional performance, strategic intent and sought outcomes.

Because of the relatively stable past environment, planning in HEIs may have been of secondary importance to other functions. Planning staff were seen and perhaps saw themselves as a group of analysts, data modellers and possibly generalist administrators. For senior leaders to plan effectively in a changing environment, they may increasingly look for a more professionalised strategic planning function to support and aid those in leadership roles. The responses described here show many institutions have appointed directors of strategy (instead of or as well as heads of planning).

However, in adopting a functional map or an organizational model for SP (or IR), the danger is to believe it is a function, which is or can be functionally defined and bounded, or that there is a 'one size fits all' solution or a maturity model along which different forms of SP organisation can be placed and assessed. In a changing situation, these attempts at definition may be a mistake, or at least premature, as the function cannot freeze or predict how it might evolve. We can look for one model or a set of models that meet all universities' needs by seeking to examine external common practice to decide what to apply elsewhere. The Association for Institutional Research in the USA, for example, published a 'Statement of Aspirational Practice for Institutional Research' (Swing and Ross, 2016), which attempted to offer a prescription for building and supporting an institutional research function. This suggested that the function of SP (or IR) could be bounded and described and was maturing in an agreed and unified direction.

The problem with this and similar guides is that every university faces a unique set of challenges and has its own history and culture, different levels of functional maturity and differing ideas about strategy. Just as strategy is contingent, so the SP and IR functions in each place may be highly contingent. It may precisely be the core identifying strength of the strategic planning (or IR) function that it is unbounded, agile and adaptable to local priorities, design and requirements.

Each university needs to look at its own context and develop an SP model that meets its own challenges. Describing a normative scope of work or an ideal organisation structure that would work for any type of university SP (or IR) function would, based on this interpretation of the results, be meaningless and temporary. The highly contingent approach seen here could, though, create a lack of clarity about what SP's (or IR's) role actually is. It is possible to conclude that the wide variety of roles allocated to SP offices means the role of SP is unclear; that what could or should be done in SP (or located elsewhere) could be a matter of dispute and that, therefore, the identity of the function is problematic.

Given universities in the UK and Australia all have an SP (or IR) function and most but not all locate a core of related activities with that function means it is clearly serving an identifiable purpose in each place. Local pragmatism is creating a function which varies in size and scope, beyond the core, and that is creating different forms of SP office. Or to put it another way, there is no one way to be a strategic planner. The survey activity reported on here provides a menu of activities which could be and are being located together in strategy and planning units but which do not have to be. This presents those who design the scope and structure of university professional services with some clear choices, whether to locate all or some of the activities described in the above taxonomy together in SP (or not). The way the function is constructed could facilitate or constrain the different elements. This flexible approach ensures that there is a clear rationale for the proposed scope of the SP function and that this is not a standardised model which SP (or IR) tries to foist on any particular university. It may be that the strength and uniqueness of strategy and planning lies in its not being precisely functionally bounded.

If it is the case that what is observed is functional adaptability rather than immaturity, then the link between strategy, organisational scope and structure needs further research to make the institutional-level causality between strategy, structure and function more evident. If what is observed is a function on the move in a single more unified direction, which will see it become more similar and coherent through time, then further research will help identify the direction of travel to answer the question: What will the SP (or IR) function in HE look like in the future?

References

Ansoff, H.I. (1979) *Strategic Management*, Basingstoke: Palgrave Macmillan.

Deem, R., Hillyard, S., & Reed, M. (2007) *Knowledge, Higher Education and the New Managerialism: The Changing Management of UK Universities*, Oxford: Oxford University Press.

Dressel, P.L. (1981) The shaping of institutional research and planning. *Research in Higher Education*, 14, pp. 229–258.

Drucker, P.F. (1999) *Managing for Results*, Abingdon: Routledge.

Higher Education Funding Council for England (HEFCE) (2000) Strategic Planning in the HE Sector: A Guide for Governors, Heads of Institutions and Senior Managers, Ref: 00/24, Bristol: HEFCE.

Middaugh, M.F. (1990) The Nature and Scope of Institutional Research. In J.B. Presley (Ed.) Organizing Effective Institutional Research Offices, *New Directions for Institutional Research*, No. 66 (pp. 35–48), San Francisco: Jossey-Bass.

Mintzberg, H. Ahlstrand, B., & Lampel, J. (2005) *Strategy Bites Back: It Is Far More, and Less, Than You Ever Imagined*, New Jersey: Pearson Prentice Hall.

Porter, M. (2002) *Competitive Strategy: Techniques for Analyzing Industries and Competitors*, New York: Free Press.

Presley J.B. (1990) Putting the building blocks into place for effective institutional research. In P.T. Terenzini and E.E. Chaffee (series eds.) and J.B. Presley (vol. ed.), *New Directions for Institutional Research: No. 66. Organizing Effective Institutional Research Offices* (pp. 103–106). San Francisco: Jossey-Bass.

Saupe, J.L. (1990) The Functions of Institutional Research. Association of Institutional Research, Tallahassee, Florida. Retrieved 12/08/2016 from http://files.eric.ed.gov/fulltext/ED319327.pdf.

Steering Committee for Efficiency Studies in Universities (Chairman Sir Alex Jarratt). Report. London CVCP, 1985.

Strike, T., & Labbe, J. (2016) Exploding the Myth: Literary Analysis of Universities' Strategic Plans. In R. Pritchard, A. Pausits, & J. Williams (Eds.) *Positioning Higher Education Institutions: from here to there* (pp. 125–140), Rotterdam: Sense Publishers.

Swing, R.L., Jones, D., and Ross, L.E. (2016) The AIR National Survey of Institutional Research Offices. Association for Institutional Research, Tallahassee, Florida. Retrieved 13/07/2016 from www.airweb.org/nationalsurvey.

Swing, R.L., and Ross, L.E. (2016) Statement of Aspirational Practice for Institutional Research. Association for Institutional Research, Tallahassee, Florida. Retrieved 13/07/2016 from www.airweb.org/Resources/ImprovingAndTransformingPost secondaryEducation/Documents/Statement%20of%20Aspirational%20Practice%20for%20IR%20Report.pdf.

Terenzini, P.T. (1993) On the nature of institutional research and the knowledge and skills it requires, *Research in Higher Education*, 34, pp. 1–10.

Tight, M. (2012) Higher education research 2000–2010: Changing journal publication patterns, *Higher Education Research & Development*, 31(5), pp. 723–740.

Ulrich, D. (1997) *Human Resource Champions: The Next Agenda for Adding Value and Delivering Results*, Boston: Harvard Business School Press.

Volkwein. J.F. (1999) The four faces of institutional research. In J.F. Volkwein (Ed.) *What Is Institutional Research All About? A Critical and Comparative Assessment of the Profession* (pp. 9–19). New Directions for Institutional Research, no. 104. San Francisco: Jossey-Bass.

Volkwein. J.F. (2008) The foundations and evolution of institutional research. In D. Terkla (Ed.) *Institutional Research: More Than Just Data* (pp. 5–20). New Directions for Higher Education, no. 141. San Francisco: Jossey-Bass.

Watson, D. (2000) *Managing Strategy*, Buckingham: Open University Press.

Whitchurch, C., & Gordon, G. (2011) Some implications of a diversifying workforce for governance and management, *Tertiary Education and Management*, 17(1), pp. 65–77.

Chapter 3

Developing institutional strategy

John Pritchard

Introduction

The focus of this chapter is on the role of the strategic planner in enabling the development of a new or substantively revised institutional strategy. The aim is to provide an overview of approaches, principles and examples that will be helpful in undertaking this role. The chapter emphasises the importance of enabling effective strategic thinking, and the active engagement of stakeholders.

Although the primary focus is on the development of an overarching institution-wide strategy, the content is also intended to be useful to those involved in enabling the development of specific strategies such as those relating to research, education, the student experience, support operations or estates.

The chapter begins with an appraisal of what constitutes institutional strategy with reference to relevant texts. The subsequent section complements this overview by setting out a framework which summarises the main elements of strategic thinking in a higher education context. The main section of the chapter comprises of a digest of ten principles which are presented as signposts to guide those embarking on the strategy development journey. This section sets out a series of practical approaches and examples which will add value in managing the strategy development process. The chapter concludes with a brief reflection on the implications of strategy development and on the changing role of strategic planners.

Understanding strategy

Developing an effective institutional strategy is a qualitatively different undertaking to simply producing a new strategic plan document. In itself, the production of a published strategic plan will not provide the basis for achieving aspirational aims or securing sustained improvements in institutional performance. Although this may seem self-evident, it is surprising how frequently the former is seen as synonymous with the latter. The publication of a strategic plan should be seen as one output which arises from a much more fundamental process of strategic thinking and engagement which goes to the very heart of how a university is configured, developed and managed.

The question of what constitutes an institutional strategy is a basic and fundamental one which strategic planners must consider. Fumasoli and Lepori (2011) have observed that 'strategy' is a contentious issue in higher education literature. The application of the term in everyday university life is also not without complication or ambiguity. There may be a number of contextual reasons for this, but it is also the case that the term 'strategy' is frequently used loosely without sufficient reflection on what it actually entails. The psychologist Kurt Lewin once remarked that 'there is nothing as practical as a good theory' (in Dwivedi et al., 2009). Experience suggests that in relation to higher education strategy, a little bit of organisational theory, if applied thoughtfully, can go a long way. The potential range of theories can be daunting, so in this section a few key insights are highlighted.

Strategy and planning are distinct

Planning can be characterised as a detached, formal and analytical approach to achieving a desired future. Mintzberg (1994) argues that while planning fulfils a useful institutional function, it is fundamentally different to the capabilities required to enable the strategy development process itself, which is seen as more emergent, creative and multi-faceted. Similarly, McKeown (2012) highlights the vital importance of engaging in creative and critical thinking before embarking on the more routine activities of planning and scheduling. This way of thinking and acting opens up a much broader range of perspectives than in the analytical tradition which has perhaps typically characterised the strategic planning profession in UK higher education.

By taking account of the political, psychological and cultural dimensions of institutional strategy, strategic planners can develop a wider role as influential university change agents. The importance of these 'softer' dimensions of strategy are highlighted by Shattock (2010) in his discussion of university management. Strategic planners are urged to read, for example, Mintzberg et al. (1998) to gain a deeper insight into the implications of the distinction between planning and strategy for their roles.

Strategy functions at many levels

Strategy is concerned with an organisation's overall scope, how it will compete, and operationally how corporate and business-level strategies are delivered. Johnson et al. (2014), for example, set out a three-tiered strategy model which can be easily adapted and used when working in a university context. He describes that:

- Strategic position is concerned with the impact on strategy of the external environment, the organisation's goals, culture and resources and capabilities.
- Strategic choices are concerned with the directions in which strategy might move and the methods by which strategy might be pursued.

- Strategy in action is about how strategies are formed and how they are implemented.

Conceptualising strategy in these ways can provide a useful working framework for the strategic planner, and the practical value of the strategy in action dimension is illustrated later in this chapter.

Johnson et al. (2014) also highlight the important relationship between institutional strategy and culture. The 'cultural web' is a conceptual yet highly practical model which can be used to explore how different elements of an institution's culture (stories, symbols, power structures, organisational structures, control systems and rituals and routines) impact on university strategy.

Strategy is about establishing insight and a coherent grounded response

Strategy is often an overused and poorly defined term in universities and other organisations. A common misapprehension is that strategy is about big-picture overall direction, divorced from any specific action. All too frequently, strategies are defined simply in terms of an aspiration to be excellent or world class.

In contrast, Rumelt (2012) maintains that there are three essential elements of an effective strategy: an insightful diagnosis of the fundamental challenges which an organisation faces in a competitive environment, a clear guiding policy to address these challenges, and a coherent and appropriately resourced action plan. Failure to pay sufficient attention to each of these three dimensions dramatically increases the chances of failure. Conversely, choosing to dedicate sufficient time in all three aspects, particularly in determining coherent guiding policies and practical actions, will significantly increase the likelihood that the strategy and its implementation will be successful.

Strategy is about choices and positioning

The environment in which higher education institutions operate has changed fundamentally over the last ten years. The context in which institutions find themselves is highly competitive, and in a context of competing demands and constrained resources, fundamental choices have to be made (see Chapter 1). In this context, strategy may been seen as a process which addresses a number of deceptively simple questions:

- Where are we now?
- What do we want to do?
- What do we think is possible?
- What do we need to do to achieve our goals?
- When should we react to new opportunities and adapt our plans?

McKeown (2012) discusses a range of issues and techniques which are likely to be helpful in addressing such questions.

Strategy is about organisational change

Strategy is fundamentally about securing desired changes in organisational outcomes. As such, the processes by which people engage in organisational change are a defining characteristic of the strategy process. However, such outcomes are unlikely to be realised unless careful thought is given to the processes by which people are engaged in the strategy process and how they experience organisational change. Understanding the psychological and emotional dynamics associated with strategic change and being able to navigate the associated micro politics are essential prerequisites for successful strategy development. The work of authors such as Quirke (2012) and Hodges (2016) will be helpful to strategic planners, especially in facilitating dialogue in relation to contentious issues of critical institutional significance.

Thinking strategically

Strategy development is primarily about thinking strategically. Strategic planners have an important role to play in helping institutional leaders and colleagues across the institution to develop this capability. Arguably, the most strategic action which strategic planners can take is to encourage colleagues to reevaluate their assumptions and think more deeply and systematically about the challenges facing the institutions in which they work. Effective strategic thinking opens up new possibilities and provides clarity in relation to those options which should be prioritised or rejected (Rhodes in Garratt, 2003). The resources identified above and in the main sections of this chapter provide a rich framework for thinking strategically and offer a range of approaches which can be adapted to meet specific challenges.

Elverson (2014) maintains that thinking strategically is essentially a matter of thinking 'big, deep and long'. Adapting this formulation for a higher education setting, some of the main dimensions of strategic thinking can be understood through the articulation of a number of key questions. These are set out in Table 3.1.

A defining characteristic of this type of thinking is the capacity to identify and evaluate a range of possible but plausible scenarios. This requires the ability to tolerate a high level of ambiguity and uncertainty. Part of the skill of the strategic planner in this context is to help colleagues accept this uncertainty as an integral characteristic of the process so that potential options are not dismissed prematurely. Table 3.2 presents a categorisation of uncertainty associated with potential scenarios which may be useful in this respect.

A number of sophisticated methods for undertaking scenario planning are available, such as the online guide to scenario planning produced by the government's

Table 3.1 Dimensions of strategic thinking

Dimension	Critical questions
Big	• How does the university interact with other HEIs, organisations in other sectors and the wider external environment? • How do students, academic staff in other HEIs and external stakeholders perceive the university? • What are the critical challenges in the competitive and funding environment for the sector?
Deep	• Is there a need to review the mission and values of the university? • How can we think more deeply about the fundamental ways in which the university is operating? • What are the unspoken assumptions regarding the university's processes, structures and culture? • Is the university operating on the basis of an interpretation of the past, or in anticipation of the future?
Long	• How far into the future are we looking? Do we need to look further ahead? • What are the long-term trends or events which could disrupt the positioning and sustainability of the university? • What are the alternative futures for the university? • What is the long-term vision for the university?

Adapted from Elverson (2014).

Table 3.2 Levels of uncertainty

Low uncertainty. Future outcomes are relatively predictable.	Limited set of possible future outcomes, one of which will occur.
Outcomes indeterminate, but bounded in a range.	A limitless range of possible outcomes. Highest level of uncertainty.

Adapted from Gordon (2008).

Horizon Scanning Centre. Nevertheless, higher education strategic planners should not be afraid to support more straightforward forms of scenario thinking. Simply asking 'what if?' questions in relation to the operating environment can add significant value. Indeed, the value of such thinking about possible scenarios or alternative futures is underlined by the extent to which many UK HE institutions and other organisations were unprepared in advance for the outcome of the EU referendum. Greater use of scenario thinking would have prompted useful contingency planning in relation to short-term operational matters, as well as deeper reflection on strategic issues concerning local, regional and international engagement. Such short-term and long-term benefits are typical of effective scenario thinking.

Finally, in thinking as a strategic planner, the following reflection may be helpful:

> To think like a strategic planner is to see possibilities that can be shaped into situations that are desirable. You have to be able to notice what is happening

around you. You should be able to notice historic trends that open up new opportunities and you need to be able to play a kind of multi-dimensional chess, imagining several moves ahead what your next move should be now. . . . Skilled strategists accept the world is complex and still figure out what to do now to shape events.

McKeown (2012, p. 25)

Navigating the territory

There is no simple map or guide that will ensure that the strategic planner is able to successfully navigate the unpredictable currents of institutional strategy. Nevertheless, those embarking on this journey may find it useful to consider the following suggestions as helpful signposts. The ten guidelines which are set out below are based on the author's personal experience in developing strategies in a variety of institutional settings. They are also informed by the good practice discussions which took place at an inaugural meeting of the HESPA Strategy Network in June 2016.

Develop close working relationships with senior leaders

The role of the strategic planner is not to determine institutional strategies but to act as a critical enabler and facilitator. Strategies must be led by vice-chancellors, presidents or principals and their senior teams, with the council or board of governors having ultimate responsibility for setting the strategic direction of the university. It is therefore imperative to establish close working relationships with institutional leaders from the outset (see Chapter 7). This requires the strategic planner to establish himself or herself as a trusted individual who is able support the co-ordination of the strategy process, enable an evidence-based approach and, where appropriate, act as a critical friend in highlighting potential pitfalls and weaknesses of proposed approaches. Demonstrating an awareness of good practice, a sensitivity to institutional politics and a constructive pragmatic approach are key qualities in this respect.

Engage and communicate

At all stages of the strategy development process, it is important to think about engaging with relevant individuals, groups and organisations. One of the most effective ways in which to do this is to undertake a systematic stakeholder analysis. If strategies are to be successful, those leading and supporting them need to know who is going to be affected, who is going to be influential and who needs to be involved. As Hodges (2016) emphasises, the ability to categorise and understand the needs of stakeholders is crucial in this respect. The benefits of understanding stakeholder needs in a systematic way are summarised in Table 3.3.

Table 3.3 The needs of stakeholders

Strategy benefit	Approach
Buy-in	Strategy leaders and managers can use the opinions of the stakeholders to shape strategies at an early stage, thereby increasing the level of support from the outset.
Quality of strategic thinking	Engagement of stakeholders, including those with influence and those who might otherwise be overlooked, can increase the actual quality of the strategies.
Anticipation of issues	By communicating with stakeholders early and frequently, strategy leaders can anticipate what people's reaction to the proposed strategy might be, and build into their strategies the actions that will increase the likelihood of support.
Resources	Gaining support from powerful stakeholders (both internal and external to the university) can help to win more resources to enable the implementation of the strategy.

Adapted from Hodges (2016, p. 172).

Consistent with the approach advocated by Hodges, there are three main steps in undertaking a strategy stakeholder analysis.

1   Identify key stakeholders (perhaps through a group exercise)

- Who will be affected by this strategy?
- Who will be responsible for making it happen?
- Who will be accountable for it?
- Who will benefit from the potential changes?
- Who can influence the strategy?

2   Analyse stakeholders

- How much influence do they have to shape or block the strategy?
- What is their interest in the strategy and expected changes?
- How supportive are they likely to be?
- What is their experience of the consequences of the strategy likely to be?

3   Manage stakeholders

The final stage is to evaluate the answers to the above questions to determine the nature and extent of engagement with stakeholders that should take place. The templates in Tables 3.4 and 3.5 may be useful in this respect.

It is recommended that the overarching stakeholder analysis is complemented by a detailed assessment of any aspect of the strategy process which is likely to have a major bearing on the student and staff experience, resources or external reputation. It is good practice for stakeholder analysis and action plans to be reviewed and updated throughout the strategy development and implementation process.

Table 3.4 Stakeholder analysis templates

Individual or team	Role in strategy process (i.e. leader, influencer, participant)	Level of impact (i.e. degree to which strategy may affect them)	Degree of likely support (high/medium/ low)	Level of influ-ence (high/ medium/low)	Issues/ reasons

Table 3.5 Stakeholder action planning template

Stakeholder	Role	Action	Action category	Action owner	Timing	Performance measures	Feedback
Stakeholder 1							
Stakeholder 2							
Stakeholder 3							

Staff	Students	Governance	External
• 4,700 academic and non-academic staff in 13 locations across the four UK nations • 5,600 Associate Lecturers (ALs) all across the UK	• 138,000 students (headcount) 67,000 (FTEs). • Located across the four nations of the UK, in the EU and outside the EU	• Senate • Strategic Planning and Resources Committee • Council	• Funding bodies in the four nations of the UK • Commercial partners • Employers
Engaged through • Online discussion forums (Yammer, IdeaScale) • Senior team workshops • Supported discussions in each unit • Cross-university workshops • Associate Lecturer webinars and discussions with the AL Executive and AL Assembly	**Engaged through** • Online student consultative forum • Discussion with the OU Students Association • Students attending cross-university workshops	**Engaged through** • Formal meetings • Workshops • Discussions with individuals or small groups of members	**Engaged through** • Discussion event with a range of partners, funders, employers and other stakeholders

Figure 3.1 Modes of strategy engagement at The Open University
Case study diagram: Anna Barber, The Open University

Once stakeholders have been identified, the process and channels of engagement can be determined. The approach adopted by The Open University is an example of good practice in this respect. During 2015/16, The Open University developed its new strategic plan, 'Students First: Strategy for Growth'. The key characteristic of the strategy process was the focus of the new vice-chancellor on extensive stakeholder engagement in all stages of development. The different approaches to engagement are illustrated in Figure 3.1.

Staff in communications and external relations departments can be productively engaged in the strategy process from the outset so that they may provide professional advice on wider aspects of internal and external communications. In this respect it may be useful to consider appointing a member of the communications team to support the strategy process on a dedicated basis.

Specific communication and engagement tools which may also be useful are:

- the use of workshops, small group discussions, professionally facilitated meetings and world café discussions to open up dialogue and prompt new thinking across the institution (see Weisbord and Janoff [2007] and www.theworldcafe.com);
- the use of a strategy development intranet site;
- regular town hall meetings to provide opportunities for updates and discussion;
- managed consultation processes on key elements of the strategy;
- email updates and rolling responses to 'frequently asked questions'; and
- the use of a 'strategy on a page' diagram which summarises the main areas of the strategy, implementation priorities and the relationship between the various elements.

Define work streams

Most strategy development processes entail the management of a complex array of competing imperatives. One practical step that can be undertaken at the start of the process is to work with institutional leaders to define the key areas of work which will be undertaken.

It will be helpful to define each work stream in the following specific terms:

- the main challenges and imperatives which are to be addressed;
- the required deliverables (typically a strategy statement which addresses agreed priorities);
- leadership and operational management responsibilities; and
- reporting timescales.

It will be useful for the definition of these work streams to be undertaken in a systematic way and for particular consideration to be given the interrelated dimensions of each work stream.

Establish active governance and management

The strategy development process should be managed actively by those with primary leadership responsibility and overseen as a co-ordinated programme of development. It will be important for the established governance and committee structures to be engaged fully (see Chapter 7). This will require close liaison with governance/secretariat services to ensure that an appropriate schedule of committee dates is established for the year ahead, with a clear set of expectations regarding the level of involvement, consultation and decision making expected at each stage of the process.

Particular consideration should be given to the contrasting roles and requirements of different committees and constituencies. This may include considering the potential to hold joint meetings on major areas of development (e.g. a joint council/governing body and senate/academic board meeting). One particular approach which can add value is to convene special meetings which make use of workshops and small group discussions in order to allow individuals from across the institution to discuss critical issues in depth.

An iterative process of development, such that draft proposals and strategy papers are presented prior to the presentation of formal strategy documents for approval, can help achieve greater understanding and ownership.

Effective engagement with the main governing committee structure can usefully be complemented by the establishment of a small co-ordinating strategy development group or programme board. Typically this would be chaired by the vice-chancellor, principal or president and would comprise a small number of senior staff such as the deputy vice-chancellor, director of finance, the director of communications, registrar or chief operating officer and members of the strategic planning office. This group should meet regularly to ensure that all work streams are on track and to review drafts of the strategy.

Another approach is to establish a parallel process of internal business assurance. Such a process offers the opportunity to identify risks and assumptions which might otherwise be overlooked, thereby providing a welcome degree of confidence to the overall integrity and robustness of the strategy process. In all aspects of strategy development and implementation, it is helpful to establish clear lines of accountability and to be rigorous in communicating and managing the associated timescales.

Develop a strong evidence base

One of the great strengths of the strategic planners is their capacity to support effective evidence-based decision making with information and analysis (see Chapter 11). The opportunity to play an active role in the wider strategy process therefore provides an ideal basis upon which strategic planners can demonstrate the added value and insight which they are able to offer.

University strategies should always be underpinned by a robust evidence base and will be enhanced significantly by the insights derived from the skilful deployment of analytical techniques. Evidence regarding the competitive environment, the strategies and approaches of comparator institutions, changing patterns of student demand, the academic labour market, the higher education funding environment and the wider operating environment can, for example, be analysed.

One specific approach that is likely to be useful in this context is to establish a peer set of national and/or international institutions for benchmarking purposes. The approach taken by these institutions can then be reviewed in relation to each strategy area. This will help to ensure that the strategy process is externally orientated, informed by good practice and open to innovation. The responsibility for establishing an appropriate evidence base can rest with named strategy leads. The strategic planning team can play a useful role in developing a set of peer institutions, commissioning additional analyses (it may be appropriate for some comparator work to be undertaken by research students), and in undertaking specific elements of the benchmarking or analysis.

Determine priorities

Developing effective strategy is also about prioritisation and choices. The ability to prioritise one aim over another, allocate resources in one part of a university in preference to another or to decide to follow a particular implementation approach in relation to many others which might have been considered is crucial. There can be an inherent tendency in the strategy process to rush the process of evaluation and prioritisation in order to quickly confirm the best way forward. Quite often this initial 'best way forward' will not have been considered fully and is likely to reinforce established ways of working or the personal preferences of particular influential individuals. More specifically, initial best ways forward may not have taken due account of:

- the key institutional imperatives and challenges which need to be addressed;
- the range of options or implementation approaches which might be considered to address the key imperatives; and
- the feasibility, affordability and risks associated with the proposed approach to strategy implementation.

The strategic planner can play a valuable role in encouraging institutional leaders and others to take a systematic approach when determining priorities. The strategic planner can act as a critical friend to seek assurance in relation to the questions arising from each of the above dimensions:

- Is there clarity on the appropriate institutional imperatives and wider challenges that should be addressed? Have some imperatives been overlooked? Are we focusing too much on the established way of working and neglecting new challenges in the sector?
- What other options and implementation approaches might be considered? What are other institutions doing? What constitutes good practice in this area?
- What are the practical implementation issues which need to be anticipated in prioritising this particular option? What are the direct and indirect costs associated with this option? Are there hidden risks? What should our risk appetite be in this context – are we being too risk averse?

Addressing such questions is broadly consistent with the approach identified by Rumelt (2012). This is likely to call for an assertive approach on the part of the strategic planner and require techniques for influencing people (Gardner, 2006).

However, a determined approach to seeking assurance on these questions is time well spent and will significantly strengthen the effectiveness of the strategy.

A complementary approach to strategic prioritisation which may also be helpful is that advocated by Wright (2001). The suggested approach is discussed in some detail by Wright in his chapter 'How to Make Trade-offs', but may be summarised as follows:

- Identify the choice alternatives.
- Identify the criteria relevant to the decision.
- Weight the criteria.
- Assess each choice alternative in relation to the criteria.
- Review scores for each alternative.

Such an approach may be readily utilised to determine priorities in relation to the development of education and research portfolios.

Align strategies

One of the most challenging aspects of the development process is to ensure coherence across all elements of strategy. The likelihood of developing a coherent strategy will be greatly increased if component strategies are developed in the context of a clear, compelling and unified vision for the future development of the university. Nevertheless, there is a need to actively manage the process of strategy alignment at all stages of the development process. The strategic planner can help in the following ways:

- Encourage strategy leads to consider the implications of their proposals on other areas throughout the process (e.g. the relationship and mutual dependencies between research and education strategies, the implications of the estate strategy for financial sustainability and vice versa). The main implications can be summarised in the relevant section of the strategy document.
- Review individual strategies to identify areas which are repeatedly identified as key areas for development. There may be a case for such areas to be prioritised or for special consideration to be given to how they might be developed in a more effective way which meets the needs of multiple stakeholders.
- Review individual strategies with a view to identifying elements which appear to be in tension or contradict each other.
- Work in partnership with senior colleagues in the finance office to ensure that financial sustainability is addressed as an integral element of the development process.

Develop strategy iteratively

Strategy development is an inherently fluid and iterative process. There is a need to accept and work with this aspect of the strategy process, while also ensuring that there is a requisite degree of structure and scheduling to ensure that outputs are delivered on time.

Careful consideration will need to be given to the identification of critical pathways and interdependencies across individual strategies to ensure that papers are produced in time for relevant committee meetings.

A schedule of key milestones can be developed and reviewed on a regular basis by the strategy programme board or development group. It will almost certainly be the case that the process of development will take longer than originally envisaged. It will be more productive to allow additional time at the outset to allow full engagement in the process than to seek to impose unrealistic deadlines. Nevertheless, it will be important to ensure that individual strategy owners are committed to delivering against the schedule that has been agreed. The use of a traffic light system showing the extent to which an individual strategy is on track can help to concentrate minds.

A case study of the iterative and phased nature of the strategy development process undertaken at The Open University is provided in Figure 3.2.

In this example a deliberately iterative and transparent process was adopted, with care taken to actively engage multiple stakeholders at each stage. A clear feedback loop was established as an integral aspect of the process, and a 'you said, we did' summary of feedback was provided at the final stage of strategy approval.

Think about implementation at the development stage

It is often the case that having a vision or a set of strategic aims is confused with having a strategy. An aspiration to become world class or improve league table ranking is an intent and not a strategy. To develop a grounded strategy which has some prospect of being implemented effectively, it will be necessary to spend some time in the development phase in thinking through how aims and objectives are going to be implemented in practice. While it is not necessary to consider every aspect of implementation in detail, it is important to reflect on whether the proposed implementation approaches are feasible. The strategic planner can play a useful role in this respect by asking whether the resources and competences currently exist in the institution to implement this aspect of the strategy effectively and, if not, whether they can be obtained (Johnson et al. 2014).

A further consideration which should also be addressed in this context is that of affordability and return on investment. These questions can be applied to any implementation approach that has a bearing on the viability of a proposed strategy. This requires a firm relationship with financial appraisal, financial planning and forecasting (see Chapter 9). Significant value can be added by adopting a critical but constructive approach in seeking assurance on these issues. Time spent at this stage is likely to yield significant benefits and will greatly increase the likelihood of the strategy being implemented effectively. Once agreed, the implementation approach can be summarised in your internal strategy documentation.

The problem-solving cycle identified by Schein (1988) can be usefully adapted in relation to the strategy development process. Drawing on Schein's model, the

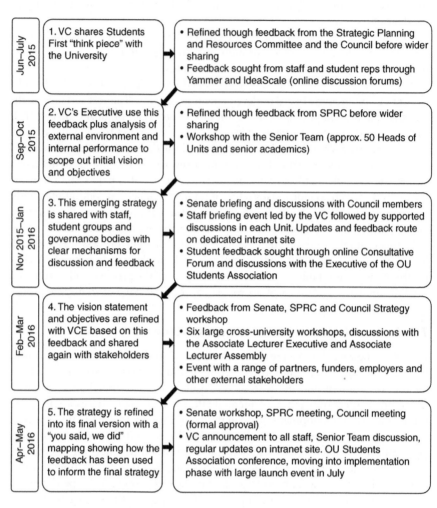

Jun–July 2015	1. VC shares Students First "think piece" with the University	• Refined though feedback from the Strategic Planning and Resources Committee and the Council before wider sharing • Feedback sought from staff and student reps through Yammer and IdeaScale (online discussion forums)
Sep–Oct 2015	2. VC's Executive use this feedback plus analysis of external environment and internal performance to scope out initial vision and objectives	• Refined though feedback from SPRC before wider sharing • Workshop with the Senior Team (approx. 50 Heads of Units and senior academics)
Nov 2015–Jan 2016	3. This emerging strategy is shared with staff, student groups and governance bodies with clear mechanisms for discussion and feedback	• Senate briefing and discussions with Council members • Staff briefing event led by the VC followed by supported discussions in each Unit. Updates and feedback route on dedicated intranet site • Student feedback sought through online Consultative Forum and discussions with the Executive of the OU Students Association
Feb–Mar 2016	4. The vision statement and objectives are refined with VCE based on this feedback and shared again with stakeholders	• Feedback from Senate, SPRC and Council Strategy workshop • Six large cross-university workshops, discussions with the Associate Lecturer Executive and Associate Lecturer Assembly • Event with a range of partners, funders, employers and other external stakeholders
Apr–May 2016	5. The strategy is refined into its final version with a "you said, we did" mapping showing how the feedback has been used to inform the final strategy	• Senate workshop, SPRC meeting, Council meeting (formal approval) • VC announcement to all staff, Senior Team discussion, regular updates on intranet site. OU Students Association conference, moving into implementation phase with large launch event in July

Figure 3.2 Iterative strategy development at The Open University

Case study diagram: Anna Barber, The Open University

first cycle of strategy development may be characterised as comprising the following three stages:

1. Identifying the strategic imperative or 'problem'
2. Producing proposals for a solution
3. Forecasting consequences, testing proposals

The forecasting of consequences of the strategy solution is frequently overlooked and may lead to the reformulation of proposals or even the redefinition of the original strategic imperative.

The second stage of the strategy development process comprises:

4.   Action planning
5.   Taking action steps
6.   Evaluating outcomes

The evaluation of the outcomes of the implemented strategy may also lead to a redefinition of the original strategic imperative. A mature approach to development and implementation will be characterised by a willingness to reevaluate agreed strategies in light of experience and the application of this development cycle.

A diagram illustrating Schein's problem-solving circle can be accessed at www. slideshare.net/sandhyajohnson/the-consulting-process-models (slide 3). The framework which Schein sets out here can be followed in working through the extent to which a strategic imperative (in Schein's terms, a 'felt need') is logically formulated and translated into a specific action plan. Working through the cycles of problem solving which Schein identifies will help to clarify whether each stage of your strategic thinking remains appropriate.

Make strategy relevant to everyday roles

Strategy development can sometimes be seen as abstract and removed from the reality of university life. In taking forward the development and implementation of a new strategy, it is helpful to provide lots of practical examples of the specific implications for people's roles. At the development stage there is likely to be a much greater degree of buy-in if people can see how they might benefit from a new way of working or a new direction. For example, in the case of developing a new research strategy (see Chapter 6), it will be helpful to think about how members of staff might benefit in terms of the amount of time they have available to undertake their research, the additional support they might receive from professional services and the benefits they might expect in terms of their career progression.

Where possible, connections can be highlighted between a person's day-to-day working life and the various elements of the new university strategy. Helping colleagues to see how they might benefit personally by the new strategy will help to foster interest and engagement, thereby increasing the prospect of more effective implementation.

Establishing a strategy framework

Typically, an overarching university strategy comprises a vision which is underpinned by a series of interrelated academic and enabling strategies, as shown below in Figure 3.3. In turn, these strategies are underpinned by a series of implementation plans.

A useful action that can be taken at an early stage in the process is to establish a template for the development of individual strategies. The use of such templates not only provides a degree of consistency in documentation but more

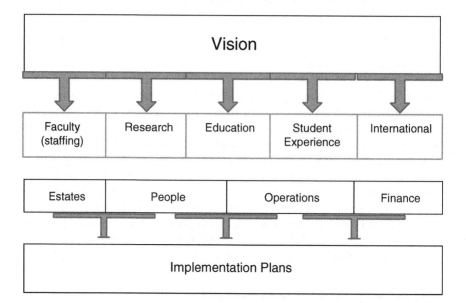

Figure 3.3 Strategy framework

fundamentally helps to influence the strategy development process itself. In providing a structure for the strategy document, the template sets expectations about key dimensions which should be explicitly considered, such as the external context and evidence about the current position. This can help institutional leaders to think more strategically from the outset.

An example of a strategy template (adopted at Durham University) is set out below, along with commentary on the purpose and benefits of each aspect. This template can be adapted to suit the priorities of an individual institution. Concern regarding the potential uniformity which might arise from the use of such a template may be mitigated by adapting the template to suit the circumstances of an individual institution. Further, an analysis by Strike and Labbe (2016) provides compelling evidence which contradicts the commonly held view that all strategic plans are essentially the same. Strike and Labbe demonstrate that the wide variety of choices which are made in relation to the content and presentation of published strategic plans reflects a deeper underlying diversity in institutional character and priorities.

Following the UK parliamentary convention, it may be helpful to produce individual strategies in green paper and white paper forms. A green paper is essentially a draft for discussion which allows the opportunity for committees and other stakeholders to comment on work in progress and the direction of travel. White papers are the final versions which are presented for approval, subject to specific amendments.

A strategy template

1. Context

This should provide a brief analysis of the sector and wider external context, including the implications of key drivers in relation to changing markets, competitor strategies, funding and the policy environment. PESTLE, scenario planning and benchmark analysis are all likely to be useful in this context. A succinct commentary on fundamental institutional challenges may also be provided here.

2. Goal

A statement which confirms what the overall strategy is seeking to achieve, e.g. to strengthen the university as an institution in which world-leading and world-changing research and engagement is created and sustained.

3. Strategic aims

Typically, between three and five high-level outcome-orientated aims, e.g. to establish a critical mass of world-leading research outputs within and across all core academic units in the university.

4. Gap analysis

A reflective commentary which identifies the gap between the stated aims and the institution's performance to date. This may be omitted at the white paper stage.

5. Strategy into action

If strategy is to be more than a surface-level statement of aspirations, it must address how aims and objectives are going to be translated into practical implementation actions. A critical section of the strategy template is therefore 'Strategy into Action'. This section should set out the specific objectives which will underpin the broad aims and the proposed implementation approach or policy which will translate the objectives into practical actions.

The number of objectives and associated implementation approaches or policies will vary depending on the strategy in question, although ten objectives would seem to be a reasonable upper limit. In keeping with the thinking advocated by Rumelt (2012), it is recommended as good practice to identify a small number of high-priority actions which will be critical in driving forward the success of the strategy. Such actions can usefully be identified in the strategy template and subsequently be collated and assessed for overall coherence and feasibility. An example is shown in Table 3.6, with the critical importance of this particular implementation approach signalled by the word 'PRIORITY'.

Table 3.6 Capturing strategic objectives

Objective	Implementation approach or policy
Maximise the supply of high-quality research engagement and impact activities.	Review of policy and processes relating to knowledge exchange and commercialisation activities, ensuring appropriate incentivisation. PRIORITY

6. Key performance indicators (KPIs)

The identification of effective KPIs is an important element of the strategy process (see Chapter 12). There is a risk that senior colleagues may underestimate the level of thinking which is required to produce effective KPIs and overlook potential pitfalls. Issues of criticality (measuring what is central to the strategy objective in question) and feasibility (the practicality of data collection) must be considered carefully.

7. Dependencies

One of the value-adding roles of strategic planners is to help institutional leaders think through the implications which individual strategies have in relation to each other. It is quite easy for those with responsibility for leading strategy in an identified area to focus simply on their own area without considering dependencies, sequencing, capacity and overall coherence. Identifying some of the main dependencies at the development stage will help to provide a strong basis for an achievable programme of strategy development.

For example, in the education strategy there may be an intent for student number growth. The planned growth in teaching capacity implies a concomitant increase in faculty headcount. This has the potential to support achievement of sustainable critical mass in areas where this growth aligns with a need for additional research capacity.

8. Risk analysis

It is useful to identify the positive contribution which the strategy will make in relation to mitigating the institution's primary risks (for example, with cross-reference to the register of key strategic risks). Similarly, there will also be value in understanding and evaluating the major risks associated with the implementation of the new strategy (see Chapter 8). It would be expected that additional risks would be less serious than those associated with maintaining the status quo, and it will be useful to highlight this when presenting strategies for discussion and approval. This section should summarise the risks which the strategy will address as well as the risks associated with the implementation of the strategy itself.

This section can provide a springboard for subsequent discussions which can add real value to the strategy development process. For example, there is likely to be value in facilitating workshop discussions with senior management teams and board members on risk appetite and management in relation to the new institutional strategy.

9. Equality and diversity analysis

Mainstreaming thinking on institutional actions to strengthen equality and diversity within the strategy process will add value to the development process. This section should provide a summary of expected equality and diversity benefits of the proposed strategy and the implications and risks which might be encountered in relation to implementation of the new strategy. For example, recruitment, retention and promotion plans may be intended to improve recruitment, retention and promotion policies and will mean that staff will have the opportunity to work in diverse teams.

Concluding remarks

The role of the strategic planner in higher education has changed substantially in recent years. Profound changes driven by increased competition, unforeseen political events, funding pressures and globalisation are unfolding across the international higher education sector. The challenges arising from these changes require HEIs to reimagine their future development in fundamentally different ways. Strategic planners have a unique opportunity to position themselves as essential partners, advisors and facilitators in the process of change as institutions seek to compete, collaborate and develop from different national contexts. While the future is necessarily uncertain, establishing a more thorough, professional approach to institutional strategy development will be essential if the journey ahead is to be navigated successfully.

References

Dwivedi, Y.K., Lal, B., Williams, M.D., Scott, L.S., and Wade, M. (2009), *Handbook of Research on Contemporary Theoretical Models in Information Systems*. London: Information Science Reference.

Elverson, D. (2014), Strategic Thinking. Workshop presentation given on 3 July 2014 at Durham University on behalf of Understanding Modern Government.

Fumasoli, T. and Lepori, B. (2011), Patterns of Strategies in Swiss Higher Education Institutions. *Higher Education*, 61, Issue 2, pp. 157–178.

Gardner, H. (2006), *Changing Minds*. Boston, MA: Harvard Business School Press.

Garratt, B. (2003), *Developing Strategic Thought: A Collection of the Best Thinking on Business Strategy*. London: Profile.

Gordon, A. (2008), How to Build and Use Scenarios: Presentation to the World Futures Society at Washington, D.C. www.slideshare.net/adgo/scenario-building-workshop-how-to-build-and-use-scenarios [Accessed 21/09/16]

Hodges, J. (2016), *Managing and Leading People through Organizational Change: The Theory and Practice of Sustaining Change through People*. London: Kogan Page.

Horizon Scanning Centre, Government Office for Science. Scenario Planning Guidance Note. http://webarchive.nationalarchives.gov.uk/20140108140803/, www.bis.gov.uk/assets/foresight/docs/horizon-scanning-centre/foresight_scenario_planning.pdf [Accessed 21/09/16]

Johnson, G., Whittington, R., Scholes, K., Angwin, D., and Regnér, P. (2014), *Exploring Strategy*. London: Harlow.

McKeown, M. (2012), *The Strategy Book*. Harlow: Prentice Hall.

Mintzberg, H. (1994), *The Rise and Fall of Strategic Planning: Reconceiving Roles for Planning, Plans and Planners*. New York: Free Press.

Mintzberg, H., Ahlstrand, B., and Lampel, J. (1998), *Strategy Safari: The Complete Guide through the Wilds of Strategic Management*. Harlow: Prentice Hall.

Quirke, R. (2012), *Making the Connections: Using Internal Communication to Turn Strategy into Action* (2nd Ed.). Aldershot: Gower.

Rumelt, R. (2012), *Good Strategy Bad Strategy: The Difference and Why It Matters*. London: Profile.

Schein, E.H. (1988), *Process Consultation*, Vol. 1 (Rev. Ed.). Reading, MA: Addison-Wesley.

Shattock, M. (2010), *Managing Successful Universities* (2nd Ed.) Maidenhead: McGraw-Hill, Society for Research into Higher Education & Open University Press.

Strike, T., and Labbe, J. (2016), 'Exploding the myth: A literary analysis of universities' strategic plans' in *Positioning Higher Education Institutions: From Here to There*, (pp. 125–140), edited by R.M.O. Pritchard, A. Pausits and J. Williams. Rotterdam: Sense.

Weisbord, M., and Janoff, S. (2007), *Don't Just Do Something, Stand There! Ten Principles for Leading Meetings That Matter*. San Francisco: Berrett-Koehler.

World Café. www.theworldcafe.com [Accessed 20/09/16]

Wright, G. (2001), *Strategic Decision Making*. Chichester: Wiley.

Part 2

Integrated planning

Chapter 4

The planning cycle
A strategic conversation

Steve Chadwick and Olivia Kew-Fickus

Introduction

This chapter explores the role of the planning cycle in delivering institutional strategy in higher education. It considers both the 'why' and the 'how' of the planning cycle. The first half focuses on the purpose, approach and inherent tensions within the planning process. The role of the planning cycle as a venue for strategic conversations that lead to structured and considered decision-making is emphasised. The second half presents the elements and architecture of an effective planning cycle, recognising that there is no single right way to run it. It also considers the challenges to conducting an effective planning process, including both those inherent in the process and those which emerge from the increasing marketisation and instability of the HE environment. The planning cycle sits within the broader framework provided by the institutional strategy (explored in Chapter 3). This chapter draws on the authors' experiences as practitioners at various universities, set against reflections from key academic texts.

The purpose of the planning process

The annual planning cycle is the route through which higher education institutions (HEIs) take their strategic intentions and translate them into targets, budgets and activities in order to make strategy happen. It brings together and balances institutional with departmental needs and visions, short-term efficacy with long-term sustainability and resources with reputation. The best planning processes facilitate structured, strategic conversations that consider challenging issues in the round and deliver decisions deemed reasonable, transparent and – most importantly – actionable by the key stakeholders.

As such, the planning cycle is an integral part of the continuous strategy-making process. Effective strategies identify a direction and goals, and also a means of getting there (Rumelt, 2011). However, some university strategy documents focus on the first part – the direction and goals – and say relatively little about the means of getting there. When they do consider the 'how', these often take the shape of a few large initiatives, which by their very nature are one-off, time-bound and focused on discrete areas of activity. This is not necessarily a symptom of poor strategy-making so much as fundamental to the nature of higher education institutions: complex and multi-faceted, composed of disciplines which often have strikingly different needs, and characterised by distributed decision-making rooted in the professional expertise and autonomy of the academy (Hardy et al., 1983; Mintzberg and Rose, 2007; Shattock, 2010). For HEIs, therefore, the 'how to get there' elements of the strategy will be numerous and need to be co-produced with the input of the wider academic population as well as those with particular management roles. However, strategies can fail at the implementation stage because they do not take this final step of making strategy concrete and all-encompassing through a planning cycle which translates top-down direction-setting into tangible actions.

An annual planning cycle which requires the various academic and professional services units to drive forward the institution's strategic plan at the local level is commonly used in many HEIs. Such plans need to reflect and embed any top-down or central initiatives, turning them into business as usual, or to collect and assimilate unit and departmental plans into the central steering and resource allocation, as shown in Figure 4.1.

Following Mintzberg (1994a, 1994b), one of the classic thinkers in this field, planning adds value when it is structured but not overly formulaic. The planning cycle should aid strategic thinking, and be embedded into the organisation,

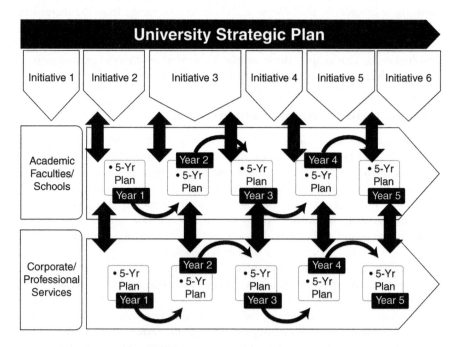

Figure 4.1 An integrated annual planning cycle

rather than creating plans for their own sakes. Where the planning cycle adds value is in:

- engaging all parts and activities of the institution;
- providing analysis and asking the right questions to support decision-making and catalyse strategic thinking;
- converting the often messy and emergent world of strategy into firm targets, objectives and budgets;
- deciding on investment priorities and resource distribution;
- identifying good ideas and practice, particularly if they emerge from below rather than above, and, conversely, embedding top-down initiatives into business as usual;
- delivering accountability and managing risk;
- integrating and coordinating across the breadth of university activity and clearly communicating outcomes to all stakeholders.

The annual planning process is not primarily about seismic change, but about shifts, whether incremental or disruptive. It keeps the whole moving forward coherently, by challenging both the parts of the HEI that are resistant to necessary change and those that wish to drive ahead, sometimes without proper consideration of how their own strategies contribute to the institution's. This is not a simple process, but it is an important one. HEIs which cannot marshal their resources effectively at all levels will increasingly be challenged not only for success but for survival because, wherever on the globe they are located, the environment they are operating in is becoming significantly more competitive.

Annual planning in times of crisis

In a world where the past is no longer a reasonable indicator of the future, looking forward in a considered, strategic way and having a means to ensure that strategy gets implemented is no longer a nice-to-have, but is fundamental to institutional survival.

The past two decades have seen the increased massification of higher education. The question of how to pay for the concomitant growth of HE has been a challenge for governments around the world. State-funded provision is affordable when 5% of 18- to 21-year-olds go to university. Once that percentage reaches 20%, 40% or even 50%, providing a high-quality education in a financially sustainable way becomes a major challenge, no matter how rich or developed the country.

Since the financial crisis of 2008, higher education in many Western countries has been facing existential questions. In the US, student debt has become an election issue and state-funded systems have been paralysed by budgetary impasses. Some politicians have called for students to be actively discouraged from studying 'liberal arts', with preference for vocational degree tracks. In Australia, uncapping of student numbers has led to increased competition between universities and concerns about quality. In many European countries, fees have been kept low or are publicly funded, but this has meant universities have been starved of resources and unable to offer a high-quality student experience.

Internationally, therefore, we are seeing a move away from higher education sectors funded solely by government grants. Rather, funding increasingly follows the student, and in that more market-oriented environment HEIs are developing a more strategic approach to ensure they can compete effectively nationally and globally. This brings its own challenges both to institutions and their students.

In England, HE places are now largely unregulated. Even in devolved nations, where student number controls have prevailed, competitive forces are being felt increasingly keenly. Some universities have seen numbers soar, perhaps above sustainable levels; others have seen them plummet, threatening their sustainability for very different reasons. Government policy has repeatedly lowered the barriers for new providers of higher education. The international student market, where the UK has punched above its weight for many years, is also being exposed to increasingly competitive forces not only from other English-speaking countries, but from rapidly growing HE provision in China, India, Africa, South America and the Middle East. The UK's changing relationship with the EU and shifting immigration policy have increased uncertainty further.

Alongside this, expectations are changing. Students and government are increasingly questioning the value-for-money of a degree. There is debate about the purpose of higher education: is learning for the sake of learning an unaffordable extravagance, and should universities focus just on 'employability skills'? Is higher education predominantly a public or private good? The quality of teaching is coming under increasing scrutiny, and universities are being asked to do more to make good their claims of contributing to social mobility.

The research sphere is in no less flux. Government demands research to deliver 'impact', and the changing shape of the UK research infrastructure aligns research ever more closely with prosperity and well-being. Research budgets are under pressure. Co-funding prevails, large capital grants have the potential to unbalance the research ecosystem, and non-university research institutes have emerged. Universities and academics are expected to be public actors, not ivory towers, working with stakeholders and able to prove their contributions to the economy, society and culture.

Strategic conversations

As Mintzberg, Ahlstrand and Lampel (1998) argue, the more unpredictable and confusing the external world, the more flexible and 'emergent' strategy-making needs to be, adapting to the emerging situation. Strategy-making will also be increasingly more challenging in a constrained and competitive environment, where 'satisficing' rather than optimisation will be required.

The planning process is a fundamental part of developing emergent strategy. While in the past a formulaic approach to planning might have worked, prevailing conditions in HE mean that a more nuanced approach must be taken to respond to rapidly emerging challenges and opportunities. The planning process should be a yearlong, structured, purposeful strategic conversation within which the implementation of institutional strategy is hammered out. This conversation should not be formulaic, but creative, bringing together top-down strategic direction with bottom-up vision of how the different areas can best flourish, and working out what this means in an environment of constrained resources. It is a venue for exercising judgement and making decisions, interpreting evidence, testing goals and working out how to move the university forward.

Increasingly in the literature the concept of 'strategic conversation' between key, informed stakeholders has emerged as a much richer route to strategy-making than more bounded processes (Van der Heijden, 1996). There are numerous benefits to a purposeful strategic conversation.

- It is inclusive, involving key actors and thereby gaining their buy-in and increasing the credibility of the process (Groysberg and Slind, 2012).
- Because of this inclusivity, a strategic conversation will consider the organisation as a whole, pulling focus regularly from the local (bottom-up) to the totality (top-down) and back again (Liedtka, 1998).
- A strategic conversation can encompass many types of input. It can be intuitive and analytical, recognising that both toolkits are critical for good decision-making (Mintzberg, 1994b), and it can draw on evidence ranging from detailed quantitative analysis to qualitative market intelligence to nascent kernels of ideas. Good analysis can also create new and challenging insights (Nichols, 2006).
- It can provide space for disagreement, uncertainty and exploration of new ideas before being forced to a decision, thus enriching the decision-making process (Van der Heijden, 1996). In fact, it needs different points of view to help avoid confirmation bias, which is the phenomenon of dismissing evidence that does not align with what is expected or desired. Confirmation bias is a real danger in a rapidly changing environment, and a major contributor to bad decision-making in organisations (Bolman and Deal, 2013).
- It can think across time, drawing in lessons from the past and projecting to the future (Liedtka, 1998).
- It provides space to compromise, prioritise and find common ground, recognising that in an environment of constrained resources it is impossible to satisfy everyone.

However, just because the benefits are many, such a conversation will not just emerge naturally. It is unfortunately easy for planning processes to become, on one extreme, a series of set pieces with all real decision-making occurring elsewhere, or, on the other, unproductively confrontational. Strategic conversations must be purposeful and managed, with care given to both fostering the preconditions and shaping the activity itself.

The right actors need to be engaged

On the academic side, these will certainly include the senior academic charged with resource management, heads of academic units (at faculty or departmental level, depending on the institutional structure) and key professional advisers from strategic planning, finance, HR and, frequently, student recruitment or research management. A cognate process should occur for professional/support services, involving directors/heads of these services, taking care to align with academic priorities. Increasingly, universities also find ways to include other stakeholders, most notably students, at key points. Providing students with an opportunity to set out their priorities for additional investment, for example, enables senior management to consider resource allocation from their students' perspective. Similarly, allowing students to comment on iterations of the budget and thereby influence decision-making and understand the compromises which necessity dictates can be enormously informative.

For many institutions this will require a greater time commitment than senior staff are used to – especially since some would not naturally consider planning as a core part of their remit. Responding effectively to the challenges of surviving and thriving requires a professional, rigorous approach to management and brave decision-making, which takes time.

There are implications also for the capabilities, skills, competences and knowledge of senior staff. They must be able to think and act strategically. Not all senior teams have staff with long experience of managing complex organisations, and, if they have spent the majority of their career in higher education, they have inevitably gained whatever experience they do have in a relatively stable sector. These challenges are exacerbated by the often transitory nature of senior management teams, with a tenure in post of two to three years (particularly for senior academics) not uncommon.

The process must be structured and intentional

A strategic conversation will not emerge from a free-for-all. The discussion should be phased and follow a natural, logical sequence. The purpose and topics for each discussion should be understood (Groysberg and Slind, 2012). The documentation, evidence and analysis should be robust. Within this structure, discussions can then be creative and solutions innovative. The better the structure, the easier it will be to explore issues from all angles/perspectives. A clear structure will also give confidence that ideas are being considered both analytically and intuitively. It is vital to get this balance right so a systematic, orchestrated, logical sequence of conversations does not stifle creativity, agility and innovation.

There are various tools to help define the structure. The use of targeted and strategic questions to focus the conversation on the most important issues can be very effective. Scenario exploration is another approach, considering what might be an appropriate response in the shape of a specific new situation (Van der

Heijden, 1996). By helping people to consider a different reality, scenarios can be particularly effective in drawing people past immediate, short-term objections so they can consider the preconditions for long-term, sustainable success.

The conversation must be two-way

Often senior staff set out their vision and pass this down to the academic units and professional services for translation into reality. This vision is important and needs to be communicated and shared, so that the whole institution can work together. However, from the departmental perspective, the significant gap between this vision and reality is often stark, with internal and external obstacles looming large and leading to cynicism. On the other hand, there may be solutions and ways forward evident at department level which would not occur to those sitting more centrally. These may be relevant only to the particular discipline, or they may have resonance elsewhere in the university, if they can be shared. Central and local units need to be able to influence and shape each other's perspectives, if a realisable strategy is to emerge. In practice, this often means revising or refreshing the top-down vision, and in particular any targets which have been set by the senior management, so they are better informed by the reality on the ground.

The conversation must be constructive and between equals

The planning round is not a star chamber, but a place for co-creation of strategy (Liedtka, 1998). For this to occur there must be trust on both sides that ultimately everyone is working together for the greater institutional good. This does not always exist, replaced instead by a type of 'parent-child' transaction between central (budget-controlling) and departmental (delivery) units. The former assume the role of enforcer and the latter the role of supplicant (Berne, 1961). This is rooted in an assumption by the central units that the departments only care about themselves, and by the departments that the central units care more about control and money than academic excellence. This leads to an adversarial situation which does not provide the foundation for a creative dialogue.

There are legitimately different points of view during the planning process, but all those engaged in it should recognise that they provide each other with mutual support: faculties, schools/departments and professional services by understanding and delivering their role in meeting university priorities and targets; and senior management by removing barriers to implementation and ensuring, as far as possible, there is a rational, transparent allocation of targets and resources. Constructive challenge should work both ways, and it should be recognised that airing different points of view is the whole purpose of the conversation.

To make this work, there must be a sense of shared purpose, which is to achieve a sustainable position for the institution by shaping and implementing a clear, agreed strategy. The senior management team, and in particular the vice-chancellor/principal or president, needs to sets the right tone and create an atmosphere of mutual respect. A commitment to shared values and agreed standards of behaviour are vitally important for success.

The conversation must recognise internal politics

The effect of internal politics on coherent, rational decision-making is enormous in any large, complex organisation. Universities, with their traditionally guild-like mentality rooted in the principle of academic freedom and the acknowledged expertise of academics in their individual disciplines, are arguably more likely to be political than companies, where command-and-control may prevail. Politics in HEIs are exacerbated by multiple factors, including the tension between academic units and administrative departments; a commitment to collegiality and a strong dislike of what is often considered 'managerialism'; and strong resistance to change because 'we have done very well so far'. There is also no doubt that there are often egos at work around senior management tables. Those coming from the outside are often struck by the sense of hierarchy and the power wielded by vice-chancellors or presidents (compared say to chief executives of health trusts or local authorities).

The planning function must be particularly sensitive to internal politics, because its role is to 'join stuff up' and coordinate between multiple actors and stakeholders; for that reason it is susceptible to political fallout. Planning is therefore regularly perceived to be treading on other people's territory. (See Chapter 2 for a description of the often unbounded nature of the functions of strategic planning offices.)

Although politics are commonly treated, both in practice and in the literature, as negative, they are an enduring fact of life in most organisations. As long as they are contained and controlled, they can actually improve decision-making through debate and coalition-building (Mintzberg, 1985). The planning process must harness the institutional politics for this purpose, acting as an impartial mediator, truth-speaker and curator of the process.

The process must be transparent

Everyone should be clear what will be discussed and what has been decided. If decisions are made 'off-line', they need to be recorded and incorporated. Decisions should also be open, so that other stakeholders know, for instance, where investment has been made. Reasons for decisions should also be transparent, as far as possible, to avoid the process losing credibility.

The conversation must be evidenced

Conversations without an evidential foundation can lead to bad decision-making, as changes internally and externally are ignored or a goal is locked in without a means to achieve it. Strategic planning has a critical role to play in providing much of the evidence, often marshalling the support of other professional services (e.g. recruitment, finance). Academic departments will also bring their own evidence and insight to the table. Evidence can come in many forms, but strategic planning is often best-placed to draw it together, posing those key questions which lead to meaningful strategic conversations, an interpretation of the evidence and, ultimately, to high-quality decision-making.

Reputation and resources

So what is this strategic conversation all about? At the heart of strategic planning is striking a balance between competing priorities. This is fundamentally a compromise between reputation and resources. Each university has its own particular constraints, but each should be seeking a way to deliver academic excellence while also being sustainable.

To the question 'What do modern universities need to be successful in an increasingly turbulent environment?' there are many different answers. However, these generally boil down to the need to acquire and sustain above all else two things: reputation and resources. The academic success which drives reputation is expensive, as academic activities (when done well) are resource-intensive (Shattock, 2010).

Building or growing reputation takes time, while resource allocation is more immediate. This can be a source of significant tension – a tension which lies at the very heart of every strategic conversation. If senior decision-makers do not have an acute consciousness of this interplay and the criticality of striking the right balance between them, then any planning process is likely to produce poor outcomes, at least when judged in the light of an HEI's ability to sustain its activities in the long term.

Reputation

All HEIs, like academic staff themselves, 'trade' on reputation, in part because the quality of their offerings (education or research) cannot be seen directly until they have been experienced. Institutional reputation influences whether students want to study at, and academics want to work for, a particular HEI. For students, it directly affects their postgraduate prospects. For academics, it can be a factor in determining their opportunities for academic partnering, funding and conference invitations.

Reputation in HE is gained or lost primarily through the education and experience of students and the quality and impact of the research conducted by the academics. Occasionally HEIs can experience short-term reputational damage because of incompetent management, lax processes or failure to follow legal or financial rules. However, providing the institution maintains the quality of its education and research, such damage can be contained.

Conversely, an institution's failure to protect its reputation in education and research can genuinely result in lasting damage and, if it persists, even threaten its existence. Admittedly, an institution's reputation can sometimes be more artifice than reality since, whether positive or negative, reputation often lags behind actual performance. Nevertheless, reality will eventually catch up, particularly in today's era of social media and publicly available third-party league tables (see Chapter 13) which have speeded the process of building and destroying reputations.

The relative importance of education and research for any given HEI depends on its mission. The greater the institution's global ambition, the greater the need to excel in research, since international reputation and global rankings are heavily influenced by the quality and volume of research activity. This is because there are commonly accepted methods of measuring citations internationally, but none for student satisfaction, retention rates or entry qualifications.

Nevertheless, neither a global research powerhouse nor a provincial teaching institution can afford to neglect teaching quality and its student experience. Producing satisfied students who can compete successfully in the job market, develop into future leaders, make a valuable contribution to society and act as ambassadors and advocates for their alma mater will enhance the reputation of any HEI.

In countries where domestic league tables rankings are largely determined by measures related to teaching and learning (which is certainly the case in the UK), providing a high-quality education can also support international student recruitment, since some overseas sponsors refer to the domestic as well as international rankings when deciding where to send their students.

Resources

The challenge with reputation is that influencing it takes time and requires resources:

- money (cash or affordable borrowing),
- people (enough of them with the right skills and competencies) and
- things (buildings, space, equipment, infrastructure, systems, processes and tools).

If an HEI can invest in a sufficient number of high-calibre people and things, it is better positioned to sustain and enhance its long-term reputation. To take advantage of this situation, senior leaders need to understand their institution's business model and how to exploit it.

We might illustrate this balance between reputation and resources as shown in Figure 4.2.

Traditionally, HEIs have focused on the generation of income, unlike commercial enterprises where 'profit' or 'margin' are what matters. Because HEIs have a

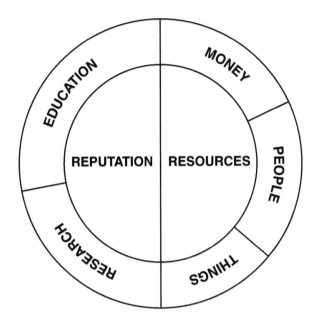

Figure 4.2 Relationship between reputation and resources

long history of receiving income (e.g. from government or funding bodies), few universities have robust means of tracking the cost of their activities. In a more competitive environment, the whole notion of 'margin' for future sustainability is becoming increasingly important.

Any HEI interested in cultivating a global reputation must produce high-quality research. However, research sponsors are reluctant to pay more than the direct costs of conducting the research project. As a result, it is rare for research activity to generate any 'margin' and in most cases research funding does not cover the full economic cost of the activity. In the UK, according to HEFCE data (2016), 73.9% of the cost of research was funded in 2014/15; in other words, for every £1 spent on research by UK universities, about 25p must be found from non-research funding sources (e.g. student fees, philanthropy). This message is increasingly well understood by senior teams.

So how does an HEI generate that subsidy? In the majority of cases the answer is to recruit sufficient numbers of students who pay more in fees than it costs to teach them. This 'margin' is then used to subsidise other things, including research activity, which in turn drives global reputation – that very same global reputation which enables an HEI to recruit high-fee-paying students to fund their research in the first place. This 'ecosystem' lies at the heart of a research-intensive university's business model, as it does in just about any sector in the commercial world.

The pressure has been no less intense for more teaching-oriented universities. For these institutions, competition from new, multinational, private providers with the ability to invest in high-quality accommodation and facilities can be fierce. They are also affected by growth strategies of universities 'above' them in the food chain, many of which have benefitted disproportionately from government capital investment targeted on research-intensive institutions. Higher fees and (compared to the more research-intensive institutions) relatively low costs provide an opportunity to invest in their estate and facilities and catch up with their richer research-intensive cousins. These institutions must also protect their market share; in a competitive marketplace few institutions can afford to see their competitors gain market share at their expense.

In an increasingly competitive environment for HE, the scrabble for resources for investment or to cover funding gaps can result in institutions focusing heavily on generating cash. If cash is in short supply, the obvious solution is to grow the student population, especially easy in a time when there is an explicit policy drive to increase the proportion of young people in HE. It is relatively easy to take more students. In the short term this approach helps generate a healthy margin, which funds capital and academic investments. Any self-respecting governing body will pay close attention to the size of the surplus and the affordability of investment strategies, so it is easy to see how in the short term growth is considered a winning strategy by senior leaders and governors.

However, generating 'margin' by simply growing the student population is fraught with problems. Frequently, the race to grow the surplus means lowering the quality of the intake and damaging the student experience, through large class sizes, overcrowding, timetabling clashes, poor service and less individual attention. How many HEIs plan such growth carefully and ensure they have sufficiently qualified academic staff to teach them, buildings to accommodate them, facilities to satisfy them or administrative staff to support them?

Moreover, if the university's activities require investment in high-cost facilities in science, engineering and/or clinical disciplines – most of which require subsidy on a recurrent basis – the need to grow the student population in low-cost subject areas will only increase. This can put pressure on an HEI's ability to offer an outstanding student experience unless the expansion is carefully planned, and can put the institution in direct competition with others, including increasingly the for-profit providers, seeking to maximise their low-cost numbers. This has been a common challenge for many research-intensive UK universities in the recent past.

A balanced process

The tension between short-term financial gain and long-term reputational impact is not a bad thing. What is bad is if annual planning processes are not consciously designed so that at critical decision-making points there is acknowledgement of this tension and a genuine exploration of the long-term effects on reputation and sustainability of a short-term scrabble for cash.

Growth is easier than taking a serious look at costs or fundamentally changing the business model, and thus it comes to be seen almost universally as the solution. Cost reduction on a major scale is never easy, and doing it well takes great care and huge senior management commitment. Similarly, an approach which reconfigures the whole institutional business model by rationalising provision and ceasing activity in some disciplines is just as demanding. Therefore few university management teams want to adopt such an approach in any really serious way.

What is needed is a mature approach to planning. Growth is not a sustainable position for many HEIs in a fiercely competitive environment. Rather they must create enough 'space' in the strategic conversation to allow the tensions referred to above to be recognised, acknowledged and fully explored before decisions are made. The planning processes should therefore ensure that at critical decision points the short-term financial imperatives are not automatically allowed to override and obscure the longer-term reputational impact. If the decision is still made to pursue short-term strategies to maximise financial gain, the institution should, at the very least, plan how to manage possible impacts on reputation. Failure to do so effectively will have major consequences on the institution's sustainability further down the line.

Key features of a planning process

There are of course many ways to run an annual planning round, and there is no 'right or wrong' way. Its precise nature, key features, workflows and so forth will depend on the HEI's mission, culture, risk appetite, its senior leadership team and its specific circumstances. What follows is therefore not a recipe for success but rather a number of features which work effectively in a range of HEIs and which are hopefully useful to anyone designing or reviewing the 'strategic conversation' in their own university.

Comprehensive

The process needs to be comprehensive in the sense that it involves all academic and administrative units, including research centres/institutes and language centres, and specifically any to whom the university provides significant funding. This would include student guilds or unions.

Integrated

Institutions generally have well-developed processes for dealing with discrete aspects of their activities. The problem is that these activities are often managed in uncoordinated silos. A fiercely competitive environment does not allow the luxury of such inefficiency. The annual planning process is an opportunity to join these activities up and 'glue' them together. It should therefore encompass the academic, administrative, financial, human resource, risk management, capital and infrastructure aspects of the HEI's activities. In some cases these can form an integral part of the discussions at the planning meetings themselves; where other processes run in parallel, they need to be carefully coordinated so that there is two-way communication and passing of information/data/decisions at appropriate points.

A typical example would be the development of capital and infrastructure plans. It is difficult to see how the mainstream planning process itself could incorporate these. They require detailed discussion with expert estates and financial input. It would be too time-consuming to conduct these within the main planning meetings. However, the two processes can work effectively in parallel as long as the capital and infrastructure plans take full account of the student, research, staffing and so forth plans at appropriate points in the cycle.

The strategic planning function might want to consider, for example, the following indicative list of activities/processes and how they can be integrated into the 'strategic conversation':

- academic strategies to maintain and enhance reputation for education and research;
- performance monitoring using KPIs/KPTs (including the metrics used in any annual review of courses);
- student number planning;
- research income;
- academic enterprise income (short courses, consultancy etc.);
- workforce plans;
- estates, space, equipment and other infrastructure;
- financial budgets and projections;
- project and programme management plans.

Senior management setting the vision

Most HEIs will set a vision at the beginning of a strategy development process, but it ought to be revisited more frequently as part of the annual planning cycle. Many HEIs will hold a regular (usually annual) event where the senior team take time out from the business as usual and consider in detail the external environment and what the competitor or peer institutions are doing, review progress against their strategy and either confirm or adjust institutional priorities and targets.

As a rule, these events are scheduled at the beginning of a new academic year and at the start of the annual planning process. Their purpose is to determine and/ or confirm the size, shape and nature of the university for the next few years and to thereby 'frame' the planning that will take place throughout the institution. As with the planning process itself, the discussions at such events need to be structured, well informed and expertly chaired so that they produce the outputs and outcomes that provide clarity for those engaged in the planning process.

This requires thorough preparatory work both by the senior team themselves (on those topics for which they each carry ultimate responsibility) and by the colleagues who support them. Not only should the discussion papers or presentations be informed by hard data, but the nature of the discussions themselves and the decisions which need to be taken, carefully considered. Typically, the senior team will review progress using KPIs and structure discussions around major themes in their strategy. Some take the opportunity to use traditional management tools such as a PESTLE or SWOT analysis. However, when working with senior academics for whom the notion of a university as business is abhorrent, such methods need introducing with great care.

A key output from this event is often a planning framework, a document which provides a high-level summary of institutional strategic priorities and targets organised by key themes and which contains guidance for those involved in the planning process. Such an overview document sets out what the institution will achieve within the planning period and thereby acts as the benchmark against which any targets agreed during the planning round can be compared. Consequently, it is important that this document is widely shared.

The planning process should empower academic and professional service units to do their own planning within that overall framework. Academic and professional services staff know their own disciplines/areas better than anyone else. They know the competition, what they are doing, how their discipline/function is evolving, what they need to do to best serve the needs of students, what research sponsors are most likely to fund and so on. They are also on the front line and will need to deliver against university goals. Empowering them to plan for themselves and to determine not only how best to meet university targets, but the level at which they are set in the first place, means they are far more likely to have a genuine sense of 'ownership'. The planning process therefore needs to encourage and facilitate sound planning by all units in the university.

Academic-led strategy

An annual planning process which starts with next year's financial surplus and sets targets to achieve a particular financial outcome has started at the wrong place. At some universities, this approach has led to the student populations in certain disciplines growing beyond what is desirable from an academic perspective, simply because they are 'cash cows' and the market will allow them to grow. In such cases the 'ecosystem' is out of balance.

If, however, we approach the question of optimum size and shape from an academic perspective, we could well reach a totally different conclusion. For example, how big can the student population grow before a department starts to find it difficult to provide a high-quality learning environment for all students? Or, as the staff population grows, at what point will it become very difficult to maintain the quality of teaching? Or can a department grow substantially and still maintain an appropriate sense of belonging? How big does the staff population need to be to ensure an academic department has the critical mass for high-quality research? If a department significantly exceeds the optimum staff population, will research quality suffer?

There is clearly no simple answer to these questions. Nevertheless, consideration of them is equally as important in the strategic conversation as the question about how we meet next year's surplus target. Failure to make academic strategy central to decision-making almost invariably leads later to the need for remedial action, which can sometimes take years before it takes effect. In today's aggressively competitive environment, few institutions can afford to operate on such lengthy timescales.

Clear responsibility and accountability

Ensuring clear lines of responsibility and accountability is not easy in a university setting, as there is often not a simple linear relationship between a task and who is responsible for it. For example, recruitment involves both academic units and professional services. Academics must design, deliver, and often present at open days about academic courses which students find attractive, while the actual process of making offers and maintaining good customer relations with applicants generally sits with central administrative units.

How responsibility/accountability is played out will vary. In some institutions, academic managers (e.g. deans, heads of schools/departments) are held responsible for achieving academic targets (including student intakes) while professional services are held responsible for delivering a high-quality service to academics. Even where professional services lead on strategies (e.g. for estates or IT), it is clear these are serving the education or research objectives of the institution and in that sense are a supporting function. In other HEIs the achievement of targets and objectives is treated as a shared responsibility between academic and administrative units. It is of course possible to link achievement of objectives to personal development reviews as well as financial or other incentives and/or major celebrations of success (both formal and/or informal).

A good planning process will comprise a series of 'touch points' during the course of the year in which deans of faculty and heads of professional services meet with the senior team and effectively give account for their contribution to institutional targets and objectives. This is an important step in itself in helping colleagues take ownership for the achievement of targets and objectives. If the tone and format of these meetings are right (see below), no dean or director will want to see the indicators in their area moving in the wrong direction, and it becomes a matter of professional pride not to have to repeatedly defend poor performance.

Five-year planning horizon

It is impossible to plan effectively using a one-year time horizon, and yet it has been common to have annual planning rounds that focus on determining next year's budget. Increasingly, HEIs are moving away from this to a longer timeline. Certainly, if the planning process is to be integrated with capital and infrastructure planning (which often requires significant lead-in times) it is important to look further ahead. In practice this means that student numbers, workforce plans, research targets and so forth must use at least a five-year time horizon. Much longer than this and it becomes difficult to plan anything with a reasonable degree of accuracy.

Evidence-based decision-making

Horizon scanning during the vision-setting event, the review of performance for the university and individual departments, the setting of targets for student recruitment, research and academic enterprise, and the allocation of budgets at an appropriate level: all of these require good management information if they are to be done properly. Such information should be predetermined and designed with efficient, effective decision-making in mind. That includes which data is important, the definitions of the data, the levels of aggregation to use, the mapping of internal structures to externally used categories and so on. No one should be allowed to turn up to planning meetings with data/analyses they have done themselves using their own definitions. That is too distracting since the time allotted for such meetings is too valuable to spend trying to understand data, disputing its accuracy or the reliability of the analysis.

No back door

All major decisions around resourcing should be taken as part of an agreed planning process if it is to have credibility. It should not be possible for persistent, influential colleagues to beat a direct path to the president/principal/vice-chancellor's door and get decisions for major investment taken outside the strategic conversation. This requires discipline among the senior management team. It does not preclude the existence of a strategic development fund which the senior team can deploy to support strategic initiatives, but the process by which that fund is accessed should be transparent and well-publicised, and discussions about its use should be part of the mainstream planning process.

Structured sequence of meetings

Some HEIs have one meeting a year to 'do the planning'. However, if we are to integrate so many aspects of planning into a coherent whole, and if it is to take the form of a genuine 'strategic conversation' conducted in a phased, structured manner, then sufficient time needs to be devoted to the process. The sequencing of the key topics will vary depending on admissions and funding timetables. In the UK, fine-tuning student intake targets for the following year will occur after the current year's recruitment is known, for example, which is usually in the autumn term. In the US, expected enrolments are available earlier as conditional offers are less prevalent, but state-derived funding for public universities is increasingly known only much later in the cycle, as austerity and politics collude to add uncertainty to this funding source.

A typical planning cycle might well look something like that shown in Figure 4.3.

Typical Integrated Planning Process: Schedule of Meetings

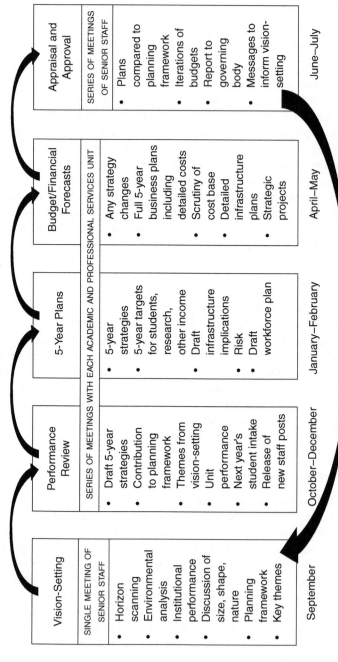

Vision-Setting	Performance Review	5-Year Plans	Budget/Financial Forecasts	Appraisal and Approval
SINGLE MEETING OF SENIOR STAFF	SERIES OF MEETINGS WITH EACH ACADEMIC AND PROFESSIONAL SERVICES UNIT			SERIES OF MEETINGS OF SENIOR STAFF
• Horizon scanning • Environmental analysis • Institutional performance • Discussion of size, shape, nature • Planning framework • Key themes	• Draft 5-year strategies • Contribution to planning framework • Themes from vision-setting • Unit performance • Next year's student intake • Release of new staff posts	• 5-year strategies • 5-year targets for students, research, other income • Draft infrastructure implications • Risk • Draft workforce plan	• Any strategy changes • Full 5-year business plans including detailed costs • Scrutiny of cost base • Detailed infrastructure plans • Strategic projects	• Plans compared to planning framework • Iterations of budgets • Report to governing body • Messages to inform vision-setting
September	October–December	January–February	April–May	June–July

Figure 4.3 Typical integrated planning process

Realism

Problems arise for institutions if targets are set too ambitiously. This is a particular temptation in a competitive marketplace. Academic leaders are afraid their competitors will gain market share, which puts pressure on staff to demonstrate growth. Inevitably this leads to underachievement against budgets and financial projections, which in turn results in the need for in-year intake or budgetary 'adjustments', including compensatory over-recruitment in other areas or significant in-year cost-cutting. All of this will be unplanned activity. Over-recruitment can create problems in terms of capacity, class sizes, and accommodation, while in-year cost-cutting can affect the institution's ability to recruit staff or lead to slashed non-staff budgets. It is far better to plan realistically and prepare for lower income levels so that if cost reductions or efficiencies are necessary, these can be identified and planned for in advance.

Co-creation of plans

If plans are set by academic units and then scrutinised by a central team, or vice versa, this can easily exacerbate the 'us and them' divide which can so easily exist in universities. The process must allow for open dialogue and input into the development of plans as they emerge from both academic and professional service units. There are various ways to do this: through the use of a 'business partners' model where professional services staff assist academic units as they develop various aspects of their plans; by having more informal planning meetings before the main 'strategic conversation' meetings in which professional services staff can contribute, providing analyses and support in the run-up to the main planning meetings; having academic colleagues provide input to professional services as they develop their plans, possibly by attending awaydays and commenting on drafts of PS plans; or by the sharing of plans on intranet sites. Whatever method is used, the key thing is to allow input from other parts of the HEI before plans are finalised.

Use of clear transparent processes and simple documentation

If the purpose of a planning process is to generate an ongoing 'strategic conversation', then all the documentation provided as part of that process should be designed specifically to that end. Long bodies of text from which it is difficult to extract key data or messages are rarely helpful, and such documents are very difficult to keep updated. One alternative is to use 'strategy thumbnails'. These are short, summary documents which contain key information regarding the size, shape and nature of a given academic unit or professional service. Typically they would contain:

- key facts and/or achievements for the past year;
- details of performance against the university's KPIs;

- a summary of the five-year strategy;
- a list of strategic objectives;
- five-year targets for student numbers, research activity and other income;
- a projection of staff posts;
- income and expenditure projections etc.

Thumbnails can be supported by operational plans and more detailed figures, but during a two- to three-hour meeting which will cover several topics, it is simply not possible to properly consider very long, detailed documents. Thumbnails are also much easier to update, and senior staff can keep these short summaries with them as a reminder in all dealings with the unit.

Clear and consistent communication

If the planning process is not to be a 'black hole' for staff, it is important for the senior team to communicate regularly to a range of stakeholders throughout the cycle. This usually means using a variety of formats including reports on the outcome of the vision-setting stage, often in the form of a message from the vice-chancellor to all staff; regular internal newsletter updates to inform staff of progress and key decisions; emails to inform line managers of decisions taken at major planning meetings; formal reports at key stages in the process to committees and/or statutory bodies; notes of all meetings tracking both university-wide and unit-specific issues and decisions; and an internal resource site with access to all guidance, notes, templates, analyses and so forth.

How to shape a contextual approach

The previous section outlines a number of elements of a robust planning process. This final section picks up the question of how to consider these contextual factors in shaping a planning process.

In most HEIs, there will be a number of factors which make implementing a planning process challenging. They include the capabilities of the key actors/ stakeholders, the culture around how the institution makes decisions (transparently or behind closed doors, based on evidence or preference, through debate or by fiat, willingness to accept risk), and the balance of power between actors, as seen in mechanisms such as budget setting. Institutional politics can derail the best-laid planning process – not only politics between academic units, but also politics between professional services – as can an institutional culture not amenable to the premises of a strategic conversation. All of these raise a fundamentally important question: How ready is the HEI to have strategic conversations?

Readiness will be affected by a number of factors. In many instances, behaviours which may not be conducive to strategic conversations will have emerged for very legitimate reasons. In a crisis situation action may have been required before full evidence could be amassed. Sometimes a new vice-chancellor/president inherits some weakness in the senior leadership and has to act more by fiat than through the shared executive to implement things he or she thinks are right. In some cases, the personal characteristics of the academic lead will shape the process. The ability of the professional services to work together, rather than in silos, is also a factor. These kinds of cultural barriers are difficult to overcome, and implementing a robust planning process may take time. In very few HEIs does a planning process emerge fully formed and remain unchanged year after year.

Another factor is degree of urgency. HEIs with large surpluses and/or cash reserves may feel less exposed than those with large levels of debt or razor-thin margins. Some have a long history of success at recruiting students, generating research income, or international activity, for instance, and may be complacent about the level of challenge emerging in the environment. Some are very obviously exposed to strong competitive forces, while others are currently more isolated from the same, perhaps due to geography or reputation. However, these universities will have other challenges, whether of resourcing, demographics, logistics or global competition. Even the world's great universities will not remain immune from external forces forever. It is therefore incumbent on the planning function to gather evidence and help focus attention on these challenges and generate an appropriate level of urgency at a sufficiently early stage.

Each institution's niche will shape the kinds of challenges it faces and the balance of conversation needed in a strategic planning process. The profile of different income elements will shape both the emphasis of the conversation and decisions. A 'recruiting' university will spend much more time considering student numbers, while a research-intensive 'selecting' university will focus more heavily on research funding and metrics. A university which relies on commercial income, perhaps from conferences or publishing, will be acutely aware of the factors influencing those markets and the different forces at play there to those which affect their core academic business. HEIs in partnerships to deliver certain aspects of their offering, such as distance learning, will again need to consider somewhat different factors. All universities need to consider how to attract and retain the best staff, but the discussion around this may look very different in areas where the main constraining factor is cost of housing versus those where geographical isolation or civic malaise is the challenge. These factors will determine the shape and timing of various parts of the strategic conversation.

Next steps

The emerging environment for higher education demands considered, joined-up, strategic decision-making. This creates a more complex and more challenging situation, but also one which is much more interesting.

This chapter does not aim to provide a template which will work in all institutions but rather to offer insights into the key elements which make for effective planning. Strategic planning is an institutional endeavour, not a process owned exclusively by the director of strategy and planning. Any particular institutional approach to it should be shaped through consultation and discussion internally – a strategic conversation about strategic conversations, so to speak! In the next few years, few HEIs will be able to navigate the increasingly stormy seas of higher education without effective strategic conversations.

References

Berne, E. (1961). *Transactional analysis in psychotherapy: A systematic individual and social psychiatry*. New York: Grove Press.

Bolman, L.G. and Deal, T.E. (2013). *Reframing organizations: Artistry, choice, and leadership*. 3rd edition. Hoboken: Wiley.

Groysberg, B. and Slind, M. (2012). 'Leadership is conversation', *Harvard Business Review*, 90(6), pp. 76–84.

Hardy, C., Langley, A., Mintzberg, H., and Rose, J. (1983). 'Strategy formation in the university setting', *The Review of Higher Education*, Summer, 6(4), pp. 407–433.

HEFCE (2016). 'TRAC income and costs by activity 2014–15', May, www.hefce. ac.uk/data/Year/2016/tracincome/Title,108872,en.html (Accessed: 24 October 2016).

Liedtka, J.M. (1998). 'Linking strategic thinking with strategic planning', *Strategy & Leadership*, September/October, 26(4), pp. 30–35.

Mintzberg, H. (1985). 'The organization as political arena', *Journal of Management Studies*, 22(2), pp. 133–154.

Mintzberg, H. (1994a). 'Rethinking strategic planning part I: Pitfalls and fallacies', *Long Range Planning*, 27(3), pp. 12–21.

Mintzberg, H. (1994b). 'Rethinking strategic planning part II: New roles for planners', *Long Range Planning*, 27(3), pp. 22–30.

Mintzberg, H., Ahlstand, B., and Lampel, J. (1998). *Strategy safari: The complete guide through the wilds of strategic management*. London: Financial Times Prentice Hall.

Mintzberg, H. and Rose, J. (2007). 'Strategic management upside down', in Mintzberg, H., ed., *Tracking strategies: Towards a general theory*. Oxford: Oxford University Press, pp. 283–317.

Nichols, C. (2006). 'Facilitating good strategic conversations: A 6P facilitation framework', Converse, pp 16–18, April, www.ashridge.org.uk/faculty-research/research/publications/facilitating-good-strategic-conversations/ (Accessed: 9 August 2016).

Rumelt, R. (2011). *Good strategy bad strategy: The difference and why it matters*. London: Profile Books.

Shattock, M. (2010). *Managing successful universities*. Berkshire: Open University Press.

Van der Heijden, K. (1996). *Scenarios: The art of strategic conversation*. Chichester: Wiley.

Chapter 5

Student number planning

Lucy Hodson

Introduction

Chapter 3 in this book grappled with how an HEI sets its strategy, and Chapter 4 described the annual dialogue between academic departments, professional services and the centre, and the tools and techniques which are involved in that strategic conversation.

This chapter provides an overview of the building blocks and mechanics of how student number planning responds to – or frustrates – those strategic designs. It looks at the challenge of planning for and delivering the required student numbers.

This chapter looks particularly at the issues which a department of strategy and planning has to address when assisting both the senior leadership team and the constituent academic units in undertaking student number planning.

An overview of policy changes which have affected student number planning

University strategic planners are, as shown in Chapter 2, a flexible breed. A look back over the last ten years gives an interesting perspective on the challenges strategic planners in the UK context have had to face in terms of delivering planned student numbers which are both compliant with government legislation led by changing political imperatives, and in line with institutional strategies. Table 5.1 provides an overview of the political and policy changes experienced in the UK HE system in relation to student number planning in the previous ten years.

Student numbers – the lifeblood of a university

Student number planning is a fundamental part of the role of the strategic planner. The strategy and planning office is in most but not all HEIs looked to for target setting, for predicting student numbers, for counting the students in during the year, reporting on numbers to senior and academic management and for submitting statutory returns on student numbers during and at the end of the year.

Table 5.1 Policy factors affecting student numbers in the UK HE system

Academic year	Factor affecting student numbers
2005–6	High numbers of applications were generated the year before top-up fees were raised from £1,000 to £3,000. Until and including 2011/12, HEIs received substantial state funding for undergraduate tuition, via a block grant.
2006–7	Lower recruitment as a result of lower deferrals from the previous year, and higher fees. Wales retained fees at £1,000 and Scotland abolished fees for 'young' students.
2007–8	Gradual impact of high numbers of 18-year-olds, aspirational expansion of HE participation, increasing grade inflation at A level meant that a greater proportion of offers had to be honoured, and enabled strategic expansion of mid-tier universities. Wales introduced top-up fees.
2008–9	Increasing numbers of students led to English government overspend on student support. HEIs were required not to recruit over their 2008/9 levels for 2009/10 to ensure that the student support budget was not overspent. Maturing of the EU market delivered higher numbers of EU students.
2009–10	Strict student number caps in England; led to greater than expected recruitment in Wales and Scotland, as English universities which normally recruited in Clearing found that they were full.
2010–11	Student number cap more strictly enforced; HEFCE set the exact number with penalties per student. Still rising grade inflation at A level meant that HEIs were offering very cautiously. Many HEIs reduced franchise numbers (which were counted in the number cap) and EU recruitment. White paper published in November 2010 introduced the idea of higher fees (£6,000–9,000) for 2012/13.
2011–12	Pre-high fees bumper year in terms of applications. A-level grade inflation still happening. Students who would otherwise have deferred decide to apply to avoid higher fees; and all HEIs fill their places very quickly. HEIs in England and Wales almost universally, in April 2011, choose to set their student fees for 2012 at the highest amount allowable at £9,000 per annum. Student number caps also apply in Wales (to limit HEFCW grant spend), and Scotland (operating a system of limited number of free places).
2012–13	Student number control (SNC) for all FT UG Home/EU students except those entering with A-level grades of AAB+ or equivalent (limited equivalences allowed). Many HEIs taken by surprise by downturn in applications coupled with sudden A-level grade deflation, which meant fewer students took up offers, or were eligible for the English AAB+ cap exemption (and lack of experience from Russell Group universities in Clearing).

2013–14	Continuation of SNC, but now at ABB+; however, strict penalties for going over the limit still apply. Selecting HEIs still need to fill their capped quotas of sub-ABB+ and get more knowledgeable about attracting Clearing students. HEIs assume fees will not be inflated so recruiting more students is the only way to address annually rising costs. A new competitive streak enters the sector; HEIs which had not had big marketing departments now appoint directors and teams. New and bigger planning teams emerge, as growing recruitment and building reputation become priorities – both needing a strategy informed by data analysis.
2014–15	Same SNC, but with a broader definition of ABB+ for exempted students, and a much less punitive threshold and fine. Impact of UKVI and Confirmation of Acceptance for Studies (CAS) forms on international students starts hitting HEI's overall student numbers. Chancellor announces that the number cap will come off for 2015/16 in English HEIs. Competitive efforts redouble.
2015–16	Student number cap is lifted completely in England; a financial cap remains nominally in Wales, although maintained for private providers. While the greater competitiveness is noticeable, the big change came the previous year when the tolerance threshold on student recruitment was sufficiently lax to allow effective freedom of recruitment. White paper published November 2015 – fees could rise from 2017/18, dependent on achieving a quality threshold. UCAS responds to very different Clearing environment by offering 'Precision Marketing' facility, whereby HEIs can call students who have registered for Clearing. UCAS notes first year of zero growth in applications from UK – growth only in EU numbers of applications (pre-Brexit).
2016–17	No cap on student numbers. Perturbation enters into the system through the UK's vote to leave the EU. While government sources guarantee fee loan to EU students for those coming in 2016/17, some impact already felt.
2017/18	English universities who have achieved TEF1 (QAA clean bill of health) can apply inflation to their fee. Lower demographics, and lower EU applications (depending on fee and loan settlement during the Brexit period) may impact recruitment. Private providers so far have not been seen to take students away from mainstream HEIs, but it may still happen.

Strategic planners in HE can feel they need be expert in many areas which might seem the preserve of academics within their university: teenage psychology, international politics, epidemiology, public policy interpretation and implementation, social group theory, advanced demographics since WWII, the fortunes of premier league football clubs and the ever-changing memes of popular culture. And a few skills that might be regarded as unique and inherent – clairvoyance, instinctual foresight and the strength of character to be a lone voice of reason.

Strategic planners care for the fortunes of their HEI while HE strategy changes and as policy U-turns whirl about them. They are depended on by senior managers, finance directors and accommodation halls providers alike to set a course and predict outcomes despite ever-changing recruitment environments.

Student number planning – the building blocks

Students are the lifeblood of a university. From their presence – the differing lengths of time they spend at an HEI, the different levels of fees they pay, their various academic and other needs and expenditure – flows income for the estate, to meet the costs of academic staff, professional service staff, infrastructure renewal, and from secondary spend a whole range of potentially profit-making activities around the campus. From their changing numbers and needs, students challenge an HEI to respond and adapt to be able to meet new demands in some areas, or reduce oversupply of academic delivery in other areas.

Strategic planners (and funders and policy makers) define and codify different kinds of students to facilitate the planning and forecasting processes. And how they code defines to some extent how they think students will behave.

The basic terminology used in UK HE planning (some of it influenced by HESA) includes the following concepts, key to the student number planner's arsenal:

> Mode: the manner of study. The most common distinctions are whether students are studying full-time, part-time or as distance learners.
> Level: the level of progression at which the student is studying – at undergraduate, postgraduate taught or postgraduate research (doctoral student) level. At its most simple, levels 4, 5 and 6 relate to the three years of an undergraduate degree (students may exit at each level with sub-degree qualifications) and level 7 for postgraduate qualifications.
> Status: usually to do with fee but can be a number of different categories – UK/EU (EU may develop its separate categories), Islands (a slightly different fee status) and Overseas.

A good strategic planner has an acute awareness of the balance of students and the mix of mode, level and status in her or his institution. Broadly speaking, out-of-town campus universities tend to specialise in full-time undergraduates, offering a residential experience, while city-centre modern HEIs may have a greater mix of part-time students. A research-intensive university will also tend to have more postgraduates and research students as a proportion of the student body; and those with successful and prestigious business/law schools will tend to have larger overseas populations.

FT UG UK/EU (full-time home and EU undergraduate students)

This group includes full-time undergraduates from the UK or from the European Union – the largest student grouping for the majority of broad-based HEIs in the UK. Most of these students are between 18 and 21 when they start to study. The home/EU status – at least until the UK government makes an announcement – signifies that the students are (nominally) publicly fundable, may attract some grant, but most importantly will pay a £9,000 to £9,250 fee per year (unless domiciled in Scotland attending a Scottish university), for which they can access government loans and/or grants for student support.

The fees they bring are not as high as overseas, but the cost of acquisition and retention substantially lower. Many HEIs have more than 80% of their students in this category – and the 80/20 rule often applies, as strategic planners apply 20% of their effort on this 80% of student number planning for this generally predictable group, with 80% of their planning effort dedicated to other, less predictable and less modellable student groups.

PT UG UK/EU (part-time home and EU undergraduate students)

These students can be studying at any range of intensity – from retired people attending a weekly evening class, to motivated career-changers attending classes three evenings a week and achieving their degrees in almost the same time as it takes to achieve a full-time degree. Part-time students bring their own special planning challenges, as they tend to start their programmes at different times, may suspend study for a while, may vary intensity and may never complete – all of which characteristics affect how securely numbers and fees can be predicted.

FT UG OS (overseas undergraduates)

This group of students have been vitally important to the UK HE sector for some time – ever since Mrs Thatcher ended state subsidy to those outside the UK, so that HEIs started charging unregulated (i.e. higher) fees for overseas students.

In addition to the higher fee, overseas students are important in terms of maintaining or growing student numbers. Many HEIs are coming up against their capacity for growth from UK students, and overseas markets are a way to expand student numbers at quality.

For the strategic planner in mid-ranking HEIs, overseas numbers predictions – particularly in the last two to three years – have often been the product of the triumph of hope over experience. Each year, it seems, is the year when that key partnership with that important sending overseas institution will come good and produce a flurry of international UG students; and every year there is some international incident, event or key academic departure which means that the connection does not quite mature that year, and there is underperformance against prediction.

In very successfully recruiting universities – in the world top 100 in the international third-party league tables (see Chapter 13) who can attract government-sponsored students from East Asia particularly – another challenge is maintaining a good balance of nationalities in subject cohorts.

A complication for many is that progression agreements with overseas universities may send students into Years 2 or 3 of their programme, meaning they are only in the institution for 1 or 2 years; this difference of timing and length of stay must be factored into student number forecasts.

FT PGT (full-time postgraduate taught students)

Whether UK/EU (usually a lower fee, possibly some related government grant) or overseas, these students are usually on the books for one to two years. Fee setting is outside the scope of this chapter – but in the UK, PGT students carry non-regulated fees. There is an opportunity to charge higher fees, but given the relatively low demand from UK students, few HEIs charge enough for PGT provision to be really sustainable based only on UK numbers. Given the small numbers of UK students enrolled in many PGT programmes and therefore the high staff per funded credit ratio, the PGT market is even more susceptible to economic trends than the undergraduate market, and to fashions in what it makes sense for students to study. A sustainable PGT strategy for many HEIs will be focused on the overseas market.

PGR (postgraduate research students)

Research students are another dimension altogether. In the past they have been drawn not necessarily by the overall success and image of the HEI or even academic department but by a particular academic supervisor. Increasingly, though, research students are recruited in cohorts to doctoral training centres (DTCs). Completion rates predictions and funding for PGR are subject to the most elaborate of formulas; for this reason, strategic planners tend to model the number of funded full-time PhDs, where doctoral students are required to finish within four years and therefore behave more or less predictably.

Other student categories

There are a wide range of other students at HEIs who are in some way non-standard. These can range from FT UG students who are studying at collaborative partner institutions, to distant learning students taught either by employed lecturers or contracted out companies, to students undertaking validated courses at partner institutions, and students at branch campuses overseas. Some HEIs are managing to deliver so-called accelerated degrees (a full degree in two years rather than three) – but continued government attempts to increase the number of offerings here have not met with great success, as most HEIs find them too expensive to teach.

Strategic planners may need to carefully model and predict individual student numbers in some of these cases – particularly if there is a per capita overhead cost to the university such as library access – but in other cases may simply use a volume driver to predict fee income for high-level planning. These types of students do not use the UCAS application route; data about applications to enrolments ratios is sparse, and there may be a considerable last-minute walk-in factor. The more unusual the student type, the greater the difficulty for the planner – it requires strategic planners to cope with a greater and more varied student body. Expertise in a particular student type in a strategy and planning office may well derive from the specialism of their particular institution.

Student number planning – the process

Chapter 4 dealt with a description of the planning round – the process by which internal strategy and ambition meets external realities, trends and circumstance to produce ambitious but realistic student number, financial and academic plans for the next year and beyond.

A set of historical student numbers, broken down into the categories described above, will in all likelihood be in existence in the HEI for the last few years. Based on the institutional strategy and academic department's own plans, a five-year student number forecast will then be developed, assessing likely new intakes each year and then will probably draw on historic progression and non-completion rates to calculate the student cohorts expected. It is this five-year student number plan, consisting of actual and forecast student numbers – probably built up from programme level – which forms the starting point of the student number planning process; it rolls forward year on year, and its relationship to what is realistic and achievable is key to the success of a range of other processes at a university: fee income forecasts, timetabling teaching, estate planning, future requirements for residential student accommodation, academic workforce planning and brand/marketing.

The student number planning model is updated at the beginning of the new academic year as new students and returners register in September, with adjustments made for students set to arrive during the year (midyear starts are an increasing phenomenon).

Intake targets for the in-year recruitment round by department, as established through the previous planning round, provide the framework for the marketing and schools liaison functions to go out and promote the HEI and its programmes.

A conversation begins with academic units, in that they are asked to provide their achievable intake targets for the next year and for the plan period. Academic units are asked to justify their optimism or pessimism against their academic plan.

Forecasts are often sense checked by the strategy and planning office – a summing-up exercise against previous recruitment experience, applications per place, intake tariffs, market share and competitor strength are used to ensure goals are in line with the strategy, and are, as far as possible, realistic, sufficiently ambitious and achievable.

Targets from the previous planning round are confirmed in time for the bulk of offer-making for FT UG students. This process enables offers to be monitored where any external or internal caps are in place. A government-imposed student number cap is still in place in Scotland for instance; space requirements may impose caps on other disciplines; guidelines might be in place about how big certain areas should be to protect staff-student ratios, to ensure the student experience, for laboratory capacity and so on. Discussions may continue about the planned next year and future years targets as required.

A census of applications is taken, for FT UG, in January at the UCAS deadline. This census can be used, if necessary, for sense checking budget setting and accommodation modelling. First drafts of the teaching timetable for next year can be drawn up, as historical data converting applications to likely enrolments can be used.

Further sense checks can be taken for other student populations later in the year – as overseas and postgraduate students have later and less predictable application to enrolment patterns.

Targets are used to set income forecasts. In many cases the strategy and planning function will co-ordinate the process of fee setting, and if not will maintain an up-to-date fee list, and can model income forecasts from the student number forecasts. Through a conversation between the planning and finance functions, this can inform budget setting (see Chapter 9). The budget can be the format in which agreed five-year student enrolment figures are reported back to academic units, if they are not reported separately as forecasts.

Student number planning – factors to take into account

There are a considerable number of factors which need to be taken into account when undertaking modelling on student numbers to obtain an accurate forecast. This is important for two reasons:

- Planning/predicting student numbers on a year-by-year basis as part of the annual budget cycle;
- Assisting the HEI to get where it wants to be in terms of its student number profile in the mid to long term.

The concepts of 'selecting' versus 'recruiting' HEIs have a huge impact on the ability to confidently plan numbers, and to reach a planned number rather than a designed range. Strategic planners need to think about certainty and likelihood in relation to their own HEI's position in the market when designing a model for student number forecasting.

In a truly selecting HEI it will be possible always to reach target on programmes, even if application numbers have fallen, by reducing the grade offer through UCAS or the tariff points required in Clearing.

The varying factors which might be taken into account by a university planner when building up the five-year view of planned/predicted student numbers are:

University strategy

Most HEIs in the UK are seeking to grow FT UG UK/EU students; which was not necessarily the case before the higher fee regime. The extraordinary but predictable outcome in 2011, whereby nearly all HEIs classed themselves as exceptional and therefore were allowed to charge £9,000 for an FT UG student, rapidly changed the planning horizon. The lifting of the SNC but freezing of the fee level led to the development of growth strategies and ambition in most HEIs. The fact that so-called inflationary increases will apply (in England) to fees from 2017 may slow down the universal need to grow numbers just to pay the bills.

UK demography

The UK has entered deep into the trough cycle 'echo boom' as the baby-boomers' children now start to leave university and the children of those born in the era of easy birth control start entering HE; the numbers of 18- to 21-year-olds are not set to pick up again from 2024 in England and 2028 in Wales. Planners may dig more deeply into the data to see which of their key recruiting heartlands are affected, linking up with feeder schools to see evidence of falling or increasing rolls at school, and how this is might pan out at subject level.

University so-called quality

This has differential impacts depending whether an HEI is recruiting or selecting. This is important in a contracting local market – as HEIs which set traditionally high tariff points on entry have the choice to maintain quality or to relax their offer – perhaps at offer, interview or when A-level performance is confirmed – to ensure that student number targets are met or quality maintained, even if applications have not increased in line with strategy.

Distance from urban centres and whether there is a natural hinterland

In many urban centres, a certain proportion of the local population will naturally move into the local HEI – usually the local modern HEI, wherever that HEI may be reputationally. Semi-rural campus-based HEIs are dependent on the travelling market, and more susceptible to fluctuations in reputation, and to the plans and fortunes of competitors.

Subject mix

Strategic planners are able to access data from their own institution and the sector, which shows which subjects are in decline and which are on the up among 16- to 18-year-olds in full-time education, and patterns of applications to HE. The continuing decline of applications to modern languages in the UK is, for example, well documented, while applications for computer science continue to grow. Evidence of demand may therefore drive the areas where the HEI wishes to grow student numbers; but they may wish to control numbers in other areas where space (laboratories, studios) can be an issue.

Changes to fee regimes from one year to the next

The small, inflation-linked hike in fees from £9,000 to £9,250 from 2016 to 2017 entry in England, particularly as for the majority of students this will be covered by a fee loan, is unlikely to affect entry patterns – unlike the move from £3,000 to £9,000 fees from 2011 entry to 2012.

One-off events

Particular perturbations might hit an individual HEI's recruitment positively or negatively: the local football club makes it into premier league, a spate of gun crime reported in the home city, or a hiccup in the performance in the NSS causing league table movement – these are all issues which can affect application and conversion patterns.

Changing status and ease of movement of students

At the time of writing, a hard Brexit is expected, meaning that a concession to allow EU students to access a full three years of student loan funding at home prices seems unlikely as a permanent solution; carefully nurtured EU strategies are in tatters. There may be a further tightening of the strict regulations for overseas students whereby HEIs are expected to keep tabs on overseas students at all times. UKVI Tier 4 licences represent a risk when they can be revoked if above a certain percentage of overseas students who are offered places and apply for visas are rejected.

Internally, strategic planners need to be aware of any regulation change, and new innovations in programmes, which might mean that there are more or fewer repeaters, or more students doing one- or two-year programmes.

Student number predictions in-cycle – achieving the magic number

The ability to be able to predict over the course of a recruitment cycle how many students will eventually enrol and be counted is a considerable skill, one that can be underrated, but a significant badge of honour for strategic planners if they can do it well. To do this in-year prediction, strategic planners must seize and analyse the data as follows:

Application numbers

In the UK, the Universities and Colleges Admissions Service (UCAS) plays a huge part in UK universities being able to predict eventual enrolments up to 11 months ahead.

UK/EU and increasingly overseas students use the UCAS system, most often before they have achieved their final school leaving qualifications, to apply to up to five different courses at UK universities.

Universities are able to use historic ratios between the numbers of applications received at given points in the UCAS application cycle (it starts in September each year) to start predicting how many students will enrol the following September.

A dip in applications in October/November – showing a deviation from the previous year – can highlight a problem with overall positioning that can be difficult to reverse during the recruitment cycle.

Offer rate and conversion

The offer rate will have been assumed through the annual planning and target-setting cycle (see above). Planners will have advised those staff/departments who make offers to students submitting applications, that offer rates need to be lower or higher depending on the numbers of students which are required to enrol; planned offer rates are also likely to vary between subjects/programmes. A lower than planned offer rate emerging through the cycle, however, might signal that applications are generally of a lower standard, making it impossible to offer places on some of the more demanding courses, and indicating that the HEI may no longer be attracting the same highly qualified cohort as before.

As soon as offers start being made by the university to applicants – any time from October onwards – planners monitor how many offers are being accepted, and being 'converted' from a Conditional or Unconditional Offer to Conditional Firm (offer holder) or Unconditional Firm offer holder – meaning the applicant wishes to attend that university the following September.

Conversion rates as a KPI can incorporate different data, and strategic planners need to advise on which definition makes most sense in measuring the efficacy of university strategy. They can mean the rate at which applicants accept an offer in the early stages of the recruitment cycle, or simply the number of applications divided by the number of enrolments. UCAS produces an applicant to final acceptances ratio. For a recruiting university, the conversion factor (Offer to Firm accept by the candidate) shows effectively whether the university was a first, second or lower choice for the applicant, depending on the alacrity with which the applicant might accept the offer. The changing conversion factor, when compared to previous years, might be a first window onto the changing behaviour of other HEIs.

For many mid-table recruiting HEIs, conversion rates have taken a hit in the UK because higher-ranking selecting Russell Group universities, pursuing expansionist plans, have been making offers early in cycle to students whose predicted grades would not have merited an offer in earlier years, and which candidates are accepting quickly.

Confirmation once school leaving results are received

The eventual conversion factor from application to enrolment is also dependent on what proportion of applicants are likely to achieve their predicted grades in their final school assessments.

HEIs can over- or undershoot a planned target depending on whether or not there has been steady year-on-year grade inflation at A level. A sharp halt in the year-on-year grade inflation at A level in 2012 was one of a number of factors which led to a number of Russell Group civic universities under-recruiting that year.

In the UK, for FT UG students, UCAS still predominantly operates a prequalification admissions system. There was an attempt to introduce post-qualification admissions for 2016 about four years ago, but the sector rejected the proposal.

In the UK, teachers predict the achievements of their students at A level, or similar final qualifying exam – and most universities take the view that teachers over-predict by two grades and work out likely student success rates. Both for HEIs that need to keep within a certain quota, or want to control entry for a whole host of reasons, and for HEIs that are keen to expand or are concerned about meeting financial targets, the confirmation process offers a helping hand. Many students will not have achieved the offer they have been made – depending on the need to control or grow student numbers, an exercise is taken at Confirmation at which HEIs hold hard to their offers, or soften the requirement to let more students in. Under the previous system of SNC (student number control) it was essential to control admissions; under marketisation, the confirmation process is an important point in the student number planning journey, as it informs HEIs by how far published entry offers may need to be flexed to achieve planned student numbers. And for strategic planners – dealing with the most certain bit of data in the whole recruitment cycle – it's an ideal time to make sure the HEI comes in on target by having a very clear strategy set out for different scenarios based on results and applicant behaviour.

Clearing applicants

If all has not been achieved at Confirmation, there is always Clearing – where unplaced applicants can apply to any university with spaces. Planners have to predict at the beginning of a recruitment cycle how many students their HEI may wish to or be able to pick up in Clearing. Clearing has become a very different exercise than it was five years ago; more students are using it for direct entry in the UCAS system, and more highly qualified entrants are using it as a method of testing out whether they might be able to get into a top Russell Group university. To use Clearing as a way of coming in on target, strategic planners are involved at the planning stages and provide input into developing Clearing verbal offer targets and enrolment targets, based on historical conversion rates. Clearing is now entirely a respectable activity both for an applicant and an HEI – it is recruiting direct entrants who have not gone through UCAS, and the mechanics are changing with more use of online offer-making and newly developed UCAS cold-calling lists. The whoop of joy from an applicant at the end of the phone when receiving a Clearing offer is a thing of the past – Clearing applicants are noting the offer, moving on and shopping around for the best offer they can get in what they perceive to be a hierarchy of choice.

Post-Clearing drop-off

Another key point in the cycle for planners is after all the main dialogue points with applicants have happened and there is still time for minds to change, family circumstances to alter, finances to be hit – and for the student to decide not to attend after all. This August to October pre-entry attrition rate can vary between institutions – and can be between 2% and 10%, and may be more in certain subjects.

For populations applying for FT UG entry less likely to use UCAS, or students using UCAS but who may have their other options outside the system (such as EU students applying to a UK university as an insurance against getting into a free, but capped, university system in their own country), predicting enrolment is not easy. A typical in-year conversion to a Conditional Firm does not mean that the applicant is therefore holding no other offers from any other institution, or has no other options for his or her post-18 life. Planners may take a particular group of students – EU for instance – and apply historic conversion rates to this cohort from application to enrol, and treat cautiously any signs of burgeoning conversion rates.

Overseas students apply much later in the cycle; for some, school results come much earlier in relation to the UK academic calendar. Planners will need to use historic conversion rates from the beginning of the cycle, but also incorporate quite intimate knowledge of individual partnerships which might be delivering student numbers to specific subject areas.

Postgraduate taught students

PGT students generally apply much later in the cycle. While there is a UCAS postgraduate application portal, it is not universally used, and therefore institutions have much less intelligence than with the undergraduate system whether the applicant is applying to other universities. The lateness and lack of assurance about what else an applicant is looking at make it a significantly greater challenge for the planner to provide reassurance about numbers of students in these categories. Historic application to enrolments rates can be a help – but this type of student can also be affected most by economic and other factors.

Returners

It's not only new intake which student number planners are forecasting, it's the returning students. These populations are possibly more predictable – as historical trends can show the proportions of students who leave in their first year, and in the second and third year. However, even here things are changing. HEIs may change their progression rules – possibly as a result of advice from a quality assurance agency; the profile of students could be subtly changing as the external environment changes. One notable development is the very significant rise in the numbers of students entering HE with vocational qualifications. Equivalent vocational qualifications are by their nature more applied/practical than A levels, and some students may struggle with the more academic demands of the first year of an undergraduate degree; there may be a higher attrition rate for cohorts of students with higher numbers of students with equivalent qualifications. Increasingly, planners are drawing on learning analytics to help them develop more robust predictions around student attrition.

Students transferring between institutions

What has not really happened yet is a noticeable increase in student mobility within their period of study – that is transfer between institutions due to students exercising a choice to take their fee with them to another place during their time as a student. There are always transfers between institutions, usually for pastoral reasons and in small numbers, but the market rhetoric and a system with fees and choices may foster greater mobility between institutions – encouraging students to vote with their feet – and this has yet really to impact on planning processes.

Student number planning tools

Strategy and planning offices avail themselves of a range of analytical software tools to predict the eventual outcome of a series of human choices as expressed on the student's UCAS form.

Most have either created for themselves, or commissioned, a student number planning model. It can, for example, be based on Cognos, built by SQL or be a sophisticated Excel spreadsheet. Even if the product has been sourced from one of the increasing numbers of firms selling solutions to HE, the institution will inevitably have to spend time customising the model for its own purposes.

A number of considerations have to be borne in mind when building this model. In terms of the usability of the model, it must have a user interface which is understandable to the academic community and to senior management. It must have a simple data capture facility, and it must have the capacity to undertake scenario modelling over five years.

Examples of the variances which need to be built into the model to ensure that robust and realistic plans emerge are:

- Full awareness of the behaviour of students on four-year programmes; whether students start at Foundation Level and finish in Year 3, or whether they start in Year 1 and progress to Integrated Masters. These considerations help to calculate the total number of students in each year in a department and even a programme.
- Awareness of the behaviour of repeating students. The Year 1 figures in the model need to be understood as including repeating year students.
- Visibility of sandwich year students, those taking a leave of absence, year abroad or year in industry.
- A link to fees and related bursary and scholarship information to be able to model associated income.
- A way of addressing joint honours degrees to attribute teaching load to each department delivering the joint honours.
- An ability to be able to forecast over/around years when there might not be any students on a niche programme.
- Student numbers at franchise provision, with a different linking into the finance system to show how the validation fee will be broken between the departments.
- Students where funding is derived differently from most UG students, such as nurses funded by Health Trust arrangements.
- Any lower credit bearing activity if it is likely to make a significant difference to the department bottom line, such as continuous professional development (CPD).
- The impact of specific government initiatives such as degree apprenticeships.
- The fact that some programmes have regular intake into Years 2 and 3. The model needs to be able to cope with accepting new entrants into any year.
- An ability to factor in growth in new programmes and to model the effect of teaching out deleted programmes.

The visibility of these different variances helps academic units, when under-taking their student number planning, to see and understand how varieties in the length and type of programmes contribute to overall high-level planning numbers.

Targets and forecasts – the politics

Even before the higher fee of £9,000 per annum was introduced, student numbers on spreadsheets marching forward into the future were the tools and fuel of presidents and vice-chancellor's visions and new strategic plans. Even if it was unrealistic, under a capped environment, to posit significant growth in UK/EU numbers, student number forecasts could show growth in international student numbers.

And here is where strategic planners started to find themselves in political positions required to show or give validity to plans for steady growth in numbers, or growth followed by sustained high numbers over a sequence of years, caused by the need to be able to obtain loans or raise other finance.

So intake targets and student number forecasts became things to be traded as currency in the facilities war among English universities in particular. Ambitious senior teams – anxious to replace aging building stocks in time to attract students away from their rival university – can exert pressure on the planners to predict optimistically and ambitiously or to give credibility to such predictions. Planners can find themselves asked to sign off ten-year forecasts – which by Year 3 or 4 may bear scant resemblance to any known or predictable reality.

The new managerialism in HE – whatever the planning community broadly may think of it – also forces a new definition of target onto the sector. While performance-related pay in the sector is still relatively rare, performance-related promotion is common.

Excellent performance can be hard to demonstrate – meeting student number targets or intake quality is a tangible measure of success. If a target is merely therefore a forecast, based on years of previous data on how student applicants behave, with some adjustment to take account of particular perturbations which may affect a certain year (such as a key policy change), everyone could meet target and its effectiveness as an incentivising mechanism is lost.

However, if a target is too stretching, it creates despondency and resignation if these targets are consistently not met. Worse, it makes the strategy and planning function look out of touch with how applicants are really behaving.

Importance of student number forecasting in predicting and planning an overall strategy

Most strategic planners learn pretty quickly not to put exact figures, such as forecast size of the institution, or annual income in four years' time, in a publicly published strategic plan document. However, most strategic plans will quote ambitions for their size, shape, reputation, regional presence, global reach and so on.

But because student numbers represent the health and vitality of the institution in so many ways, including its financial health, more than ever in today's UK higher education, the student numbers which underpin institutional strategies are crucial, even if they might wisely remain invisible in the strategic plans which are published on websites.

The progress towards achieving a given strategy is increasingly first and foremost measured in the profile, quality and number of students – at least for a recruiting university. Quantifying real growth is relatively straightforward; and it will be a real measure of reputation-building, positioning, planning and marketing know-how, if significant growth is indeed achieved.

The strategic planner is the first person to measure the success of a growth strategy – at the end of each recruitment cycle – in terms of overall numbers, in terms of quality and in terms of the spread of numbers and quality across the different areas of a broad-based institution.

It follows also that the planner is the first person effectively to say to the senior team that the strategy is or is not working, and might need to be revised and rethought. Too few students at a recruiting university may mean putting estates plans on hold as loan finance is not forthcoming, or that key programmes cannot happen; a larger cohort of lower tariff students who might struggle that little bit more might mean that a growing elite university that chooses to lower tariff to meet target may find itself with inadequate remedial resources, student satisfaction issues and higher rates of non-completion or lower numbers of students with good honours on graduation.

Bottom-up student number planning

A key question is to what extent academic units are 'let loose' on the student number planning process. Some institutions set their intentions centrally and then cascade targets through modelling. Others build up an institutional view based on input from their academic units plans.

The academic unit – which is usually an academic department or school, teaching one or two main subject areas, can vary hugely in size – and may set its ideal student numbers based on what the unit thinks it can attract, afford, and teach. It may develop these targets within parameters of growth or maintenance as set by the institution, and/or possibly a middle-layer academic unit such as a faculty comprising several departments.

Most units will seek to recruit a few more students than they recruited in the previous year, unless either there was a one-off shock result (positive or negative), or very clear evidence of decline or growth in a subject area. The problem here is that it is possible that the planning will be done in isolation of the overall needs and priorities of the institution, and possibly from a perspective that is based on the needs of the department and its own specialisms, rather than an interrogation of applications and enrolment patterns more widely. For example, an academic unit is unlikely to propose to end its own programmes because they are not recruiting at quality. On the other hand, modelled institutional plans when cascaded can be seen to be unrealistic when the assumptions made reach the teaching academics who know their own field and peers.

An ideal strategic conversation seeks views from a range of stakeholders, with a solid dollop of realism applied by the strategy and planning office, at a crucial stage in the forecast setting.

Challenges which are set to keep the life of the strategic planner full and interesting

The student planning round is an annual task, but no year is the same as another. The strategic planner must respond rapidly to external factors to flex models, sound alarm bells with the senior team if necessary, and influence other leaders of the need for certain action – whether immediately affecting that planning cycle, or something that will need to be built into long-term strategy.

This chapter has already listed ways in which the strategic planner has had to adapt process and assumptions over the last few years. The following developments have either started or may be due to start and could affect the planner considerably:

- The addition of an inflationary uplift to the student fee. This may mean that some growth plans may slow down. Currently in the sector a fear of bankruptcy is trumping fear of an NSS meltdown in the event of over-recruitment against capacity; this fear will be tempered by the promise of successive years of granting an inflationary uplift to the fee. However, the potential for numbers to be lost from the EU will mean that competition for UK students will continue to grow. Planners will need to watch competitors closely, even at subject level.
- The TEF Gold, Silver and Bronze awards will affect recruitment for 2018. Whether they are a serious factor in student choice will depend on the success of the narrative and promotion around them. Will an unfettered TEF mean the cachet of the Russell Group be gradually eroded, for instance?
- The TEF Gold, Silver and Bronze awards will secure universal fee inflationary uplifts awards for 2018 in England; and for the following year it is promised that differential fees may be applied. It is likely that, given the assumption that fee loans will follow these higher fees, price will be a proxy for quality as measured by the TEF, and it might be assumed, for example, very few students will choose a bronze university because it is cheaper.
- Already there are more private universities in the HE system than previously. The growth of private providers into the traditional young undergraduate space could create significant perturbations in the ability of strategic planners to predict student behaviour.

- The successful planner will work closely with learning and teaching teams in the institution to draw on learning analytics data to inform predictions of student behaviour.

Student number planning – lessons from abroad?

Australia introduced a demand-driven uncapped system of student recruitment to its universities. So far, although Malcolm Turnbull's pre-July 2016 government had mooted the possibility, there was no deregulation of fees, and this looks more uncertain given the political realities in Australia at the time of writing. An uncapped student recruitment combined with uncapped fees would be a first in world higher education. In the light of reducing funding for HE, the Group of 8 universities in Australia (equivalent to the UK Russell Group) say that the system – which has delivered five years of steady growth in student numbers as a whole – is unsustainable. Peter Coaldrake, vice-chancellor of Queensland University of Technology (Coaldrake and Stedman, 2013), saw the system as being largely self-regulating, with a natural high-water mark of 40% of the population.

It is being reported that the Australian system is seeing a greater number of students from poorer backgrounds being recruited to university, but that also the overall average quality of student entering HE is dropping, as universities relax their admissions controls to increase enrolments.

Presumably the move to a deregulated fee would introduce price into the modelling equation in a way which UK strategic planners have not yet had to grapple with. With all universities charging the same fees (or fees with only inflationary differences), planners have not had to model financial appetite or ability to pay into their take-up models. This may be a reality in Australia in the next two to three years – and UK strategic planners should take note.

Conclusion

This chapter has intended to show that it would be a mistake to see strategic planners as student number functionaries. Their roles in some institutions might previously have been to complete external student number returns to funders and regulators, and to help the institution respond to government initiatives, and to serve the director of finance with income forecasts, by ensuring that the university had about the right number of students in the right places in the forecasting model against student number controls. All this remains important. However, the strategic planner is increasingly required, driven by the changing government agenda, markets and demographics, to be able to help academic leaders to respond in strategic and data-informed ways very quickly to short- and long-term changes which could be existential in nature.

Strategic planners lose at their peril a built reputation as the experts in student number planning, forecasting and the shaping of institutions. Planners have the experience and the modelling tools. They must now nurture and develop a forward-facing focus to incorporate rapid external change, so that an extant reputation for understanding and influencing the strategic imperative of institutions' lifeblood can be best utilised to assist their institutions in facing future challenges.

References

Coaldrake, Peter, and Stedman, Laurence (2013, new edition 2016), *Raising the Stakes: Gambling with the Future of Universities.* Brisbane: University of Queensland Press. 2016 edition.

Chapter 6

Generating a research strategy for sustained success and growth

Jane Boggan, Rebecca Lambert, Elizabeth Westlake and Michael Wykes

This chapter is informed by interviews with strategic planners in a range of HE institutions including research intensives, teaching-focussed, modern-applied and specialist institutions across England, Scotland and Wales. In some HEIs, the research planning function sits in the strategy and planning office, often coupled with responsibility for the REF submission and alongside the work supporting the size and shape of the institution. In others the research planning function and REF is led through the institution's research office. In either case the critical challenge is to ensure that a close working relationship is established between the supporting departments, to develop a research strategy that is consistent with, and connected to, the institutional strategy.

Introduction

Why does research need planning, and why does that planning need an institutional strategy? Why can't institutions just trust academic colleagues to get on with it – follow their curiosity and see where it takes them? How do we answer the charge that anything else is bureaucratic meddling, that research and scholarship cannot be corralled into anything as formulaic or prescriptive as a strategy? Those who have been around the research environment as strategic planners for a long time may have some sympathy with this view. So much innovative research and impact is the outcome not just of funding opportunities, knowledge, expertise and imagination, but of bloody-mindedness and serendipity; the right people happening to be in the right place, at the right time, with the right kit. For a research strategy to be effective, then, it has to 'engineer' serendipity – creating an environment where all of those 'rights' are aligned.

Research is expensive. According to HEFCE's (2016) Review of the Financial Health of the Sector, TRAC data demonstrate that across the UK sector research activity does not cover its costs. Consequently, institutions need to prioritise how time and resources are allocated to support research, and in turn support the development of strategic aims and objectives. Those institutions that are most effective at taking those tough decisions around prioritisation of activity and focus, *know* themselves. That is, they have thought through the various options and scenarios to arrive at an optimal balance between investing in areas that are demonstrably strong, supporting areas that are identifiably weak and managing the often complex relationship with teaching. Those decisions will be informed by a thorough understanding of the institution, its aims and ambitions and its context. This understanding will usefully be informed by a combination of metrics, the subject mix and mission-type of the institution, a strong sense of the geopolitical context in which it is located – locally, nationally and globally – and an understanding of the current and future funding landscape. And one of the hallmarks of a successful research strategy is that it will have been co-created with academic and professional services colleagues so that it is recognised as distinctive and authentic across the institution and its stakeholders.

Whilst the UK sector may have been the first, it is not the only one to be subject to a national exercise to assess research quality. Approaches vary from the Australian and Hong Kong models, which are much like the UK REF process; the New Zealand model, which focusses on individual researchers; through to the German Excellence Initiative, which, to a UK audience, has elements that look more like applications for major research grant funding. Much like the REF, these processes all allow participating institutions to benchmark themselves against their peers, and incentivise effective research planning through rewarding excellence.

The sections below explore the different elements that inform the development of a research strategy.

Data and metrics

The HE sector has evolved significantly in its understanding and use of data to inform strategic decision-making. There is now a wealth of data available to aid the strategic planner in understanding research performance more comprehensively.

As might be expected, in the UK REF data are the starting point for many institutions. Responses to Lord Stern's review of REF 2014 (DBEIS, 2016) indicate that institutions consider that REF provides a valuable tool both as a regular external benchmark of research quality but also as a framework for more frequent internal evaluation. The review reports that:

> many, but not all, universities state that they use the REF intensively to manage research performance as the assessment process and results provide an independent measure and driver of research quality. Universities can get a broad picture of their strengths and weaknesses from the REF results; the external scrutiny and benchmarking complement internal performance management and aid strategic planning and decision-making.

This was certainly borne out by all of the institutions surveyed to inform this chapter.

But REF data are by no means the 'be all and end all'. As any strategic planner will know, the key to comprehensive understanding is the triangulation of multiple sources of information. It is important therefore that REF data are supplemented with additional data. A well-defined suite of metrics could constitute a standard sector 'data pack' for research. This includes at least the following datasets:

- REF outcomes
- Research income
- Research grant application and award activity
- PGR applications, enrolments and completions
- Publication activity, such as by frequency, type, publisher
- Bibliometric data, such as citations

Most of these datasets (the exceptions being application and awards data, and bibliometrics data) are easily and freely available to strategic planners in the UK via the online database 'Heidi Plus', the result of a joint project between HESA and Jisc which provides 'access to extensive [comparative] data and the latest visualisation technology to promote efficient decision making' (www.hesa.ac.uk/pr/3767-press-release-223).

Application and award data – which provide valuable insight into an institution's likely income pipeline, and which are the only 'leading' or forward-looking indicators in the standard data pack referenced above – are a largely internal dataset and therefore performance cannot be benchmarked against competitors.[1] The lack of comparative data in this sphere remains a bugbear for many strategic planners.[2]

For a growing number of institutions, the 'standard data-pack' marks a minimum range of metrics. The increased level of sophistication that strategic planners bring to interpreting and analysing data drives competitive advantage, particularly when it comes to implementing strategy (for more on this, see Chapter 11 on business intelligence).

The commercial sector has contributed to the advancement of this analytical capability, through targeted (and expensive) consultancy or the development of (marginally less expensive) data-rich, self-service research performance tools. These performance tools draw on publishers' increasingly comprehensive publication datasets, and allow strategic planners to interrogate co-authorship patterns, geo-specific partnerships and disciplinary areas where their field-weighted citations are the most impactful. By linking social media to bibliometric data, institutions and individual academics alike can see where, when, by whom and how often their research is consumed. Across the Russell Group in particular, a broader range of bibliometrics generated by these performance tools (such as field-weighted citation impact, outputs in top percentiles, h-indices) are gaining traction as 'standard' research metrics informing institutional strategy.[3]

Even the third-party league table compilers (see Chapter 13) have jumped on the research metrics bandwagon; institutions can now purchase academic reputation data or an in-depth analysis of league table performance to inform understanding of institutional performance. Whilst these tools and solutions are expensive (and have little market competition), many institutions have invested in one or more products to provide insights into their own and competitors' performance.

Whatever the institution's approach to data and metrics, there is nonetheless a need for strategic planners to use them wisely to understand their institution and, from this, identify strengths and weaknesses. James Wilsdon's (2015) report, *The Metric Tide* (see Chapter 14), provides a detailed consideration of the value and limitations of metrics in assessing research performance. Planners have myriad ways of analysing the available data to begin to 'get to know' their institution, and as noted above, the level of sophistication attached to an approach can drive competitive advantage.

A simple matrix style analysis (see Figure 6.1) is a good starting point for those seeking to make an initial assessment of institutional strengths and weaknesses to inform research strategy.

Institutions will need to determine for themselves the key criteria driving their own version of 'success', but once identified then research areas can be allocated relative positioning on a matrix as above. For many institutions, upper quartile performance within a group of selected peers was a starter for ten. It is recognised that research activity is complex, and multiple matrices can be used to give a more holistic view of performance across a number of areas. Whilst the above matrix is a rather stark RAG assessment, it should not be seen that those areas in the top right are key candidates for investment and those in the bottom left for immediate closure – we all know the reality is far more nuanced. What this gives is a point of

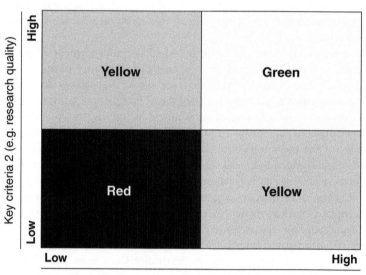

Figure 6.1 A quality matrix

departure for strategic planners in developing a strategy that seeks to sustain and foster areas of strength, and build plans to address and develop areas of weakness. The key is determining the appropriate balance between investment as 'reward' for strong performance and investment to develop. It is also about recognising that, for the vast majority of institutions, a world in which all subjects fall 'top right' is simply unachievable.

The data and metrics we have highlighted above, whether freely accessible via sector platforms, or via commercial products with a weighty price tag, are by definition lagging indicators of historical activity and scale, from which we are trying to extrapolate a plan for future direction. The next and more challenging task is to balance the institutional view we get from the metrics with a more qualitatively informed 'outward look' that is effectively contextualised, future-proofed, agile and understands risk. The survey undertaken for this chapter indicates that there is variable expertise and practice when it comes to the more forward-looking, contextualised activity.

Contextual factors

Geopolitical context

Whether the institution is located in a devolved administration, a new city region, within touching distance of other HEIs in an urban conurbation or a lone provider in a large rural area, location will have a bearing on the institutional research strategy. For institutions in the devolved administrations of the UK (and other countries where there are similar arrangements), there can be a tension between the aspirations and requirements of the devolved assembly, which will have priorities and funding mechanisms that differ from the rest of the country. Conversely, those institutions benefit from a closer proximity and easier access to their funding councils and local assembly. Furthermore, these distinctive environments do not just provide the context in which research operates; they are also the subject of an evolving research agenda in their own right.

Depending on the scope of the strategy, regional considerations are often more significant for knowledge exchange. A global outlook with respect to collaboration opportunities, reputation building, performance benchmarking and strategic alliances is becoming an increasingly fundamental focus of research strategies.

Mission groups and regional networks

The importance of networks, such as mission groups, is growing. For example, in the UK the Russell Group or the University Alliance, or regional groupings like the N8, GW4 and Midlands Innovation, was also explored with the survey group. Generally, institutions regarded such networks as a means to deliver strategic aims, including those relating to research, often through a mixture of research collaboration and collective bargaining power.

Two of the UK post-92 institutions interviewed noted particularly the importance of the University Alliance to developing relationships with funders, gaining access (through collaboration) to DTC funding and to the development of research networks. The GW4 (comprising Bath, Bristol, Cardiff and Exeter) has had a similarly important role, with DTCs cited as an important driver for and benefit from participation. Equally, the alliances deliver benefits of increased critical mass and convening power (with respect to external speakers/visitors) and the collective ability to respond to government initiatives. Likewise, Midlands Innovation (comprising Aston, Birmingham, Leicester, Loughborough, Nottingham and Warwick) has had successes for its constituent institutions with respect to large-scale research and innovation (e.g. multimillion-pound investment to establish the Energy Research Accelerator and the Manufacturing Technology Centre).

Where institutions are able to offer complementary strengths and deliver significant critical mass through such collaborations, and define their contribution clearly enough to publicise the outcomes, networks of this kind are very valuable. Their significance is increasing in England with the growing regional devolution agenda, and with N8 being strongly positioned within the Northern Powerhouse, and Midlands Innovation aligning itself with the recently launched Midlands Engine. Equally, the Scottish Funding Council's (SFC) long-term policy of encouraging and supporting 'research pooling' has been successfully tested through joint submissions to RAE 2008 and REF 2014.

Research funding landscape

A central aim of institutional research strategies will be to maintain, increase and diversify funding for research. This imperative is driven primarily by the high cost of research, particularly in the STEM areas, as well as the need to ensure that the activity is sustainable. However, if institutions are not going to be at the mercy of the ebbs and flows of funder and government strategic priorities, it is essential to develop the capacity to evaluate the external context through systematic intelligence gathering to anticipate and improve their success in securing funding. Institutional approaches vary in how to make this work, but it does require a collaborative effort, typically involving strategic planning teams, public affairs officers and senior academics (through networks of learned societies, subject associations and funding body committees and boards). The challenge is to establish effective systems for capturing, thinking about and using what is effectively tacit knowledge.

A key question for institutions will be whether their evaluation of their particular research strengths leads them to available funding, or if the available funding leads them to develop their strategy. Grand or global challenges, priority areas for innovation, regional or EU priorities and those of specific charities, trusts and foundations provide a wealth of options for the specific aims of institutions' research strategies. Clearly, the more successful strategies will be characterised by the union of anticipation and opportunity, particularly when the research questions are in harmony with academics' interests and institutional mission. And when related funding, especially for doctoral training centres, is so closely correlated with grant capture, success will breed success. Indeed, the 'convening power' of a clear research strategy is not to be underestimated, as institutions will be able to diversify income streams with private sector and philanthropic sources.

It may be argued that the priority areas and sheer volume of funding for STEM makes strategy development a more straightforward task: you've either got critical mass, the latest MRI scanner and a clear funding track record in a particular area or not; you are either within the 'managed group' of a particular funding body or you are not; and isn't it perfectly reasonable that any one country should seek to concentrate funding for expensive equipment and focus resources in a small number of 'centres of excellence'? On the other hand, the brilliant idea of a single humanities academic, perhaps with no funding track record or need for specific resources, could potentially unlock a seven-figure grant – especially from the enlightened European Research Council. In developing sustainable research strategies, therefore, broad-spectrum institutions will need to remain dynamic and opportunistic, with a healthy appetite and capacity for the unexpected against what is 'in-plan'. It would be a mistake, however, to think that there are no surprises with STEM, and indeed when actively diversifying income, especially from philanthropic sources, an institution may well end up with funding for something which it had no intention of researching at all. Ultimately, institutions should ensure that their research strategies follow the overall direction of their institutional objectives and that they are consistent with their values.

Collaboration

It is something of a truism to say that collaboration is at the heart of how science works, although in post-Brexit Britain the statement might be worth repetition. Collaboration takes many forms and whilst, from a planning perspective, it may be about developing single disciplinary areas, more often at an institutional level we are thinking about how to support or encourage inter- or multi-disciplinary research.

Interdisciplinarity

The importance, as well as the challenge, of promoting and supporting interdisciplinarity was a clear imperative across the institutions surveyed. Many institutions implement a range of initiatives to bring people together. For large institutions it requires a concerted effort to overcome what are often complex and dispersed subject communities in which the identification of partners can be challenging and where structural (as well as financial) barriers can operate against any collaborative imperative. Such initiatives range from internal networks with seed-corn funding for sandpit activities, provision of 'collision space' and seminars, to major multimillion-pound investments in buildings to bring staff together into interdisciplinary teams. Dedicated professional services support for interdisciplinary activities and funding applications was often cited as an essential underpinning element.

The survey indicated that HEIs have developed strategies to a greater or lesser extent to support collaborative research (including within single disciplines as well as inter- or multi-disciplinary research), broadly differentiated into the following categories:

- Research themes and institutes
- International collaborations
- Collaboration with non-academic partners

Research themes, institutes and centres

For many institutions, having identified their areas of research strength, the next step is to establish a set of broad research themes as an organising principle by which they present the public face of the 'peaks of excellence' in their research portfolio – a means of branding the distinctiveness of their research, often clustered around major societal problems. An extension of this kind of virtual clustering is to make a strategic investment in interdisciplinary research institutes or centres as a way of consolidating successful interdepartmental, interdisciplinary activities in formal branded structures, with staff, space, equipment and time.

Where this work is a centrally led top-down initiative, it is common for a particular tension to emerge between the aspiration to identify areas of research strength and the wish to be inclusive. The aspiration to publicly present or focus investment in research strength needs careful handling within the institution not to have a demoralising or demotivating effect on those researchers whose work is not included within the areas identified for focus and investment.

When this is a 'bottom-up' approach – where a group of academic colleagues with cognate interests wish to brand themselves as a centre – this activity tends to be managed through an institutional policy on the setting up (and closing down) of a research centre. Without a degree of oversight and vigilance, however, there is a tendency towards a proliferation of collaborative groupings, not all of which will meet the criteria of critical mass and high-quality research.

International collaborations

While internal and local collaboration is significant, all of the respondent Russell Group institutions and the more established post-92 institutions in the UK emphasised the importance of international collaborations as both a driver and indicator of research quality. Formal partnership arrangements with institutions which were perceived as internationally excellent (whether through third-party league tables, citations data or other such measures) were seen as strategically important both to position the institution and as a lever to enhance research quality. Harder to map comprehensively but equally important are the relationships that individual academics have with international colleagues. Increasingly, commercially available publication datasets are enabling strategic planners to map and evaluate the geographical spread of collaborative and co-authored research outputs and to identify key territories and institutions.

Collaboration with non-academic partners

In the UK the development of impact through REF 2014 is one of the changes in recent years to have affected the most fundamental shift in the research ecosystem. It has transformed an activity that had perhaps been something of a Cinderella hitherto. REF 2014 galvanised institutions into prioritising the allocation of time, resources and credit to this activity. For most institutions their latest research strategy will now incorporate knowledge exchange within its scope, and this is by definition a collaborative enterprise. Institutions have always engaged with non-academic partners such as industry, government, NGOs and public bodies or charities, and the private sector. As with other types of collaboration, this can be at the level of a formal memorandum of understanding with major institutions or can be at the level of an individual academic working with a company to develop or improve their products and services. Clearly the institutional context will, to a very large extent, determine the nature of the non-academic partners and the type of relationship that develops.

The call from the Department for Business, Energy and Industrial Strategy (DBEIS, 2015) for responses to the first round of science and innovation (S&I) audits is part of a new and growing emphasis on highly collaborative 'place-based' research. The S&I audits are based on a consortia approach combining universities, research and innovation organisations (e.g. 'Catapult' centres), local enterprise partnerships (LEPs) and their equivalents in the devolved administrations, and businesses. The aspiration is that the audits will help local organisations map their regional research and innovation strengths and identify areas of potential global competitive advantage. This 'bottom-up' approach by government builds on Sir Andrew Witty's (2013) review of universities and growth.

The annual Higher Education – Business and Community Interaction (HE-BCI) survey data, available through HEIDI, are a valuable, if limited, source of benchmark data for activity in the area of knowledge exchange. At the time of writing, HEFCE's work in the UK on a knowledge exchange performance framework is still in development, but that work has the potential to provide a valuable set of resources for strategic planners in this area (http://www.hefce.ac.uk/ke/KEportal/).

How does teaching contribute to a research strategy?

TRAC data and proposals to introduce the Teaching Excellence Framework to sit alongside the Research Excellence Framework in the UK mean that institutions need to consider the relationship between their teaching and research strategies at all times. Being closely involved in both REF and TEF strategies, strategic planners are arguably uniquely positioned to inform the decisions which each institution must take to remain successful.

The survey highlighted the enormously positive and symbiotic relationship between teaching and research which institutions discuss regularly with their students and governing bodies alike. In terms of how to develop a research strategy, the issues which strategic planners need to consider include: what is the optimal balance between teaching-only staff and those contracted to deliver teaching and research; how to recover the missing 20% of funding for research which according to TRAC is loss-making; how students are involved in and 'co-create' research; what is the relationship between the infrastructural requirements and revenue sources from research and learning activities; how to plan capital investment to create distinctive learning and research environments, and which has the prior claim on funding; what sort of indicators prove that students benefit from a 'research-led' education; and what are the implications for governance structures? And now that UK institutions will be operating both a REF and a TEF, and potentially at subject level in both exercises, what is the strength of the correlation between excellence in one and in the other?

Of course, prior to any considerations of this nature, it is important to acknowledge the simple fact that, at a national scale, revenue from research grants and contracts accounts for less than 18% of total income, and that barring a few postgraduate-dominated institutions, UG activity is the single largest source of income for every institution in the UK. Table 6.1 below shows the sources of income by type to UK institutions in 2014/15.

Whilst the situation is less stark in other countries, the relationship between teaching and research is a particularly acute question for the UK, and we address several of the questions raised above in determining how institutions develop their research strategies.

First, what is the 'right' balance between teaching-only and teaching and research staff, what are the financial issues and why do they matter? It is important to hold onto the 'so what' element of this question, since attempting to apply a minimum

Table 6.1 Sources of income 2014/15

Source	Income (£000s)	% of total
Funding body grants	5,279,035	15.9%
Tuition fees and education contracts	15,585,517	46.9%
Research grants and contracts	5,912,016	17.8%
Other income	6,062,545	18.3%
Endowment and investment income	359,559	1.1%
Total income	33,198,672	

Source: HESA

proportion of either teaching and research or teaching-only staff within an institution may lead to an inflexible regime which generates negative outcomes for students and staff alike. Whilst it is easy to say that an institution needs the 'right' balance, or that strength in both elements should be mutually reinforcing, it may well be the case that research stars are not actually those who are delivering the core-course content; that success in student recruitment may have, at least in the short term, a negative impact on research should SSRs creep upwards; or that a high proportion of teaching-only staff presents a barrier to growing your research power. And from the TRAC perspective, we may well wish to leave particular stones unturned rather than provide a detailed breakdown of the cost of delivering a history degree as opposed to one in biological sciences, say, despite the fact that institutions charge the same fee for both degrees. However, being explicit about the synergies between teaching and research, providing transparent information about the financial relationship between the two and how overall institutional finances operate will present a strong platform upon which to build critical mass. Ultimately the size and shape of the institution, the balance between teaching and research, should be adequately resourced, appreciated and enable growth in reputation.

Second, what is the evidence base for championing research-led teaching, and perhaps more importantly its inverse relationship: teaching-inspired research? The survey suggested that some of the more powerful evidence comes in the form of anecdotal accounts from individual academics, from orations at graduation ceremonies, and from a close reading of the acknowledgements to monograph publications. At the same time, the increasing quality and visibility of bibliometric indicators may mean that institutions would be able to evidence the number of research papers where all students – and not just PhD students – were named as an author. Further afield, is there evidence in high proportions of students continuing to further study, which supports the case for research-led education, or of greater numbers of students in highly skilled occupations, perhaps? The TEF may well tease out these relationships.

Finally, how might we bring together the data on teaching and research to present their interconnectedness, areas of particular strength and/or weakness?

Conclusion

In reviewing how institutions actually put their strategy together, it is possible to observe research planning from both ends of the continuum; from the work of a single inspired brain steering the way, through to a thoroughly bottom-up and consultative process, sprinkled with varying amounts of foresight activity, benchmarking and data analyses. Strategy and planning offices are often central to the development of overall institutional strategies (see Chapters 2 and 3), and hence component strategies, such as research, need to be consistent with the 'bigger picture'. Strategic planners have a central role to play in ensuring overall intelligibility and fit with the institutional strategy, and in recognising that compromises need to be made in developing a fully coherent, and achievable, strategy.

Finally, as much as they may want to be, institutions cannot be all things to all people, and an effective strategy needs to present clear priorities and accept that this means compromises elsewhere. The whistle-stop review on the preceding pages should give a sense of the range of factors in play, and the resources available to inform the decisions to be taken.

Notes

1 Some high-level institutional award data are available via RCUK annual reports, however it is a laborious manual process to extract the data and not a sustainable practice for overworked planners.
2 Jisc Heidi Lab does however have plans to pilot the development of a sector research awards database which, if it comes to fruition, would be a welcome move forward. See www.business-intelligence.ac.uk/heidi-lab/ The Snowball Metrics project may also provide a way forward. See https://www.snowballmetrics.com/
3 Concerns about the potential misuse of these data led to the academic community developing such statements as the San Francisco Declaration on Research Assessment (DORA) www.ascb.org/dora/ and the Leiden Manifesto (Bibliometrics: The Leiden Manifesto for research metrics, *Nature News*, 22 Apr 2015), and increasingly institutions are using these to inform the responsible use of bibliometric data in particular.

References

BIS (2013) Encouraging a British Revolution: Sir Andrew Witty's Review of Universities and Growth, BIS, October 2013.

DBEIS (2015) Science and Innovation Audits, Calls for Expression of Interest. https://www.gov.uk/government/publications/science-and-innovation-audits-submit-an-expression-of-interest

DBEIS (2016) Research Excellence Framework (REF) Review: Building on Success and Learning from Experience, Department for Business, Energy and Industrial Strategy, 2016.

HEFCE (2016) Financial Health of the Higher Education Sector: Financial Results and TRAC Outcomes 2014/15, HEFCE, www.hefce.ac.uk/pubs/year/2016/201604/ [accessed 22/12/2016]

Wilsdon, James (2015) The Metric Tide: Report of the Independent Review of the Role of Metrics in Research Assessment and Management, HEFCE, July 2015.

Centrality, co-ordination and connection

Part 3

Centrality, co-ordination
and connection

Chapter 7

Leadership, governance and decision-making

Tony Strike and David Swinn

Introduction

The link between strategy and planning as an office, as an organisational activity and its link to leadership, governance and decision-making can best be illustrated by asking a question: Who are the customers of a strategy and planning office? Or to put it another way, who does this function serve?

Like any large, complex organisation, higher education institutions (HEIs) have internal governance and decision-making structures. These structures will include a governing body and academic board, both with subcommittees, an academic leader who is accountable both to the governing body and other external agencies as an accountable officer (a president, vice-chancellor or principal) and often there will be an executive group which advises or exercises delegated decision-making powers on behalf of the institutional leader.

The governing body will be collectively concerned with determining the future direction of the institution, with standards of educational provision, the performance and sustainability of the institution as a whole, its long-term plans and whether or not these are being achieved, and with the risks the institution faces. For example, the Committee of University Chairmen (CUC) in the UK produced a new Code of Governance in 2014 which stated:

> The governing body ensures institutional sustainability by working with the Executive to set the institutional mission and strategy. In addition, it needs to be assured that appropriate steps are being taken to deliver them and that there are effective systems of control and risk management.
>
> (CUC Code, 2014, p. 15)

Once a strategy has been set out, the governing body will want to assess progress using an appropriate range of mechanisms which may include relevant key performance indicators (KPIs). These are the functions directly co-ordinated and supported by those with a strategy and planning functional brief, and they bring the function in contact with the corporate governance of the university.

A president, vice-chancellor or principal will have responsibility for strategic and operational decision-making. This will often mean he or she will want to set out academic priorities, to have these interpreted into operational plans, perhaps with targets and goals, and to receive reports back at the appropriate interval directly or through an executive board on progress or achievement of those priorities. To inform their priorities, they may want actionable insight on developments in the sector and external environment, on opportunities and risks, and on how their institution is performing – and to have that insight benchmarked in relation to peers or competitors. The president, vice-chancellor or principal may feel his or her success is linked to the ability to set the institution's values and culture, to develop and articulate a plan and to see his or her goals and ambitions for the institution successfully delivered. Where leaders see themselves as a facilitator or enabler of the plans of others, those plans still need to be extant in order to be supported.

This chapter seeks to set out the governance and management arrangements found in HEIs and the key relationship between those functions, often led by a university secretary, and the role of a strategy and planning department.

The governance structure

Despite the assertion in the preface to the UK's most recent Committee of University Chairmen (CUC) Higher Education Code of Governance (the Code) that "good governance is at the heart of the higher education sector in the UK, and will continue to be of the highest importance as it continues to develop", appropriate structures ('good' governance) are not in themselves an indicator of institutional success. Although the organisation of structures must suit the aims and objectives of the HEI, those structures rely on an engaged and effective membership and need to be aligned with institutional culture in order to create an environment of constructive challenge and a sense of collective ownership of strategic objectives, which will themselves have been devised in accordance with the institutional strategic plan.

> [S]uccessful universities try to ensure that governance is kept in balance between an active lay contribution, strong corporate leadership, an effective central steering core and an involved and participative senate/academic board. Where any element is weak the institution is disadvantaged.
>
> (Shattock, 2003, p. 97)

This highlights that when university governance is working well, three bodies each have a unique role and the ability to support each other and to keep each other constructively in check. The executive, led by the vice-chancellor (as accountable officer) has the management prerogative and can make decisions in relation to the running of the HEI. Powers are delegated to the vice-chancellor by council and perhaps from him or her to other officers or committees. Council remains ultimately responsible and holds the executive and the accountable officer to account. The senate is the supreme academic body and decides on academic matters; chaired by the vice-chancellor, the senate reports to the council on its activities (but see below). If the vice-chancellor wishes to set up a new academic activity, for example, the business plan and financial and risk elements will be a matter for the council, and the senate will be responsible for academic quality, standards and quality assurance. The vice-chancellor, depending on his or her delegated powers, would need authority to proceed from both bodies in this bicameral structure.

An effective strategic planning process must engage with each level of the governance structure in the appropriate way, tailored to the audience and to the role which a particular committee, business unit or individual is performing on a given matter. An effective HEI should ensure that those levels are structured in a way that fits the institution and be similarly constituted to reflect organisational culture, from bottom-up to top-down, in order to encourage and enable meaningful contributions from all the interested individuals and constituencies and create the necessary sense of 'ownership' amongst them.

Council (or the governing body)

In the UK, HEIs have historically been independent and autonomous bodies; private chartered institutions with degree-awarding powers. The council (in Scotland the court) or governing body is ultimately responsible for the whole of an HEI's affairs and is very broadly comparable to a board of company directors. However, despite recent efforts to reduce their size, governing bodies in higher education are still relatively large bodies of, usually, between 12 and 24 persons. That membership will include a majority of lay members, including the chair, drawn predominantly from other sectors outside of higher education who, with the exception of a very small minority – usually the chairs – receive no remuneration; and usually members drawn from the executive and wider staff body, for example the vice-chancellor and members of the senate or academic board. There is usually at least one student member, more often than not the president of the students' union. The members are collectively accountable as governors, and there should be no distinction made between the different categories of membership in terms of responsibility and duties. Chartered institutions in the UK have greater flexibility in terms of governing body membership than post-92 institutions, which for historical reasons are subject to stricter rules on staff and student governors. Frequently, other senior managers or members of the executive will attend meetings of council and relevant subcommittees as a matter of course, in order to provide clarification and support discussion by members. Councils are typically well constituted for their particular role of governing the institution.

However, the overall responsibility of a governing body for all institutional affairs (detailed in the UK in the CUC Code) can create a tension when viewed in conjunction with the need for those HEIs established as charities to act in accordance with their charitable objects, as expressed in their constitutional documents (where relevant). Generally, that clause will provide for education to be advanced through teaching and research, or similar. The strategic planning process, indeed the development of the strategy itself, must ensure that the academic community is engaged and so feels empowered in such a way that it facilitates delivery of those objectives, but accountability lies ultimately with the governing body.

To an extent, that can cause friction between the most senior governing body (the council) and the senior academic body (senate or academic board) which is, for example, reflected in the most recent CUC Code and the Higher Education Funding Council for England's (HEFCE's) Revised Operating Model for Quality Assessment 2016 (and Memorandum of Assurance and Accountability [MAA]). These publications place greater emphasis on the need for governing bodies to work with their senate or academic board to assure themselves that governance of academic affairs (i.e. quality assurance processes) are effective. The council has little competence and no experience of oversight of academic quality and has traditionally deferred to its senate or academic board on such matters.

It is arguable that this stronger emphasis on the role of the council or governing body over academic matters has more to do with the CUC and HEFCE reflecting the political environment in which HE in the UK is now operating, taking into account particularly the emergent HE legislation and the ongoing drive towards treating HEIs simply as providers of a product in a market and students as consumers. This rather than recognising that HEIs are through their senates or academic boards the guardians and protectors of standards and quality with degree-awarding powers that may be enshrined in royal charters. Academic governance has been somewhat neglected in the past when considering HE governance per se.

Universities formed following the 1988 Education Reform Act and 1992 Further and Higher Education Act were subject to strict models for those institutions previously funded directly from the local authority or government department. As a result, such institutions were largely established as higher education corporations or companies limited by guarantee, and the governors of these institutions had additional responsibilities as company directors in addition to the accountability requirements on governors of other universities.

Note that in Scotland HEIs are subject to a separate "Code of Good HE Governance (2013)". Scottish HEIs must comply with the 2013 code as a condition of funding from the Scottish Funding Council. In March 2016, the Scottish Parliament passed the Higher Education Governance (Scotland) Act, which brings a number of additional new requirements on institutions' governance arrangements. Both the 2013 code and 2016 act are intended to address the recommendations of the 2012 Report of the Review of [Scottish] Higher Education Governance, which was chaired by Ferdinand von Prondzynski. Although a longer document than the CUC Code, the general themes and underlying principles are very similar.

The role of the council in measuring and monitoring institutional performance can be challenging for newer lay members, who may well have a private sector background in which delivery of shareholder value, for example through sound financial performance, is the key driver of success. In a university, financial sustainability is important because it supports, in theory at least, the continued provision of the objects of the institution, that is, high-quality learning, teaching and research. As the ongoing debate about the Teaching Excellence Framework (TEF) metrics and Lord Stern's review of the Research Excellence Framework (REF) shows, effectively measuring these elements externally from the institution itself, or at all, is difficult. The attempted metrification of academe is at one level useful as information to academic leaders but arguably problematic if it becomes the pervasive way for governments or regulators to measure and regulate a whole sector. Furthermore, for the academic staff, whether an institution or indeed their respective individual discipline is performing well can be a disputed question of either or all of achieving reputation (amongst academic peers), of satisfying students, of making a financial return on their activities (subject to rules on a charity being able to make 'social investments'), of achieving the charitable objectives of their university, of furthering knowledge through discovery or in the worst cases achieving some relative institutional rank compared to other HEIs. When preparing briefings and papers for either senate or council (or the executive), the strategic planner will need to help those bodies reflect on what their goals are, how success might be evidenced and the way in which information presented may be interpreted in order to ensure that any resultant action is appropriately conceived in the wider institutional interest, that is delivery of strategy in accordance with mission, vision, identity and charitable purpose.

Strong (academic) staff satisfaction is more likely to correlate to strong local representation in the formal governance structure. The extent to which academic opinion is, or at least is perceived to be, able to shape strategy and inform the planning process through governance structures will be a key contributor to satisfaction. Governing body effectiveness (or otherwise) remains important, as it may have a significant, albeit indirect, impact if academics feel constrained as a result of its decisions, for example in setting budgets and prioritising capital spend. A successful strategic planning process will need to factor in the potential that contentious or unpopular decisions of the governing body (and senior management) will need to be carefully communicated and their rationale understood, to mitigate the risk that lower staff satisfaction precludes the development and achievement of academic objectives. Academic staff are often concerned with a tendency towards managerialism, or a tendency for academic goals to become subordinate to other objectives. Strategic planners can through engagement with the governance structures and with academic staffs help make it clear their role is entirely in support of the academic mission.

Senate or the academic board

The senate or academic board is normally responsible for the governance of academic matters, including strategies for teaching and research, student admissions and attainment, award of degrees and academic quality. The academic strategy of an institution will need to connect to other areas, particularly resources such as staffing, estates and, more broadly, finance. As a result, the health of the relationship and level of interaction between senate and the governing body are vital to effective governance and institutional success.

There are large variations in the composition of senates or academic boards across the HE sector. In many institutions in the UK, particularly post-92 and other modern universities, membership will be relatively small and prescribed, whereas in others the senate is a largely representative body in which all academic members of the executive, heads of departments and other senior academic staff are afforded ex officio membership, with a sizeable additional membership elected from the wider staff body. The larger, representative senate is a characteristic of pre-92 universities that have not undertaken reform (within the Russell Group, the size of senate ranges from around 40 to about 150 persons) and is a relic of a bygone era in academic governance and wider university management when institutions and the entire HE sector were much smaller and the business of running a university – in effect as self-governing bodies with highly active academic participation in institutional-level decision-making – was almost unrecognisable from today.

There is little that can be said in favour of this kind of large unreformed academic body – it does not involve its membership effectively in decisions, it is wasteful of resources, and critical decisions tend to move away from it to executive committees or some informal group (Shattock, 2003) because the senate is too big and unwieldy to discuss or make major decisions effectively and so it offers only the appearance of collegial academic decision-making. The academic business that should be at the heart of any senate becomes increasingly formal except when discontent arises on some sectional issue; and when this occurs it is difficult to ensure that a rational decision is reached (Shattock, 2003).

Like the council as governing body, academic boards will be supported by dedicated subcommittees dealing with teaching, research and possibly ethics. The increasing use of graduate schools means that there may be separate committees to deal with undergraduate and postgraduate (or at least postgraduate research) students while, depending on the organisational structure of the institution, senates will often receive reports from individual faculty or college boards. Where faculties and/or colleges do not report into the senate, then, regardless of the senate's size and membership, greater reliance is invariably placed on the executive – as a group or the relevant individual member – to ensure that faculty and departmental academic strategy is aligned with that of the institution, as espoused by the senate (and council), and that this contribution and interrelationship is properly communicated and understood across the institution.

Reports and guidance on governance have historically tended to focus on governing bodies (generally in response to failures). However, effective governance of academic affairs, falling within the remit of the senate or academic board, is as likely, if not more so, to contribute to institutional success, concerned as that body is with the core activities of teaching and research. In the case of charitable institutions, by discharging that function, the senate or academic board might be said to have a greater direct impact on the ability of the organisation to achieve its charitable objects, notwithstanding that this may rely on the governing body taking the necessary decisions relating to resources to support delivery.

In UK pre-92 universities, which have not revised or modernised their constitution, the senate is still established as the supreme authority in academic matters, as an equal partner with the governing body in a bicameral system. In UK post-92 universities it is the governing body which is invested with the power to direct educational strategy, with a more limited role for the academic board in making proposals to inform those decisions. The role of the senate in directing or proposing academic strategy may sit uneasily with the "unambiguous and collective accountability" (CUC Code, 2014) of the governing body for institutional activities, but the different operational arrangements are accommodated in the subsequent 'element' of the code that requires governing bodies simply to receive assurance from the senate that academic governance is effective "as specified in its governing instruments". Likewise, the MAA reiterates the need for governing bodies to receive assurance about the effectiveness of the HEI's framework for managing academic quality and maintaining standards "overseen by its senate, academic board, or equivalent", as well as delivery of charitable purpose for the public benefit.

For similar reasons – of greater accountability requirements, public and political scrutiny, and competition – growing interest from UK governing bodies in academic affairs mirrors that which has developed in recent years in the US, where governing bodies have been increasingly encouraged to engage in academic governance to a higher degree than has historically been the case. The role of the governing body in academic affairs can raise questions about the principle of academic freedom, which is enshrined in the constitutions of many universities. In a chartered institution the governing body is likely to be under a duty to uphold this principle, which is referred to in the CUC Code (and the most recent Scottish Code). Nevertheless, the governing body's responsibility for ensuring that risk management processes are adequate effectively supports the idea that major academic decisions should be subject to scrutiny and oversight from both council and senate.

The relationship between the academic board and governing body may be best summed up by David Williams, writing for the Leadership Foundation (Governor's Briefing Notes 04 – Academic Governance and Quality):

> The boundary between academic and corporate governance is an area where higher education governance is evolving, and may be expected to continue to do.

Ultimately, what matters is that council and senate are able to work together effectively; that the views of each are taken into account, respecting their distinctive roles, and similarly that the rationale underpinning the decisions of one is understood by the other. This is especially true for decisions of the governing body that will indirectly affect academic strategy and/or delivery, for example resource allocation and capital planning. Having a strategic plan, which sets out clearly the shared goals and values of the HEI, can help ensure and remind all parties that they are ultimately all seeking the same ends. A planning cycle which is clearly academically led and involves the relevant stakeholders can help promote a shared understanding of the opportunities, constraints, barriers and risks involved in making progress towards shared goals. Mutual reporting, and the sharing of relevant subcommittee reports, can help to foster the necessary sense of collegiality and openness provided that they are not so anodyne as to be meaningless or so vague as to even create suspicion. Neither should they contain any 'nasty surprises': ideally those matters of significance will have been developed with the contribution of all concerned. The imposition of strategies or initiatives that are not supported or in which the academic community has had little or no input is likely to hamper institutional progress by inhibiting academic ambition, stifling innovation and undermining delivery of strategic objectives.

The role of the president, vice-chancellor or principal

> The head of an HEI is first and foremost responsible for leadership of the academic affairs and executive management of the HEI.
>
> (HEFCE, 2016/03, p. 9)

In the UK this position is most commonly known as the vice-chancellor, although the US designations of president and principal are increasingly used – reflecting in part the globalised nature of 21st-century higher education. They are invariably an academic, although the move to more 'corporate' models of management and leadership and the growth of alternative and private providers may result in the appointment of more heads of institutions with a professional background.

Invariably, the head of an HEI will be designated by its governing body as the 'accountable officer', responsible for reporting to the funding council (HEFCE, HEFCW, SFC), on behalf of an HEI to discharge the governing body's responsibility for the use of public funds.

Historically, the vice-chancellor was primarily a scholar who chaired the senate and willed the implementation of academic strategies and policies (Jarratt Report on University Management, 1985). Over time, in response to wider sectoral changes and the evolution of universities to operate more like businesses, the role has increasingly shifted to provide strong leadership and direction. The transformation of vice-chancellors into, effectively, chief executive officers was predicted in the Jarratt Report, which stated:

> The shift to the style of chief executive, bearing responsibility for leadership and effective management of the institution, is emerging and is likely to be all the more necessary for the future . . . the use of Pro-Vice-Chancellors will be increasingly vital.
>
> (Jarratt Report pp. 26–7, quoted in Tight, 2009)

Executive boards and their role

Many higher education institutions will have an executive board, senior management team, policy and resources committee or other such steering committee that supports and advises the president, vice-chancellor or principal, including on planning and resourcing decisions. These groups may be established within the formal institutional structure of governance or operate outside it, although even in the case of the latter the local convention and practice will often treat them as a distinct stage in the formal decision-making process. The executive group can exist to advise the vice-chancellor, they can have powers delegated to them formally to make collective decisions for the vice-chancellor or given from council or they can possess only the powers of the individuals gathered where they choose to consult each other or submit to a majority view.

Strategic planners will need to understand the arrangements in their own institution, as well as the relationship of the executive group with the senate and council. Whether a report or recommendation goes to council or senate, or one of the committees of each, or to the executive board or to one of its senior or academic officers, can represent a maze for those less familiar with the internal decision-making structures of universities, and practice will vary place to place. Membership of executive boards, where they exist, will vary according to the particular institutional structure, but they are likely to include, in addition to the vice-chancellor: the deputy vice-chancellor(s) and/or pro-vice-chancellors, a chief financial officer or director of finance, the registrar or chief operating officer or university secretary (where they exist) and some institutions may include other senior professional services representatives, for example the directors of HR, estates, legal and compliance, marketing, strategy and planning and so forth. In some cases the executive group will include representation from other organs of formal governance, notably the senate or academic board. They can also include deans of faculty and can vary substantially in size from one university to the next.

The evolution of this kind of executive layer in the decision-making process has followed the broader trends towards a more managerial and corporate approach to university leadership (at basic level, for example, the adoption by UK HE governance codes of the 'comply/apply or explain' principle used in other sectors), and the need for flexible and rapid decision-making in times of change and challenge, and increased competition in the sector that have created greater complexity in the HE operating environment. However, regardless of status or membership, it is important that the executive group maintains strong links and engagement with the governance framework and must ensure that its decisions are not taken ultra vires (that is beyond its powers) or that the proposals it formulates do not preclude meaningful discussion, input and challenge from both the council as governing body and the senate or academic board (or their subcommittees) where there are academic consequences. The clerk to the council (sometimes called university secretary), who may also be the secretary to the senate or academic board, should normally attend the executive group's meetings to advise the executive and others on these matters of delegation and authority.

Courts and convocation

In England and Wales, the constitutions of many pre-1992 universities, particularly the red-brick, civic institutions, still provide for the existence of a court. Historically, the function of these bodies was to discharge the responsibilities now dealt with by the governing body/council. (It is important to note that in Scotland the governing body is called the court.) The English and Welsh courts are large (often up to 200 members) and now generally treated as ceremonial bodies whose membership is representative of the host city or region, including senior figures from politics, business and the professions, and local community groups. They are chaired by the university's chancellor, now a similarly ceremonial post with little or no meaningful role in institutional governance. In addition, membership will often include a number of representatives of the alumni body (convocation). In modern times, the powers of courts have become increasingly limited, for example to receiving annual reports and accounts and appointing the chancellor, and may be used simply as a means to raise understanding and awareness of institutional activity amongst the local and regional community.

Convocations are, or were, the official alumni body under a university's constitution, often with the chair holding ex officio membership of the governing body, and usually provide a number of members to the court.

As the business of higher education and the management and governance of universities has evolved (with an increasing national and global outlook and the development of modern practices more in keeping with companies), the traditional model of courts and convocations has become increasingly outdated, and many universities have sought to reform, reconstitute or completely disband these bodies, often preferring to embed local and regional engagement within strategic themes and adopting a more targeted, refined approach to alumni relations and development more akin to the US model.

Faculties

Faculties and departments will be primarily concerned with governance of academic affairs, whose impact will be felt more directly, although matters such as finance and capital planning are becoming of increasing interest depending on the extent of devolved budgetary responsibility and accountability. Often, usually when the faculty comprises a significant number of individual academic departments, it may have large budgetary responsibility and accountability, including discretion to flex budgets across its departments and authority to shape the strategic direction of individual units. Understanding practice in a given institution, and the relationships between departments and the faculty (and also the interrelationships between departments) is vital if a strategic planner is to effectively support the faculty and department. At institutional level, understanding the dynamic between faculties or colleges is equally if not more important to the effective implementation of institutional strategy. Successful institutions with satisfied staff will ensure that constituent departments within a faculty operate as a collegiate group, and that the faculties operate similarly at corporate level.

Deans and heads of academic departments

Individual heads of academic departments will each have an academic unit to lead. This is usually done in a collegial way with others but will involve decisions on such matters as curriculum, marketing, student numbers and student support, research priorities, staffing and staff roles, resources, workload allocation, space allocation, facilities and so on.

In some institutions cognate departments are formed into colleges or deaneries or faculties with an academic leader or chair who both represents and leads the disciplines involved.

Planning and governance

At each of the accountability levels described above, those involved will have a need for support in their leadership and decision-making, usually for information and impartial analysis. The close link between the activity of strategy and planning and the role of governance and leadership in an institution means that governance support is often a primary relationship. This is to ensure that the right issues are discussed in the right place, at the right time and supported by the right information, to facilitate effective decision-making.

It is the various decision-makers in the governance structure that the strategy and planning office supports or serves. Even where strategy and planning as a function is not involved in or is remote from the formal processes of governance support in the institution, they will often be asked to support decision-makers; although the requirements for support, insight, information and planning at different levels will vary.

The governance within academic units is vital to ensuring that local strategies prioritise activity that is aligned with institutional strategy and that central policies devised to support the achievement of its objectives are applied consistently and objectively (Shattock, 2003). However, those latter aspects demand that attention be given to non-academic elements, HR, finance, IT, ethics – matters traditionally established as being ultimately subject to the authority of the governing body. Internal audit can play an important role here, helping management to identify gaps or inconsistencies, and providing assurance to the governing body over the efficacy of local arrangements in the institutional context.

A changing climate: alternative and private providers

The governance of private HEIs is not as restricted by higher education legislation. However, where they seek degree-awarding powers and university title they must demonstrate to the relevant sector bodies, for example the Quality Assurance Agency (QAA) and HEFCE/HEFCW (or the Office for Students), and government departments that they have strong and effective governance processes to ensure academic quality and standards in order to protect students and to safeguard the quality and reputation of UK HE. Nevertheless, the role and culture of these institutions may be significantly different and perhaps narrower from that of a 'traditional', publicly funded university: moving away from being responsible to a wide range of stakeholders for the delivery of charitable objectives to a primary responsibility to shareholders for return (Copland, 2014).

That differing philosophy will pose challenges to both types of institutions in an environment in which an increasing number of publicly funded universities are, or are considering, establishing partnerships with new and alternative HE providers.

As private organisations, new and alternative providers tend to adopt a more corporate and managerial approach to institutional governance, as far removed (at least in structural terms) from the pre-1992 institutional model as any other commercial organisation. Depending on how the private provider is established, it may have governance arrangements designed to comply with the UK Corporate Code of Governance or that take into account both the Corporate Code and the CUC Code for HEIs, although the trend towards a more 'corporate' approach in traditional publicly funded HEIs means that many of these provisions will be complementary. For example parts of the 2014 CUC Code such as those relating to effectiveness reviews, remuneration and audit clearly draw on related areas of the Corporate Code, which also (along with related publications and guidance from the Financial Reporting Council) includes sections that translate usefully into an HE environment, notably decision-making, effectiveness, risk management, and for the clerk or governance team, guidance on the role of the company secretary.

Higher education institutions in the UK operate under a range of different legal entities, from royal charter corporations through limited companies and higher education corporations to trusts, although the latter model is now rare, as these bodies have tended to incorporate. These different legal statuses equate to different powers, an anomaly that has received only limited attention from government in the past. However, as the sector evolves and private sector involvement increases, the issue is likely to face closer scrutiny. For example, the restrictions placed on publicly funded universities by their charitable status might lead to increasing numbers considering establishing new structures to undertake activities that would fall outside of their charitable purpose (Universities UK, 2009).

Although the different legal statuses of UK HEIs may appear strange, the position is not unique; contrast this with the position in the US, whose 3500+ HEIs are a more developed mix of public, private not-for-profit and private for-profit institutions. In the US, these public institutions are accountable to the state and subject to only limited oversight at federal level, which has led to the development of a wide range of governance structures, while in some states private HEIs are overseen collectively by a single state governing body. Private US HEIs are autonomous and therefore subject only to general regulatory oversight, although that oversight has increased in the 21st century, and is likely to be an increasingly important concern for US governing bodies, as it has become in the UK. Such variations in governance practice at state and federal level are also present in Australia, where the system of governance generally follows more closely the traditional UK model and concerns about corporate governance more broadly (as in New Zealand, too) have similarly informed reforms in HE governance (Austin and Jones, 2016).

> Governance in most UK HEIs sits between these two approaches, accountability to the funding bodies providing a constraint not placed on private US universities, but it is much less demanding and politically interventionist than in some US states.
>
> (Schofield, 2009, p. 95)

That said, since 2009 the evolution of both the UK HE sector and the UK's wider political climate may threaten this greater freedom from political intervention, for example the establishment of UK Research and Innovation (UKRI) and broader efforts to align the missions and strategies of HEIs with industrial and regional policy, potentially leading to greater political direction of institutional strategy, and therefore planning.

Adaptability for the audience

The interdependencies between the levels of a higher education institution and across different disciplines or functions will create complexity, as costs (such as staffing and space requirements) will depend on income (student numbers or research activity), which will depend on the academic strategy. The academic strategy will be set considering national policy, competitor behaviour, existing strengths and the risks faced by a department or discipline. To the extent that strategic planners help pull together and co-ordinate the required inputs means they should be close advisers to those with leadership and governance roles.

It is, therefore, important that strategy and planning know when working on an issue who they are working for and why. Sometimes the strategic planner is an information authority where accuracy and timeliness in presenting the facts is key; sometimes a policy analyst role is expected where the strategic planner is asked to have a view; sometimes a spin doctor is required, presenting the data in the best possible light for some audience; sometimes a knowledge manager is wanted to reliably bring different elements together from various sources to a synthesis; and sometimes a researcher is sought to explain or interpret particular findings (Terenzini, 1993). For example, the governing body may want a balanced and understandable assessment of the university's performance presented in a fair and honest way, whereas an executive board may expect the strategic planner to have formed an opinion based on the data and want to hear that view, while a funder or regulator may seek reported findings based in evidential fact. Choosing and distilling information is rarely a neutral act.

This may all sound like a subtle distinction, but it is critical. Good governance requires effective processes of assurance, not merely reassurance. Governors or council members are reliant not only on information given to them by the president, vice-chancellor or principal or by his or her executive board or senior management group. The governing body must agree and have access to information on the performance of the higher education institution which they see as independent and factual and which they can understand, question and evaluate. Without this a governing body will find it hard to hold its executive to account. The quality of information a governing body receives on the performance of the institution will impact significantly on its ability to perform its role effectively.

That ability, whilst it has always been critical, will come under increasingly sharp scrutiny in the UK as a result of the Higher Education and Research Bill, which is before Parliament at the time of writing. The establishment of an Office for Students (OfS), in effect modelled on the regulators of traditional provider/consumer sectors, and the ability of politicians to remove institutional degree-awarding powers granted, in the pre-92 universities for example, by royal charter, is a severe blow to the autonomy of institutions. The introduction of the TEF and related provisions emphasising the need for greater governing body involvement in academic governance, and moves to allow significantly more political direction of the sector in activities such as outreach and widening participation, mean that both governing bodies and management will need to reflect on how institutional performance is perceived by a range of external audiences. How information is reported and presented to each of those audiences will be a key consideration for the strategic planner. Notwithstanding the many sound philosophical arguments against a system of HE that is founded on market-based principles rather than those of the public good, the strategic planner will need to ensure that the organisation is able to evaluate its position in the 'market'. Although student recruitment and generation of research income are areas in which universities are well versed in competition, governors and management can be expected to take a greater interest in institutional relationships with national and local politics, industry and regulators.

In an era of significant challenge for the HE sector as a whole, in which pressure on resources and competition between institutions continues to grow, external perceptions may have a marked impact on institutional performance. Furthermore, the recent changes in accounting standards and the resultant policy applicable to HE (FRS102 and the HE & FE SORP) will pose similar challenges of external communications to a variety of audiences with differing needs and levels of prior sectoral knowledge, and may also require careful internal communication to ensure that their effect and the underlying institutional position are understood by staff and students.

The role of and relationship with governance teams

Clerks or secretaries to council

The clerk or secretary to the governing body or council has an essential role in ensuring that institutional governance is effective at the highest level. The university secretary acts as the bridge between the executive and governors and, as such, has to help manage the relationship between the vice-chancellor and senior management and the chair of council. Whilst these may invariably be 'big' personalities with strong views and sometimes competing or conflicting interests and strategic thought, institutional success relies on this remaining constructive. Higher-profile governance failings in HE have in the past arisen because that relationship has broken down irrevocably. Not only may this cause the institution embarrassment if such an occurrence becomes publicly known, but more importantly it will impede the delivery of institutional strategy as the failing relationship becomes a distraction and the organisation deals with the aftermath.

This is not an easy task, and no one approach is necessarily better than another, but it is essential that the university secretary or clerk facilitates the conditions in which to achieve an appropriately balanced relationship, which in turn requires both parties to recognise the importance of good relationships despite the inherent tension. The vice-chancellor must be afforded sufficient freedom to lead the institution whilst remaining accountable to the governing body, and the chair must balance support for the vice-chancellor with constructive challenge. The Leadership Foundation for Higher Education's most recent Leadership and Management Survey (August 2016) found that the most common response from governors to the question of what they were looking for from the chair of the governing body was "an effective relationship with the senior management team" (47%) and, where appropriate, challenging and prompting the vice-chancellor and senior managers.

The university secretary sits at the interface between the institution and its governing body at both cultural and structural level and must consider the area in which they are operating on any given issue. The university secretary must ensure that as management delivers strategy the needs of the governing body (and its subcommittees) – the information it requires and how it should be presented – are taken into account. Often, governors will – and indeed should – come with their own views about how strategy should be designed and implemented, which may be at odds with those of the vice-chancellor and senior management. Care and sensitivity is therefore required to ensure that governors feel valued and that their views are considered – even if ultimately discounted – but that they do not stray into operational, management discussions, which is neither appropriate nor conducive to a healthy executive-governing body relationship. Likewise, the university secretary will need to work in close liaison with the vice-chancellor to ensure that management decisions do not circumvent the authority of the governing body.

In discharging these functions, the clerk or secretary will rely on strong contributions from strategy and planning. In practice, the manner in which this is done will vary greatly. The UK HEI's can have a unitary registrar, to whom most if not all professional services (including strategy and planning, as well as governance) report and which is usually combined with the role of secretary. Or the distinct position of university secretary as clerk to the council may exist, which has meant that universities must support the individuals within those revised structures in establishing effective systems to ensure that the clerk or secretary remains informed about the work of management and therefore able to effectively support and direct the business of the council. Both models have their strengths and weaknesses. Where the secretary is also a line manager of professional services, it is important to avoid conflicts of interest, independence of reporting of fact to the governing body and separate lines of report to the chair of council and the vice-chancellor.

Where the clerk or university secretary exists separately and is responsible to the chair of council, he or she will need to work closely with the vice-chancellor and senior management. Where there is an executive committee, the university secretary should attend meetings to ensure that they are kept abreast of institutional developments and that the views and needs of the governing body are considered in executive-level discussions and decision-making and the governing regulations on competence and delegation are complied with. A further complication may arise where, as is often the case, the university secretary or registrar (in either form) is also the secretary to the academic board or senate, which is chaired by the vice-chancellor. This may assist in developing new and refined systems of academic governance and assurance to discharge a larger role for governors in this area, but it further demonstrates the challenge and potential for conflicts.

Governance officers

Below the level of the university secretary or clerk to the board of governors, universities will employ professional staff to manage the day-to-day business of institutional governance. Usually in a distinct team but of varying size, these staff must support the clerk/secretary and be cognisant of the tensions and challenges outlined above. In a few cases, this team will be co-located with or be part of the strategy and planning function, but they may equally sit as discrete corporate governance teams, be part of the vice-chancellor's core staff or lie within a larger unit responsible for compliance in its widest sense, that is incorporating matters such as risk, insurance, internal audit, legal and Freedom of Information (FoI) and in some cases health and safety, equality and diversity, academic appeals and information security, for example. The strategic planner must take a keen interest in the distinctions between management and governors and the needs and responsibilities of each of them and/or work closely with the governance team in preparing information for the governing body (or other audiences) that meet its particular requirements. For example, the strategy and planning team may work with the council and senate on a strategic plan. Following the creation of the plan, a series of objectives and key performance indicators (KPIs), based on critical success factors for the university, may be devised and reported to the university executive board and senate and council. The purpose of these reports may be to assess how well the aspirations in the strategic plan have been translated into actions within the university and faculty objectives. The council and senate may have views on the appropriateness of the KPIs, the monitoring of progress by the university executive and the level of consultation that faculties had in setting objectives and devising KPIs. Without a very close working relationship between strategy and planning and the governance team, these objectives will be almost impossible to achieve successfully. Encouraging the flow of strategic intentions so that targets and KPIs become fully aligned with risks – a process which is ongoing – and eventually can be traced down through faculties and departments to personal objectives takes a close bond between strategy and planning and the governance and decision-making structures of universities.

Individuals are more likely to engage with the governance of the institution and be willing to give their time and effort if the structures and processes are purposeful, linked to strategy and are conducted and organised efficiently (Shattock, 2003). The role of the committee secretary, working in tandem with a strong chair, cannot be underestimated. The secretary must ensure that business is focused on decision-making within a given remit (not ultra vires) and resultant action, avoiding circular discussion that does not resolve the matter at hand. This requires a degree of sensitivity, particularly when members or those outside the process but with an interest in the outcome feel that they should be considering an issue over which the committee has no authority. An alternative perspective would be that such a use of the governance structure can facilitate engagement and aid communication on a given matter, but the secretary must ensure that business is prioritised accordingly – and guard against the governance structures being used for campaigns or by pressure groups instead of for strong internal communication. It is also important to ensure the role of the committee is clear to its members, that it has clear recommendations to make decisions within its powers and that it is well served with the information or data it needs to make those decisions in the most informed way.

Bibliography

Austin, I., & Jones, G. A. (2016). Governance of higher education: Global perspectives, theories and practices. New York: Routledge

Copland, G. (2014) Governance in a Changing Environment: Thought piece. London: The Leadership Foundation for Higher Education, available at: https://www.lfhe. ac.uk/en/research-resources/research-hub/2014-research/copland-thought-piece. cfm accessed 12/05/2017

Council of University Chairs (2014) The Higher Education Code of Governance, available at: http://www.universitychairs.ac.uk/wp-content/uploads/2015/02/Code-Final.pdf accessed 12/05/2017

Financial Reporting Council (2011) Guidance on Board Effectiveness, available at: https://www.frc.org.uk/Our-Work/Publications/Corporate-Governance/Guidance-on-Board-Effectiveness.pdf accessed 12/05/2017

Financial Reporting Council (2016). The UK Corporate Governance Code UK Corporate Code.

Greatbatch, D. (2015) Governor's Views of Their Institutions, Leadership and Governance – Higher Education Leadership and Management Survey. London: The Leadership Foundation for Higher Education, available at: https://www.lfhe.ac.uk/en/research-resources/publications-hub/HELMs/governors-views-of-their-institutions-leadership-and-governance.cfm accessed 12/05/2017

Higher Education Funding Council for England, Memorandum of Assurance and Accountability, 2016 (HEFCE 2016/12).

Higher Education Funding Council for England, Revised operating model for quality assessment, 2016 (HEFCE 2016/03).

Ross, F. (2016) Higher Education Leadership and Management Survey: The Results in Brief, London: Leadership Foundation in Higher Education

Schofield, A. (2009) What Is an Effective and High Performing Governing Body in UK Higher Education. London: Leadership Foundation for Higher Education

Schofield, A. (2013) Getting to Grips with Being a New Governor, London: Leadership Foundation for Higher Education, available at: https://www.lfhe.ac.uk/filemanager/root/site_assets/research_resources/g2g/getting_to_grips_new_governor.pdf accessed 12/05/2017

Shattock, M. (2003) Managing Successful Universities. The Society for Research into Higher Education and the Open University Press, 5, 97–108.

Stansfield, G. (2009) Developing Future University Structures: New Funding and Legal Models. Policy Commentary. London: Universities UK

Terenzini, P. T. (1993) On the Nature of Institutional Research and the Knowledge and Skills It Requires. *Research in Higher Education*, 34, 1–10.

Tight, M. (2009) The Development of Higher Education in the United Kingdom since 1945. *The Society for Research into Higher Education and the Open University Press*, 6, 134–144.

Williams, D. (2014), 'Governors' Briefing Notes 02: Governance and Management', London: Leadership Foundation for Higher Education available at: https://www.lfhe.ac.uk/en/governance-new/governance-briefing-notes/governance-briefing-note-02.cfm accessed 12/05/2017

Williams, D. (2014) 'Governors' Briefing Notes 04: Academic Governance', London: Leadership Foundation for Higher Education available at: https://www.lfhe.ac.uk/en/governance-new/governance-briefing-notes/governance-briefing-note-04.cfm accessed 12/05/2017

Chapter 8

Risk management

Rhiannon Birch, Rachel Pye, Claire McDonald and John Baker

Overview

Risk management is the discipline or process of capturing and controlling the institution's exposure to risks as it pursues its strategies and plans to achieve its goals. This chapter provides a practitioner's view of risk management in higher education. It begins with an overview of risk management and why it is important before outlining the documents and processes which characterise good risk management practice. Where relevant, this chapter draws on a recent survey undertaken by the UK Higher Education Risk Network to consider the degree of variation seen in practice across higher education institutions (HEIs). To provide a wider context, the links between risk management and business continuity are explored and the practical tools of risk management are placed in the institutional context by considering specific examples of risks which affect the higher education sector as a whole. The chapter concludes by identifying the key elements which can make risk management more effective and the potential pitfalls.

Risk management terminology

Risk management practice is full of terms, concepts and definitions, with different versions being used by different risk management frameworks. A glossary (in alphabetical order) is provided below which gives some definitions of the most frequently used terms as they are applied in HEIs.

Opportunity: a possible event that could lead to benefits, which may be advantageous. Risk management and opportunity management work together. Opportunities may be identified and managed through risk management and in many cases are 'positive risks' captured as ways to make good events happen rather than to manage the adverse effect of risk.

Risk: 'the effect of uncertainty on objectives' (ISO 31000, 2009). A risk is an uncertain event or outcome which has the potential to adversely impact on an organisation's ability to achieve its objectives. A risk is strategic in nature and should not be confused with a threat, which is more likely to be a physical event such as a power outage or flood. A risk may relate to the wider external context, to the policy or funding landscape.

Risk appetite: also known as risk tolerance. This is an expression of an organisation's attitude to risk in terms of aversion or tolerance, and the circumstances under which this may differ. The risk appetite should inform how risk is managed.

Risk assessment: an evaluation of risk in terms of the likelihood that the event may occur and the impact should the event occur. The format of the risk assessment varies depending on organisational preference but is usually informed by a matrix which sets out the levels which can be selected to express the risk assessment. The use of a matrix means that the risk assessment can be quantified, if required can be scored and the scale of the risk will be consistently flagged using a measure of severity to reflect the level of assessment.

Risk cycle: the process of identifying, evaluating and mitigating risk. The CUC Guidance (Summers and Boothroyd, 2009, p. 24) provides a basic five-stage diagram of the risk cycle. In many institutions this is developed in line with project management methodology and presented as a four-stage risk cycle which features the following steps: 1) Identify; 2) Assess, Accept, Mitigate or Treat; 3) Monitor; and 4) Report. Identifying risks should be closely aligned with strategic planning, as they are two sides to a single conversation. When an organisation identifies and agrees on its priorities, it should also consider what could prevent it from achieving them. When risks have been identified, the risk exposure should be considered. In some cases, an institution may decide to accept that a risk exists and take no further action. Where further action is required, the discussion should capture factors already in place (controls) and inform plans for mitigating and treating the risks (actions). The risks and mitigating controls/actions should be captured in a risk register which can then be used for monitoring and reporting on the management of the risks. In some instances stages 3 and 4 will happen concurrently.

Risk hierarchy: risk is managed at different levels within an organisation. The risk hierarchy captures these levels and the links between them, which allows risks to move between the levels of the hierarchy depending on the degree of exposure or the scale of the risk.

Risk management: the development and implementation of a systematic approach to the management of risk throughout an organisation. This may also be described as 'enterprise risk management'. The key principle is that risk management operates throughout the organisation and guides the process whereby risks are addressed wherever they are identified.

Risk management framework: a systematic approach which enables different types of risk to be identified and managed consistently at all levels. A mature risk management framework will cover strategic, operational and project risk, be linked with business continuity and be structured so that risks can move between levels of the risk hierarchy.

Risk mitigation: where the decision is made to actively treat a risk, the activities undertaken to manage exposure should be captured. Where there are activities which are embedded in business as usual, these are defined as 'controls', and where additional action is identified, these are identified as 'actions'. Over time as actions become embedded in organisational business, they will often become controls and will have an ongoing effect to mitigate the risk.

Risk policy: a high-level policy document which sets out an organisation's approach to managing risk. It may be several documents ('risk policy', 'risk strategy' or 'statement of risk appetite') accompanied by a broader contextual piece or a 'risk management handbook' which acts as an operational user guide linked with the risk policy documentation. It will include an expression of the organisation's risk appetite along with defined levels, categories and types of risk. It may include an overview of the risk management framework and articulate how risk will be managed and reported.

Risk register: a repository for recording risks which are grouped by virtue of their relationship with an operational area or because they are the result of a project or a strategic theme. It should capture the identification and evaluation of the risk as well as recording the exposure, that is the combination of likelihood and impact which expresses the severity of the risk and the actions to treat the risk. The risk register should be reviewed and updated regularly as a record of how risks are being managed and is part of the ongoing discussion of how strategic priorities and plans will be achieved.

Risk statement: a statement of the risk as identified initially. It may be structured as an 'if . . . then' statement to ensure that it is clear and relates to a specific issue which can be managed.

Risk treatment: there are four main options an organisation can use to manage a risk: Avoid, where possible action can be taken to avoid the risk altogether; Control, it may be possible to take action to reduce the likelihood and impact of a risk; Transfer, it may be possible to transfer the risk elsewhere; or an organisation may decide that it is not able to mitigate the risk and choose to Accept the level of exposure rather than attempting to manage the risk and reduce its exposure.

Risk universe: an overview of the context in which organisational risk management is taking place. The risk universe considers the internal and external environment and wider issues which may impact on organisational objectives.

The Higher Education Risk Management Network

In autumn 2014, the Higher Education Risk Management Network was established in the UK to provide a forum for risk management practitioners in HEIs. The network enables discussion and sharing of best practice around a range of topics and in spring 2015 undertook a survey to look at elements of risk management practice in higher education. The survey was conducted using an online questionnaire and sought information on several key areas of risk management implementation, considering both the policy and practice of risk management. Although the survey provides a partial picture of risk management in UK HEIs, where the evidence presents a clear trend, this is used to provide context for the points made in this chapter.

What is risk management?

Risk management is a technique which primarily aims to maximise the likelihood that an HEI will meet its objectives and thus improve performance. It does this by facilitating a better understanding of the risks faced by the institution and how these can be mitigated, controlled or avoided.

Risk management does not always focus on threats or negative occurrences; it can also be used to think about the degree of acceptable (or even expected) risk to maximise opportunities, by identifying the actions that would enhance the positive outcomes of a situation or project, or harness existing organisational strengths (often termed opportunity management).

Risk management can guide managers to answer questions such as "What are the things that might go wrong in this project?" or "How can we avoid these undesirable events happening and minimise the effects if they do?" Effective risk management can add value to the planning, management and governance of universities and should be embedded into normal management practices, processes, discussions and decision-making. In order to realise the benefits of risk management, many organisations, including HEIs, align risk management with wider processes including the annual planning process, strategy development and implementation, financial management, project planning and the production of business cases. Management of risk is also an integral part of cognate business management methodologies including, for example, PRINCE2, MSP and Agile for projects, disaster recovery planning for records management and information or data security protocols.

This chapter focuses on risk management where it is used to support the delivery of corporate strategy and considers the links with business continuity. However, risk management is used to support a range of practical organisational activities including health and safety and environmental management. Wherever there is a requirement to consider the implications of a decision and the factors which will contribute to its success or failure in a structured manner, risk management techniques are at work.

Why do risk management?

Risk management is increasingly viewed as a key component of the modern HE manager's toolkit. To put it bluntly, if academic leaders are not managing risk effectively, then they are not managing effectively. As the pace of change in technology and patterns of behaviour and control quickens, organisations increasingly seek to respond by doing new things and capitalising on opportunities. As a consequence there is greater uncertainty regarding the outcome or impact of actions taken. And greater uncertainty means more risk to manage. So if an HEI is serious about achieving its objectives and aspirations then it needs to take risk management seriously.

So, for an HEI there is in effect a moral obligation; if it is to deliver the experience or output promised to students and stakeholders, it will need to manage the risks that could jeopardise delivery. There is also often a regulatory obligation; for example in England the Higher Education Funding Council for England (HEFCE) has required institutions to formally manage risk since 2000 (Huber, 2011). The Memorandum of Assurance and Accountability requires publicly funded universities to ensure that they manage risk effectively and requires the annual internal audit programme to provide governors with a specific report on the efficacy of risk management procedures. It is the responsibility of the board of governors or trustees to lead on matters of risk for the organisation, including the development and approval of strategies and policies; ensuring that there are regular reviews of those policies and processes; and seeking assurance by means of suitable checks and monitoring of compliance within the organisation to be confident that the policies are being complied with by all staff.

Finally, a comprehensive and coordinated approach to the management of risk enables an organisation to be truly strategic in considering matters across its many constituent parts. It supports understanding of how issues of a certain type, or nature, or corresponding to a particular goal could prejudice or impact on its projected performance and enables effective scrutiny.

How to manage risk

Good risk management utilises a range of tools and documents which support the implementation of an overall risk management framework. In a mature risk management framework, these tools and documents are actively used as part of formal processes which work together to support the identification and management of individual risks, ensure the level of exposure is considered and that they are recorded consistently in risk registers which act as repositories for risks. The risk framework creates a structure which allows senior management to take a holistic view of the organisation and enables an organisation to consider its risk universe and to manage risks in individual areas and throughout the risk hierarchy. Key documents which form the foundation of good risk management processes typically include a risk strategy or policy, a statement of risk appetite, a risk framework which captures the risk hierarchy, and the risk register. But in order for risk management to be effective it needs to be part of the organisational culture, with corresponding support and endorsement from senior staff. The roles involved in risk management are covered in a later section.

Embedding risk management as more than a paper exercise is a challenge. In 2015/16 the University of Sheffield scoped and completed an internal audit which considered how embedded risk was in the organisation. The audit discovered that despite having good policies, a robust process and simple templates, the messages about the benefits of risk management were not widely understood and it was widely seen as a form-filling exercise which sat with the planning round. The internal audit provided recommendations intended to help revitalise risk management practices, which included engaging Council through a workshop to look at risk from a fresh perspective; providing new and revised training for academic departments to focus on the benefits of good risk management practice; and refreshing how to support risk management so that the link between strategy and risk was made clearer.

Risk strategy

The risk strategy or policy articulates an HEI's approach to managing risk. This document should clearly outline who is involved, what they will do and when in the context of the organisation structure. It may also explain the rationale for why the HEI is using risk management techniques and instruct where the evidence of risk management should be recorded, usually in a risk register. In an HE context, the risk strategy would normally be approved annually by the institution's governing body. This allows risk management to be an active part of the assurance process in line with any external regulatory requirements. The development and review of the risk strategy should also be closely linked with the HEI's strategic planning and audit functions.

Internal audit is often used to provide assurance of the quality and robustness of risk management processes. The HE Risk Network survey asked HEIs to indicate the model they used to manage their internal audit work. The data suggested that there were three main models in operation: in-house, outsourced and a dual model of internal audit. One notable comment from a respondent was that there was a difference between how internal auditors and planners as risk practitioners think about risk. The audit function often views risks as failure to achieve a particular output or goal. Whilst this may be helpful in determining which areas audit and assurance should focus on, it may not be the most useful way to think about managing risk, as it does not give explicit consideration to the causes of things going wrong. The use of 'if . . . then . . .' statements to formulate risk descriptions, rather than 'failure to . . .' can help to focus on the potential events which may hinder the achievement of objectives, thereby enabling controls to be targeted at those factors. The example below illustrates a poor formulation of risk:

Stated department objective: To improve PGT recruitment in the next year
Risk statement: Failure to improve PGT recruitment

In this example the following issues can be identified:

- The risk description simply repeats the objective, rather than identifying a specific event (or set of events) that could hinder its achievement.
- The controls and actions identified are likely to be general and limited to routine activity, without describing any particular potential cause.

A better formulation would be:

Risk statement: If the needs of current PGT students are not met then negative messages may be disseminated and prospective students may not apply.

- The risk description identifies a specific cause of potential recruitment difficulty.
- The controls section can identify targeted activity.
- Additional actions can describe a specific response.

Risk appetite

At Sheffield Hallam University, the statement of risk appetite has evolved from a narrative statement into a working guide that can be used to drive measured risk-taking and encourage behaviours needed to deliver against the university's ambitions. The risk appetite is now based around areas of strategic priority and presented as a range to reflect that almost all activities comprise, and require a balanced assessment of, both risk and reward. This range represents the parameters within which judgement should be exercised so that managers can respond in dynamic but considered ways to the level of external change that the university and sector faces.

It is widely acknowledged that the development of risk appetite is often the most difficult element of any risk management system to implement (Institute of Risk Management, 2011) and that the concept is, in general, poorly used within the higher education sector (HEFCE, 2005). However, there are benefits in defining and using a risk appetite statement which includes more conscious and consistent decision-making about taking (or avoiding) risks and improved strategic planning by identifying which risks to accept or exploit and which to avoid. Both aspects can lead to the empowerment of managers and decision-makers.

The objective of developing a risk appetite is to define the level and nature of risk that an organisation is willing to take in order to deliver its strategic objectives. The British Standard (BS31100, 2011) defines risk appetite as "the amount and type of risk that an organisation is prepared to seek, accept or tolerate". This covers the need to minimise the likelihood or impact of a threat or weakness as well as optimise the likelihood of positive outcomes arising from opportunities or organisational strengths.

There are several different approaches to defining a risk appetite. Some organisations create a qualitative statement which acts as a broad-brush guide about the level of risk-taking that is allowable or desired (see example below). Others use quantitative measures to define a risk appetite, particularly where it is relatively easy to define the value of the exposure to reputational, financial, or other risk categories. Some universities have adopted a tailored or differential approach to risk appetite for different types of risk or functional areas. Whichever approach is taken, the concept of risk appetite is only meaningful if staff are aware of its relevance and actually use it to guide decision-making. Risk appetite is an area in which governors have a legitimate interest and can usefully help in setting the context and culture around risk.

Example broad-brush risk appetite statement

"The University wishes to take appropriate risks to achieve a step change across its core areas of activity: learning and teaching and the student experience, research and business and engagement and operational effectiveness, but will of course adopt a more cautious or risk-averse attitude in matters of legislative and regulatory compliance to reduce exposures to the University's reputation, its people and its other resources and assets."

Example of a differential approach risk appetite statement

"Our overall appetite for risk-taking where people and culture could be affected is very low to medium. E.g.:

1) We do not accept risk-taking where we could fail to discharge our duty of care responsibilities or irreparably damage the staff experience (very low risk appetite).
2) We do expect staff to be prepared to take on new academic and professional challenges, and we aim to recruit, retain and develop people who thrive in an innovative environment (medium risk appetite)".

Risk registers

The most commonly used risk management document is the risk register. A well-formulated risk register facilitates risk owners in actively managing named risks and opportunities by analysing and defining them in a structured manner and providing a way of monitoring the level of risk exposure over time. A common factor in successful risk management implementation is to ensure that the influences on the risk are reviewed and reassessed regularly so that the risk register is not a static document but is updated over time and as conditions change.

A risk register is a repository for recording grouped risks; at the heart of each risk record is the risk statement, comprising a condition, cause and consequence: If . . . (a situation occurs), as a result of . . . (a root cause), then . . . (this will be the impact). The benefits of defining risks using this formulaic structure are that:

- The format applies equally well to opportunities as well as risks – indeed, in many cases a threat may be an opportunity worded in a negative way;
- Identifying the root cause helps to get to the heart of the issue and allows the risk to be managed by understanding the actions that are needed to reduce or increase the likelihood of the risk or opportunity;
- Identifying the main impact helps to understand the worst-case scenario and understand the relative priority of the risk.

Before identifying new actions which may be initiated to manage the risk, it can be helpful to analyse the risk in more detail. This can be achieved by completing additional sections on the risk register such as:

- Contributing factors: these are secondary to the root cause but could contribute to the risk/opportunity arising; as a result they may have controls or actions associated with them.
- Controls: these are existing and often systematic factors which are already in place to manage the risk. Controls normally address a particular cause or impact of the risk or provide a way of monitoring the risk. Monitoring controls look at the evidence or trend information associated with a cause or contributing factor and evaluate it to assess if the risk likelihood is within the acceptable range (this may be articulated in the risk appetite). If not, additional actions might be needed to bring it within tolerance. Controls often include intelligence gathering, analysis and exception or performance reporting.
- Assurances: these are the ways of reviewing the evidence that the controls provide, to check that the controls are effective, for example board or senior management team review or internal review/audit, and may identify the sources of evidence that can be reviewed to check that a control is working as described. In some universities a 'three lines of defence' model is used to articulate and structure assurance levels by risk type. The first line of defence consists of the actions of staff or technology intended to achieve a particular outcome. The second line of defence consists of management oversight of the effectiveness of that activity, and the third line of defence consists of independent assurance as to the veracity of internal process.
- Early warnings: these are the indicators that should be monitored to inform understanding of the level of risk at a given time. A well-defined early warning includes the threshold for taking further action.

Once any existing controls have been identified and assessed, then any additional mitigating or avoiding actions should be defined. Actions will represent the additional steps that are necessary to manage the risk, either by addressing the causes or planning for the impacts. Actions must be clearly articulated, assigned to owners and be time-bound so that their effectiveness can be measured; this in turn informs the status of the risk. For new risks there will often be no existing controls, and actions will be initiated which will develop into controls over time.

In our example in Table 8.1, this would allow you to complete the controls and actions columns of the risk register:

Table 8.1 Example of a risk register record of risk statement, controls and actions

Risk Statement	Controls	Actions
If the needs of current PGT students are not met, then negative messages may be disseminated and prospective students may not apply.	Staff-student consultative committee reviews results and outcomes.	Module evaluation questionnaires from the current academic year will be reviewed by 31 July 2017.

An essential part of the risk management process is to consider an organisation's exposure to the risk. Risk registers generally use a scoring system to indicate the perceived likelihood of the risk occurring, and the level of the potential impact if it were to do so, and combine these scores to grade the risks for ease of comparison and prioritisation. The appraisal of likelihood is sometimes supplemented by assessment of the proximity (nearness) of the risk. This two-pronged measure of probability allows mitigating actions to be prioritised according to the level of urgency. Risk registers will generally consider the exposure to each risk at three stages in the thought process: an initial evaluation of exposure to the untreated risk (the inherent or gross exposure); a review of exposure when controls are taken into account (the residual or net exposure); and a final assessment after the actions have also been taken into account (the anticipated exposure). At each stage a standard scoring system is used to indicate the likelihood and impact, which are combined to create the level of exposure to the risk.

The scoring system can be the subject of lengthy debate. Risk scoring methods can range from precise quantitative approaches to subjective colour coding. Scoring risks is an essential part of the risk management process, and the exact scoring method used will often depend on institutional precedent or executive preference. A survey of members of the HESPA risk management network revealed that whilst a 5 by 5 matrix was by far the most commonly used (by around 58% of respondents), there were a range of approaches in operation, from 3 by 3 to 10 by 10, and some with varying axes (for example likelihood on a scale of 1–3, but impact on a scale of 1–5).

Figure 8.1 provides an example of a risk scoring methodology. In the following example, the colour coding is used to inform the type of actions required. For example amber/red risks require that controls are put in place to detect the risk before it occurs. This is so that preventative actions (to minimise the likelihood) or corrective actions (to minimise the impacts) can be identified.

In managing risks, whether the matrix is roughly right or precisely wrong is less important than engagement with the process and active use of the structure which a risk management framework provides. Ensuring that there is parity in judgement across the institution is one of the challenges in effective risk management. Clear guidance in language relevant to the institution (for example numbers of students affected, or amount of income at stake) can be useful in helping managers understand what 'high' or 'critical' might mean in the context of their operation, for example quantifying a financial risk as shown in the example in Table 8.2.

In our example, the evaluation of exposure would be added to the risk statement, controls and actions to complete the risk record as shown in Table 8.3.

Some HESPA members provided anecdotes about occasions where the risk likelihood or impact was artificially inflated by a risk owner, to draw attention to personal agendas. Clear guidance and a robust process with opportunity for review and challenge should help to address this phenomenon.

Impact					
5. Catastrophic	1 / 5	2 / 5	3 / 5	4 / 5	5 / 5
4. Serious	1 / 4	2 / 4	3 / 4	4 / 4	5 / 4
3. Moderate	1 / 3	2 / 3	3 / 3	4 / 3	5 / 3
2. Minor	1 / 2	2 / 2	3 / 2	4 / 2	5 / 2
1. Negligible	1 / 1	2 / 1	3 / 1	4 / 1	5 / 1
Likelihood	1. Rare	2. Unlikely	3. Possible	4. Likely	5. Almost certain

Figure 8.1 Example of a risk scoring methodology

Table 8.2 Classification of risks by type and severity

Classification	Low	Medium	High	Very High
Impact Description	Minor	Moderate	Major	Extreme
Financial (Threats)	Negative impact on less than 1% of expenditure cap/ given budget.	Negative impact of between 1% and 4% of expenditure cap/ given budget.	Negative impact of between 5% and 24% of expenditure cap/ given budget.	Negative impact of more than 25% of expenditure cap/ given budget.

Table 8.3 Completed record in the risk register

Risk statement	Inherent risk		Controls	Residual risk		Actions
	L	I		L	I	
If the needs of current PGT students are not met, then negative messages may be disseminated and prospective students may not apply.	3	4	Staff-student consultative committee. International Student Barometer.	2	3	Module evaluation questionnaires from the current academic year will be reviewed by 31 July 2017.

(L = Likelihood, I = Impact)

Risk management training and awareness

> Do we all understand the different levels of risk? Leeds Beckett University attempted to address this during 2016 in order to align risk management more closely with the delivery of its new strategic plan. By commencing a more 'conversational' approach to embedding risk management in its culture and recognising risk management needs to operate at both the strategic and operational levels, it has been possible to develop a clear articulation between the two, which has supported increased transparency and understanding of risk management.

A major part of the strategic planner's role is to ensure that all of the parties are engaged in risk management effectively and that this is linked to the strategy and plan for the institution. This interaction may take place through regular reporting and communication, risk workshops or individual discussions. The training element of the role is an important one which can help to increase the visibility of and engagement with risk management. It is important therefore that the strategic planner has credibility in the organisation. A key aspect of this is demonstrated by a willingness not only to establish a useful framework for risk management but to get involved in the detail of specific risks at both strategic and operational levels. Being able to ask the right questions and having enough knowledge through horizon scanning to be able to challenge where needed are also vital parts of the role. Having a good understanding of the organisation and the sector, as well as an insight into emerging trends and developments, is key. The strategic planner needs to maintain integrity and act as an independent voice in risk matters. There can be a tendency in any large organisation towards 'groupthink', and it is part of the role of a strategic planner to be able to resist this and challenge current thinking or the prevailing culture if necessary.

Use of risk management software

The section above outlined how risks should be recorded for the purposes of regular review and scrutiny, which is usually managed using a risk register. The HE Risk Network survey revealed a number of ways that organisations are managing the production of their risk registers, from the use of standard Microsoft Office products to more specialised software. This data is summarised in Figure 8.2.

The use of Microsoft Office products has the advantage that there is no additional cost to most HEIs, the tools can be built using existing expertise and are bespoke to the needs of the institution and are familiar so do not require additional training. However, there are some drawbacks, regarding version control, lack of complex reporting options, and platform linkage opportunities, which have led some institutions to purchase specialist software or build custom products utilising local expertise and solutions.

The survey revealed that HEIs using a customised risk management software package feel that it enhances the risk and records management process by allowing:

- Automatic alerts to action owners within specified deadlines;
- Centralised secure storage of assurance sources and evidence;
- Multiple slice and dice reporting options to analyse risk aspects across the entire institution;
- Record review across the institution to shape consistency of practice;
- Full history report functionality to understand movements in risk exposure over time;

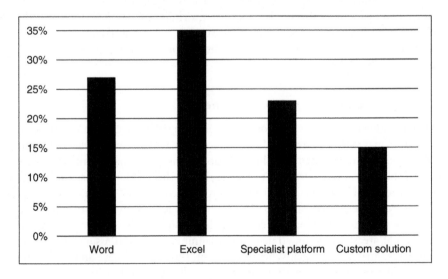

Figure 8.2 Software used in managing risk registers: HE institutions – November 2015

- Automated document reporting in legible formats;
- Cyclical review processes to drive behaviours of risk owners and managers.

Software providers identified in the survey as used by UK HEIs included Insight-4GRC, Wynyard, Covalent, and the creation of custom solutions designed by ICT services using tools like SharePoint, InfoPath and Java, or other similar programming languages.

However, it is important to note that good risk management practice depends on the development and use of a robust process with involvement and buy-in from staff across the organisation and the provision of documents which allow staff to undertake risk management effectively. While software solutions are a good way to highlight the need for effective risk management, they cannot replace an embedded process which supports effective consideration of risk.

Who manages risk? Risk management roles

Staff at many levels need to be involved in risk management, from the president/principal/vice-chancellor and chief operating officer to heads of department and project managers. In fact, to some degree, anyone with management responsibility will have to deal with risks, either as a risk owner or perhaps through carrying out activities designed to mitigate risks (risk owner or action owner).

The risk register will capture who has responsibility for managing each of the risks identified and may identify both a 'risk owner' and a 'risk manager'. The risk owner will normally be a senior member of staff with overall responsibility for the area of activity which the risk effects, and which will serve to mitigate the risk, and he or she will take responsibility for overall management of the risk. The risk manager can also be the risk owner, or might be a direct report of the risk owner, and will be responsible for overseeing or undertaking actions and activities which are intended to mitigate the risk or act and report when the risk becomes a live issue.

Strategic planners as risk practitioners

Most institutions also have someone operating as a risk management practitioner, or risk management professional, whose job it is to take responsibility for the effectiveness and consistency of the operation of the risk management framework across the institution. They don't manage risk, as this is the responsibility of the risk owners and managers, but they need to ensure that risk owners understand and exercise their responsibilities. The recent HE Risk Network survey revealed that risk management practitioners in HEIs are situated in a range of different functional areas, including strategy and planning, audit and assurance, human resources, finance and legal. Wherever they sit, they need to have an overarching view of the organisation, with good links to colleagues in departments, schools and faculties in order to facilitate the use of risk management in the governance and management of the university. Some HEIs have designated risk professional roles, though the responsibility for developing and overseeing risk management practices more often rests with strategic planning or audit professionals and forms part of their wider role. Often, the risk management policy or framework outlines the organisational responsibility and governance structures around risk, but the operational risk management activities are usually delegated to functional areas.

One of the main roles of the strategic planner when operating as a risk management practitioner (whether as a specialist role or part of a wider job) is to develop the framework and processes for risk management linked to the strategy. This would normally include defining the decision-making and reporting processes, developing scoring mechanisms and criteria and designing risk registers for use by staff who are responsible for managing risk. To be successful in this process-architect role, the risk practitioner needs to ensure that the framework is comprehensive and efficient, without being overly bureaucratic or administratively burdensome, which would undermine its effectiveness. A further element of getting the process right is to make sure it fits with and is embedded into existing processes in the institution such as annual strategic planning, project management and management reporting.

Risk Management Group

The Risk Advisory Forum at Leeds Beckett emerged as a peer review group to review the risk registers of all services and academic areas through workshop style meetings, and to make generic recommendations based on consistent understanding and application of the risk management policy and our risk appetite scores. Observations and recommendations from the Forum are captured in an annual review report to the University Executive Team for approval, which serves as additional assurance for the governing body concerning their role in oversight of risk management.

Strategic planners may have responsibility for coordinating risk management activity and reporting on risks and controls to a relevant committee such as the audit committee, senior management team or a specialist risk management group or forum. The HE Risk Network survey suggested that a range of groups were used in the universities surveyed to facilitate high-level discussions of risk management. Each of these models has pros and cons. A designated risk group can be a useful forum and ensures sufficient time to consider risks and controls, but it can be difficult to ensure that any conclusions or required actions are progressed outside of the group. Clearly, good communication mechanisms are needed to cascade information effectively. On the other hand, reporting straight to the executive committee has the advantage of drawing in the most senior individuals in the organisation and making risk management visible at the highest level. However, there is always the danger that risk management will be pushed off the agenda by other business items which are seen as more pressing. Having the buy-in and support of the chair and secretary of the executive group is therefore vital.

Governing body

As part of a sound system of risk management, corporate risk will also be reported to the institution's governing body, which should be actively engaged in the discussion of institutional risk both from the perspective of identifying risks as they emerge and recommending mitigating action. The CUC in its guide to risk management in universities (Summers and Boothroyd, 2009) suggests a set of ten key risk issues for governors and outlines a series of dilemmas which governors may face. These echo many of the issues identified in this chapter and highlight that the independent viewpoint of the governing body is a useful part of creating and embedding a strong risk culture within an institution.

The link between business processes and risk

The practical implementation of risk management is most effective when it is linked with other business processes. Two examples of this are the links between risk management and strategic planning and between risk management and business continuity.

The link between strategic planning and risk

The link between strategic plans, annual planning and risk management is a key part of an annual cycle of business planning, priority setting and performance evaluation. Risk management looks at the threats and opportunities surrounding aspects of the organisational environment and places additional emphasis on the longer-term, strategic impacts given what the institution wants to achieve by way of goals. Institutions will often seek to link their strategic plan actions, the inherent risks of those actions, key performance indicators and risk status together in a coherent way.

The link between business continuity and risk

Risk and business continuity management both consider uncertainty and threats and involve a process of gathering and analysing information that will be useful when making decisions about, or responding to, anticipated or actual disruption. Business continuity management mainly focuses on how to maintain or resume an organisation's critical functions after an incident or period of disruption; it recognises that some interruptions can be neither foreseen nor prevented and therefore concentrates on what to do when a harmful situation occurs, regardless of the cause. The traditional focus of risk management is to manage (reduce or improve) the likelihood of a foreseeable situation by focusing on causes rather than responding to the outcomes or impacts, although developing a business continuity plan is a valid risk control to apply to an outcome. A successful link between risk and business continuity management can strengthen both processes and avoid the potential pitfall of making risk management about avoiding critical failure rather than achieving strategic success.

As suggested, business continuity plans and arrangements apply from the point that, despite comprehensive risk management, some form of disruption occurs that creates actual or highly foreseeable negative impacts in the organisational environment. The impacts could be to any components of the environment, such as:

- Operations, service delivery or processes;
- Infrastructure (buildings, equipment, IT network);
- Resources (people, skills, information assets or the supply chain);
- Reputation.

Whilst a significant business continuity incident may require a dynamic assessment of the impacts on strategic objectives, this would not be a priority action within the business continuity plan. Institutions that experience a major incident will sometimes find that a new 'normal' is the eventual outcome of the long-term recovery phase, but the early stages of the response will focus on how to continue delivery of existing university processes and services at an operational level. In contrast, risk management actively considers the potential impact of a risk on the achievement of strategic objectives as a way of understanding whether, and how, the risk should be treated. However, both risk and business continuity management are ultimately concerned with assuring the long-term sustainability of the organisation and can therefore be considered to have a strategic focus.

Whilst business continuity management is heavily focused on impacts (something has happened) rather than causes (something may happen), the analysis that is needed to develop a business continuity plan will sometimes reveal risks that would benefit from mitigation or control. For example, evaluating and identifying the resources and dependencies needed to deliver a critical function may reveal a sole dependency on a particular supplier; business continuity management would consider how to mitigate this by looking for an alternative supplier so that there are options if the primary supply chain is broken or disrupted.

Finally, business continuity plans can contain predetermined options and arrangements that can be deployed to protect the components of the organisational environment from being (further) damaged or disrupted beyond agreed, acceptable thresholds. This closely aligns with the use of a risk appetite to indicate the boundaries of risk-taking.

At their heart, risk management and business continuity management are preparatory and planning activities that are completed during relatively stable operating conditions. As a result, they work together to identify issues and mitigating actions that can be implemented for a foreseeable or actual event. While the two processes are often managed separately, they are highly cognate, and best practice is for them to work together to maximise the opportunities for the organisation to realise its ambitions and minimise the possible impacts of threats.

Concluding remarks: hints and tips

Risk management is a simple technique with clear elements of best practice. To conclude, the key elements making risk management more effective and the potential pitfalls are:

- Risks need to be linked with objectives (at any level, i.e. strategic, operational, project) and should not be identified in isolation;
- Expressing risks as 'if . . . then' statements makes it easier to formulate risks usefully;
- Risks need to be sufficiently granular that you can take action, for example Brexit was not a corporate risk;
- Actions and controls should be targeted at mitigating specific concerns;
- The scoring system for assessing risks should ideally provide guidance as to how to score both likelihood and impact;
- Risk practitioners should provide regular training and support to keep risk as a 'live' management tool in the organisation;
- Engaging with internal audit to provide assurance that you are meeting best practice can be valuable in generating new ideas for best practice;
- Engaging with risk practitioners in other institutions can help you to identify new tips and techniques which you can try in your own organisational culture.

Risk management is a valuable management technique which can be undervalued as being bureaucratic. This chapter has tried to draw out how best practice can help institutions to get the most from active risk management.

References

BSI (2011), *A Code of Practice for Risk Management*, London, British Standards Institution.

HEFCE (2005), Risk management in higher education, a guide to good practice, prepared by PWC for HEFCE, available at: http://webarchive.nationalarchives.gov.uk/20100202100434/www.hefce.ac.uk/pubs/hefce/2005/05_11/accessed15/09/2016

Huber, M. (2011), *The Risk University: Risk Identification at Higher Education Institutions in England*, London, Centre for Analysis of Risk and Regulation at the London School of Economics and Political Science.

Institute of Risk Management (2011), Risk appetite and tolerance: Guidance for practitioners, Guidance Paper, September.

ISO (2009), 31000:2009, *Risk Management, Principles and Guidelines*, Geneva, International Organization for Standardization.

Summers, E. and Boothroyd, K. (2009), *Getting to Grips with Risk: Resources for Governors of UK Universities and Higher Education Colleges*, London, Leadership Foundation for Higher Education and the Committee of University Chairs.

Chapter 9

Finance, resource allocation and income forecasting

Sonia Virdee and Andrew Keeble

Introduction

Finance can seem a dark and mysterious place, complex and impenetrable where even highly numerate strategic planners may struggle to fully understand how budgets are built and how income is forecasted and allocated. This chapter has been written with the strategic planner's perspective in mind in an attempt to shed light on some of the principles of higher education institutions' finance, and how this links to institutional strategy (see Chapter 3) and the planning process (see Chapter 4). In some institutions, planning and finance teams work closely together during the planning round and in framing the strategic parameters for budget setting; in others, planning and finance exchange information but operate separately; and in the extreme, they live in different worlds and speak different languages.

This chapter outlines the different approaches taken to resource allocation and financial forecasting and hopes to demonstrate the value and insight that can be gained from the strategic planners' understanding and contribution to financial modelling and resource allocation.

Principles of resource allocation

What is resource allocation?

All HEIs allocate funds to pay for growth or to enhance their activities, and to ensure activities that by their nature are not income-generating are funded by those that are. The purpose of resource allocation, or more specifically the resource allocation model (RAM), is to ensure costs are covered and to provide a basis for decision-making on investment in the activities of greatest strategic importance to the institution as established by its strategic planning (typically for education, research and external engagement). There are a number of principles to bear in mind in designing a model for this purpose.

To work well, the RAM will allocate resources in line with actual costs and be broadly consistent with economic reality. However, the RAM is not merely an accounting mechanism, but a potentially powerful strategic tool. The RAM can and perhaps should be designed to incentivise the right behaviours for achieving desired institutional objectives as well as reflecting pure income and costs as accurately as possible. It is this design dialogue that links academic and financial planning in the context of the strategic plan. For example, a RAM that allocates estates costs based strictly on the usage and cost of space would disadvantage space-intensive disciplines and/or might act as a disincentive for academic departments looking to increase student contact hours due to the additional cost of booking teaching rooms. Increased contact hours may be an important objective in the education strategy as a means of improving the student experience. Directly apportioning costs, in this case space, might be seen as the fairest approach; however, it may be more appropriate to allow an element of 'rough justice' in the allocation of income and costs in order to incentivise behaviours that align with institutional priorities.

If developed and communicated properly, the RAM is central to promoting understanding of the institution's finances and the levers that can be pulled to improve performance. A reasonably simple, transparent model can be a very valuable tool in building broad engagement with the institution's financial mission and in underpinning a well-functioning planning process.

Strategic planners and finance directors need the RAM to work well as a planning tool at the institutional and school/departmental level. It should show the financial starting point before plans are made and the degree of gain or shortfall against planning targets. It should then enable scenario testing of plans and their associated costs and income to show how those targets may be reached in future years, thus providing the basis for financial decision making.

Financial strategy

The strategic plan

The strategic plan sets the context for financial planning and the financial strategy of the institution (and they are often contained within the same document), with the aim of achieving financial sustainability – a position whereby the institution generates sufficient cash to finance its operations and strategic needs over the medium to long term, including its investment in human and physical resources. Changes in the way HE is funded have impacted the financial strategies of institutions in England through the reduction in grant income and increased reliance on fee income (see Figure 9.1), resulting in increased volatility in funding levels and increased risk.

The strategic plan and its enabling supporting strategies will set the direction of the institution as approved by the governing body and will provide it and the executive board with the information required to monitor the institution's progress against its financial and other strategic objectives. The financial strategy and the strategic plan will generally operate hand in hand in helping

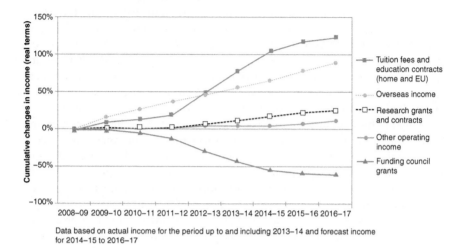

Data based on actual income for the period up to and including 2013–14 and forecast income for 2014–15 to 2016–17

Figure 9.1 Cumulative change in HE income

Source: HEFCE

the governing body to balance investment in the delivery of the institution's objectives and in ensuring financial sustainability, including some or all of the following (FSSG, 2016):

- Generating sufficient income in order to invest in infrastructure, facilities and services and in teaching, research and knowledge exchange as informed by the priorities set out in the strategic plan. This may take the form of capital investment in buildings or systems or revenue investment in additional staff;
- Making provision for repayments on loans that the institution may have taken out in order to invest in new facilities, and planning for future capital development and how it would be funded;
- Assuring external agencies, such as banks and other actual or potential sources of funding, and giving confidence in continued investment in the institution;
- Considering operating costs, both from the perspective of incorporating increased costs such as to salaries and pensions, and consideration of efficiency gains and areas where costs are expected to reduce;
- Increasing financial resilience by increasing the level of surplus, enabling the institution to ride through fluctuations in its income or expenditure that are outside its direct control, such as changes in the student market and student numbers;
- Considering the level of risk and the scale and nature of financial contingency planning.

Financial planning

The financial strategy will contain targets, for example for the level of institutional surplus, growth in income, increased efficiency and/or sums invested. Translating the strategy into financial planning and demonstrating that the institution is on track to deliver its targets relies on a system of financial forecasting and monitoring. At the departmental level, forecasts will be based on income and expenditure and their treatment in the RAM (see below). At the institutional level, a range of factors will inform the overall financial position and how it will change over time, and these factors will need to be modelled in order to establish the overall financial envelope for the institution.

Financial planning assumptions are used to differing degrees in all institutions and are a useful way of objectively framing key strategic drivers for the institution over the planning period. These assumptions can be used to develop a top-down, whole institution financial forecast which demonstrates at the macro level how the institution will meet its financial targets as set by its governing body, and will show what funds are available for investment (e.g. in staff) or, conversely, the level of savings required by the institution. Financial planning assumptions probably work best where they are first considered independently from the scenarios that result from them. This approach provides an opportunity for unconstrained, blue-sky thinking about the factors driving financial performance. This objectivity is lost when planning assumptions are considered alongside their financial outcomes, and the process can become deterministic, driven by the desire to deliver a particular level of surplus (or to minimise the need for cost savings).

For example, a scenario that assumes large increases in staff and pension costs and a decline in international and EU numbers together with increased competition for home students is a pessimistic, but not unreasonable, scenario to model, and one that most institutions would find challenging. If it is accepted by the institution, it would be likely to imply some serious changes, perhaps even the closing of disciplines. More optimistic planning assumptions would set the context for investment and growth. Without the top-level planning assumptions, the natural tendency is for optimism at the discipline level and for the development of plans for investment and budget forecasts that deliver financial sustainability. The planning assumptions provide an important counterpoint against which departmental plans should be tensioned.

Finance and strategic planning teams can work well together in compiling financial planning assumptions which include realistic but challenging forecasts that are consistent with the institution's strategic plan. These can take a variety of forms depending on what is considered important and relevant for the institution, and a suggested checklist is provided in Table 9.1. Key assumptions include changes in student numbers, student progression from year to year and staff-student ratio expressed as target figures or percentage change at the institutional level (see Chapter 5). When fed into the university's financial

Table 9.1 Financial planning assumptions, checklist of possible headings

Income

Funding council grants (including HEFCE, Higher Education Innovation Fund, Student Opportunity Fund, capital funding)
Student numbers
Retention/progression
Tuition fees
Tuition fees yield (net income forecast as % of gross [approved] fees due to fee waiver discounts offered)
Impact of volatility on student numbers and fee levels (e.g. Brexit)
Research grants and contracts (volume growth and overheads)
Campus services (student residences, catering, conferences)

Expenditure

Pay costs (e.g. cost of living increases, pension costs, apprenticeship levy)
Non-staff costs (e.g. departmental operating budgets, professional services budgets, access agreement spend, scholarships)

Contingencies and Provisions

Contingency for shortfall in student recruitment
Provision for student-staff ratios (e.g. target ratios and associated additional staff FTE required)

Financial Metrics

Surplus or cash generation target
Capital expenditure
Capital funding
New borrowing
Borrowing costs

model, these income and expenditure assumptions will shape the financial forecast and provide a means by which inputs can be tweaked to show a range of scenarios, for example less student number growth or more conservative borrowing.

How much surplus is enough?

The level of surplus that is sufficient for the institution will be that which provides for its financial sustainability, and is a key metric that will be discussed with and agreed upon by the governing body. In the UK, HEFCE reports annually on the operating surpluses of HE institutions, and it noted in 2016 that the sector was sound overall but showed increased variability in the performance of individual institutions, with the gap between the lowest and highest performing on financial measures continuing to grow. The current overall operating surplus of 4.3% (ignoring exceptional factors) looks good, however HEFCE sounded a note of caution that this level of surplus is not sufficient to cover the full costs of research, and many institutions are projecting a fall in surpluses and an increase in borrowing.

Types of RAM

Contribution and full cost models

Broadly, resource allocation models fall into two types: contribution models and full cost models. These financial models are applied to the academic units in the institution, that is academic departments or schools, or to whole faculties, depending on where the financial accountability lies within the institution. Faculty-level budgets will tend to mask differences in performance among underlying discipline areas; however, this approach is common in large universities where financial planning is devolved to the faculties. From the strategic planner's perspective, a discipline-level view of financial performance, where provided directly through the RAM or through other, more granular supplementary financial reporting, is a very useful if not essential planning tool.

Both contribution and full cost models allocate all of the income (fees, research income, consultancy etc.) earned by income-generating areas to that unit; the difference is in how costs, in particular central institutional costs (such as library and HR costs) are treated.

Full cost models

Full cost models allocate all of the costs of the institution, including central/professional services costs, to income-generating areas in proportion with agreed cost drivers such as numbers of students, numbers of staff, space used and income. This gives a surplus or deficit for each academic unit. Some full cost models are developed further to provide for full economic costs and are designed to demonstrate long-term financial sustainability.

Contribution models

Contribution models attribute (usually by formula) only costs directly incurred by the academic unit, and the degree to which income exceeds costs will determine the contribution the department is making to the pool of central costs, including central support/professional services. This is illustrated by the sample departmental budget in Table 9.2. The so-called contribution is the total income less the direct costs; in this case the academic unit has covered the indirect costs attributed to it and shows a small overall surplus. In these models, direct costs of academic and other income-generating departments are regarded as variable while the pool of central costs are regarded as being relatively fixed.

How income is allocated

Most institutions have insufficient connectivity between the student information system and the finance system for income to be allocated module by module in

Table 9.2 Illustrative departmental income and expenditure statement
(based on an actual academic department at the University of Essex)

INCOME:	£K
Teaching Income	
Teaching Grant	275.0
HEU Teaching Fees	4,019.2
Overseas Teaching Fees	1,365.0
Other Teaching Income	0.0
Total	**5,659.2**
Research Income	
Research Grant (QR)	510.8
Research Tuition Fees	164.7
Research Contracts	474.2
Other Research Income	2.0
Total	**1,151.7**
Other Income	9.8
TOTAL INCOME	**6,820.7**
EXPENDITURE:	
Staff	
University Funded	2,246.7
Externally Funded	283.3
Total	**2,530.0**
Non-Staff	
University Funded	316.1
Externally Funded	93.2
Total	**409.3**
Other Direct Costs	
Faculty Office Costs	85.9
HEU Recruitment Costs	285.6
Overseas Recruitment Costs	122.4
Total	**493.9**
TOTAL DIRECT EXPENDITURE	**3,433.2**
CONTRIBUTION	**3,387.4**
PROFESSIONAL SERVICES & CENTRAL COSTS:	
Professional Services	
Academic Support (Academic Section, Research Support, Library)	628.3

(Continued)

Table 9.2 (Continued)

INCOME:	£K
Communications, Marketing, Recruitment, Admissions	344.0
Campus Maintenance	587.0
Administration (Finance, HR, IT, Vice-Chancellor's Office, Planning)	637.7
Total	**2,197.1**
Central Costs	
Capital Programme	356.2
Student-Related (Access Agreement, Frontrunners, SU)	347.2
Staff-Related (Pension Deficiency, Severance)	81.4
Other	(20.8)
Total	**764.0**
FULL COST SURPLUS/(DEFICIT)	**426.4**

accordance with fees actually paid. Therefore, pools of income at the institution level are allocated across academic departments in proportion to data in the student number forecasts, which are usually produced by the strategy and planning department, adjusted for fee and teaching load (see Chapter 2).

There are various approaches to allocating student fee income across academic units, all of which are reliant on the input of strategic planners. The model at Queen Mary University of London, for example, allocated income purely on the basis of teaching load, income being allocated to the departments teaching the modules regardless of the home department where the student was registered. Others, such as the School of Oriental and African Studies (SOAS) and Essex, allocate a proportion of the income (20% at SOAS and 25% at Essex) based on the home department registration and the remainder by teaching load. This approach seeks to incentivise student recruitment, which is the responsibility of the home department, and recognises the higher per student costs in the 'home' departments. The Queen Mary model assumes a degree of natural adjustment, because the lion's share of modules would be taught in the home department, and tends to encourage interdisciplinarity. For some years, the model at City University allocated income by home department registration adjusted for service teaching conducted in the previous year. This had the advantage that the model could be run without the need for the new teaching load data to be assimilated, a process which relies on stable student numbers information and can delay the production of departmental budgets.

Once determined, the model for allocating income can also be used to allocate other specific costs, for example overseas recruitment agents' fees and central admissions and registry costs.

Relative merits of contribution models versus full cost models

Contribution models are simpler and more stable than full cost models, allowing departments to focus on income and costs that are under their direct control. In a full cost model, a department that has worked hard to develop a plan leading to a projected surplus can find that it has been put back into deficit in the next financial update as a consequence of changes made by other departments which have resulted in those departments absorbing a lower proportion of central costs. This volatility in the attribution of central costs is outside of the control of a department and can undermine and disincentivise good forward planning.

Contribution models are consistent with the economic principle that an activity should only be undertaken if marginal revenue exceeds marginal cost. In theory, any activity that makes a positive contribution will improve the financial performance of the department and, by making a contribution to fixed costs, the performance of the institution as a whole.

However, in some full cost models, which allocate significant central costs on the basis of student numbers, small increases in student numbers and fee income can be wiped out by the associated formula increase in central costs. For example, increasing the size of a postgraduate taught class by three additional UK/EU students paying a relatively low fee can make economic performance appear worse when, in reality, central costs are likely to change very little as a consequence of recruiting three more postgraduate students. If the institution wanted to encourage innovation in curriculum development and take a risk on initially low student numbers on a new programme, a contribution model, and not a full cost model, would incentivise the right behaviours.

As can be seen in the example above, the use of cost drivers in full cost models can be contentious, and time can be lost to arguments about allocation of costs. Such disagreements about the operation of the model tend to distract attention from more meaningful discussion of academic and financial performance and strategic planning.

The disadvantage of contribution models is that the aggregate of the contributions from the departments may be insufficient to cover the central pool of costs. Therefore, many such models look to top slice, say, 45% of income or state that the contribution must be at least equal to 45% of income. A top slice can inhibit income-earning activities that do not meet the threshold. For example, a new summer school which generates an income of £1M and a surplus of a £100K, improving the finances of the institution but falling significantly short of the target margin of 45%, would make the department's financial performance look worse and could disincentivise this type of innovation.

Few costs are actually fixed other than in the very short term. Demands for academic services and facilities will vary from year to year with student numbers. Across institutions they will vary significantly with research intensity. Additional buildings are often required for expansion, increasing borrowing and estates costs, while existing facilities will periodically require major refurbishment. Omitting consideration of these costs in setting the performance expectations of income-generating areas may result in financial shortfall.

In conclusion, both models have advantages and disadvantages. Perhaps the optimal solution is to develop a full cost model that is as simple as possible, with a minimal range of cost drivers and excluding confusing accounting adjustments, such as depreciation, to focus on a simple cash surplus. Having developed the model, it would then be advisable to test various cost allocation scenarios to find modifications which ensure that the right kind of academic behaviours and initiatives are incentivised.

Capital planning

Where does the money come from?

Although the UK government has continued to commit some capital funding for research, there is less grant funding available to support non-research-related investments (Universities UK, 2015) (see Figure 9.2). In the absence of reliable capital grant funding, institutions need to generate larger surpluses in order to fund capital spending than would have been the case in the past. These surpluses are required to

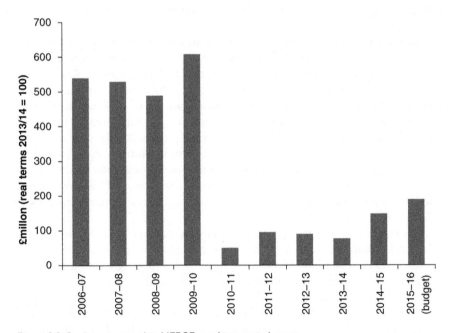

Figure 9.2 Real terms trend in HEFCE teaching capital grant

(Universities UK, 2015)

service borrowing costs (interest payments) or to build up reserves from which investments can be made. The average level of borrowing has been rising within the sector for some time. In 2001–02, the level of borrowing was 19.6% of total income, and by the end of 2014–15 this had risen to 29.6% and is projected to rise further to a high of 33.3% by the end of 2016–17 (HEFCE, 2016). Institutions are under continuous pressure to enhance the student experience and also in many cases to invest in research in order to both maintain quality and to deliver growth and enhancements.

The capital investment plan

Capital planning is about the medium and long term, and most institutions will have a capital or estates master plan which will take a 10- to 50-year view of growth and development opportunities. In addition, a more immediate 3- to 5-year capital investment plan is an important tool for determining the funding envelope for capital projects and for prioritising and monitoring projects within the planning period. Capital investment planning should be aligned with the strategic plan, with clearly articulated priorities for capital spending, such as investment in teaching facilities and student accommodation, both for enhancement and to support any growth in student numbers. Capital planning, however, also needs to accommodate more mundane, 'business as usual' investment such as major maintenance works and energy efficiency, and retain a degree of agility in order to respond to opportunities, risks or demands should they arise mid-cycle.

Strategic planners have an important role to play in contributing to the capital investment plan, through their understanding of student numbers, discipline plans and priorities, institutional priorities and KPI performance. Consistently low student satisfaction scores with library facilities, for instance, could contribute to a case for investment in a library extension; analysis of projected demand for teaching rooms might lead to investment in a new teaching block. Planners can also add value in ensuring through the planning process that the capital requirements of academic departments or schools inform institutional capital planning. A well-designed planning process will capture these requirements, refer them for further discussion, for example with estates or IT services, and for consideration and prioritisation by the relevant decision-making body, and ensure feedback to the school or department.

HE institutions are by necessity becoming increasingly proactive in planning the level of funding available during the capital planning period, discussing the balance between ambition and risk internally and with the governing body, and setting surplus targets that will underpin the agreed level of capital investment over the planning period.

Providing for all of the potential capital development projects on a 'wish list' is an unrealistic goal, and institutions often have a difficult task in balancing the level of investment that they are prepared to or able to make, whether from borrowing or from their own reserves, against the long list of worthwhile projects.

This is not a linear process; the funding envelope will be agreed first before individual projects are approved, whether the institution is prepared to invest £10M or £100M or more in its capital investment plan. However, the scale of the investment will inevitably be shaped by institutional need and by the level of ambition and the risk appetite of the governing body.

Capital planning – cash is king

In the past, many university planning or resource allocation models have reconciled to the accounting surplus or deficit in the financial statements and financial forecasts. This is the position after a charge for depreciation, which spreads the costs of capital items, such as buildings and equipment, over their useful economic life. It is a non-cash figure that seeks to show the annual cost of capital in the income and expenditure account, the main statement of institutional performance. It is not helpful for planning purposes because it does not inform the calculation of how much cash is available to be invested, for example in new projects or refurbishment of existing assets. The accounting position has been made more complex and, for planning purposes, even less helpful, by the introduction of international financial reporting standards. As a result, depreciation charges for most institutions will be even higher and capital grants which, by definition, fund assets with a long economic life are likely to be included in full as income in the year they are received, introducing much greater volatility into models of accounting surpluses and deficits.

In order to avoid this complexity and volatility, resource allocation, such as that applied by the University of Essex, now focuses on the cash surplus as opposed to the accounting surplus. This is the position before charges for depreciation and receipt of capital grants but, importantly, after interest payable, repayments of loan principal and tax. Accordingly, this cash surplus is the figure which may be added to brought forward cash balances to give the total sum that is available for new capital projects such as those emerging from the planning round, planned capital works highlighted by a condition survey of the estate, and other longer-term strategic investments.

Implementing the model

The outputs from the RAM can be used in a range of ways extending from simply informing centralised budget setting to full delegation of budgets at the faculty, school or departmental level. The RAM will inform decision making, and it is very important that financial decisions made through the planning process, for example by the planning committee or the executive, are clearly communicated in order to support transparency and engagement in the planning process.

In very large institutions, the centre can be seen to act rather like a funding council, with budget setting taking place at the faculty or school/college level based on parameters in the resource allocation model. This is a fully delegated model where, provided target surpluses are generated, authority to spend by the creation of budgets takes place closer to the point of academic delivery. Small and medium-sized institutions may adopt a mixed approach where non-pay operating budgets are calculated on a formula basis based on metrics in the model, and may include incentives around the generation of external income, with the deployment of those budgets determined at faculty or departmental level. In this case, approval to create and appoint to new and existing posts is retained at the centre, with priority being given to stronger academic performers based on indicators. These decisions will typically be taken at extended meetings of the executive or of a strategic planning committee, where plans will be approved based on the level of resource indicated as being available following the strategic budgeting process.

Integration with the planning process

The strategic planning process in institutions (see Chapter 4) will usually include a backward-looking review of recent performance across a range of strategic and financial metrics and the development of a costed forward-looking plan (see Figure 9.3). A fully integrated planning process will bring financial planning and planning for research (see Chapter 6) and for education (see Chapter 5) into a single process, whereby plans to deliver a strategy for research or to develop new curriculum areas are tensioned against the need to meet the financial targets set within the RAM. The review phase of the process, which would normally take place early in the academic year, will look at the previous year's budget outturn and early indications of recruitment relative to the forecast student numbers and budgeted income for the current year. The strength or otherwise of the department's financial performance and performance against targets or benchmarks – for example for student satisfaction, attainment outcomes and/or research income – set the context and the priorities for forward planning.

Forward planning and forecasting income

Forward planning is about promises and obligations. A department may undertake, for example, to recruit additional students, generate additional research income or improve employment outcomes for its students, articulated through its departmental plan. Its forecast income will be driven by student fee income as estimated from the projected number of full-time equivalent students registered on its courses (student FTE) and the number of students studying modules taught by the department (student load). The details of how fee and teaching grant are apportioned and forecasted will vary from institution to institution; Figure 9.4 gives an illustration of a simple allocation model.

Academic units that have sound plans which address institutional priorities and are underpinned by a healthy budget projection will be able to make the case for investment, for example in additional space, equipment or staff. However, in

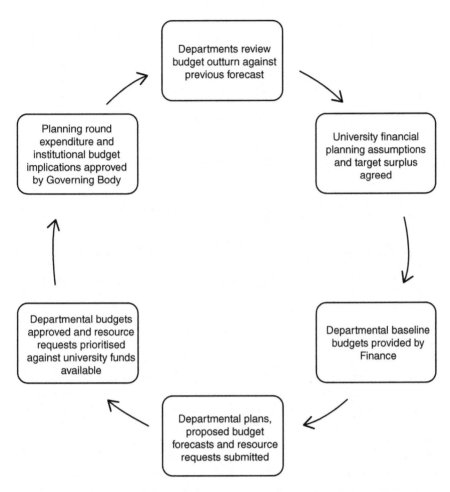

Figure 9.3 A resource allocation cycle

most institutions investment decisions are not so clear cut, and there is often an acceptance of some degree of cross-subsidy, with departments making large surpluses 'bailing out' or funding investment in less profitable disciplines. Sharing the 'spoils' in this way, rather than allowing an academic unit to 'eat what it kills,' allows the institution to sustain a broad discipline base but will undermine good planning if surpluses are not invested where they are earned and if deficit departments have no incentive to improve their financial position.

A transparent resource allocation model will show which departments are meeting the financial targets set by the institution, and where the cross-subsidy lies, and can operate as a lever for moving all academic disciplines into surplus.

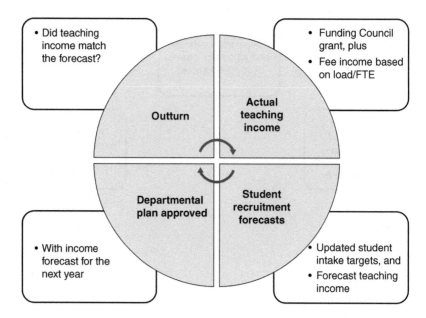

Figure 9.4 Forecasting teaching income in departments

The institutional forecast will show the level of surplus that is available, once a range of financial planning assumptions have been applied, either to support deficit departments or to invest in staff and facilities. The strength or otherwise of the departmental or faculty forecast, developed by the RAM, provides the basis for decisions at that level, and whether the departmental plan is approved and funded or not. Done properly, building and scrutinising departmental budgets through the RAM process, and scrutinising the sum of these budgets against an institutional projection, is a complex and time-consuming process. Planning committees or executive teams typically have awaydays to consider strategic plans and their associated budgets and to make resource decisions against assumed levels of performance. As the planning process is usually overseen by strategic planners, the responsibility of ensuring decisions are clear and communicated back to the academic units in response to their submitted plan usually involves input from the strategy and planning function.

Decisions made through the planning round may well be contingent on student numbers in the next academic year and other factors affecting future income. As a result it is not uncommon for some resource decisions to be less than clear cut, linked to output targets and to the resulting budget outturn and other financial indicators (such as student recruitment against target) which are not available until early in the new academic year.

Conclusions

From the strategic planner's perspective, the detailed workings of the RAM in operation in an institution and how income is forecasted and allocated is perhaps less important than how the model supports the delivery of the strategic plan. Full cost and contribution models have different properties and will operate slightly differently in the planning process. This chapter has talked a lot about behaviour, and how properties of the RAM can work with and against the strategic plan and how it can incentivise desirable behaviours (or at least help to deter undesirable behaviour).

As a minimum, strategic planners work with finance colleagues in providing the raw material for the RAM, in the form of student load and student FTE and fees. Beyond this, benefits arise from further discussion and valuable collaboration between strategic planners and finance through the planning process, for example in proposing financial planning assumptions and in undertaking associated scenario planning.

References

FSSG (2016) Mind the gap – Understanding the financial sustainability challenge: A brief guide for senior managers and Governing Body members, HEFCE. www. hefce.ac.uk/media/HEFCE,2014/Content/Funding,and,finance/Publications/ Mind,the,gap/Mind%20the%20Gap%20%20October%202016%20FINAL.PDF (accessed 17 January 2017)

HEFCE (2016) Financial health of the higher education sector, 2015–16 to 2018–19 forecasts, HEFCE. www.hefce.ac.uk/media/HEFCE,2014/Content/ Pubs/2016/201634/HEFCE2016_34.pdf (accessed 17 January 2017)

Universities UK (2015) Universities UK submission to the 2015 comprehensive spending review, September. www.universitiesuk.ac.uk/policy-and-analysis/reports/ Documents/2015/uuk-submission-2015-comprehensive-spending-review.pdf (accessed 17 January 2017)

Part 4

Analytical capacity and capability

Chapter 10

Data capability across the information landscape

Andy Youell and Dan Kidd

Introduction

Strategic planners in HE rely on access to and the ability to analyse a wide range of data for much of what they seek to do within their institutions. This chapter builds on the work of the HE Data & Information Improvement Programme (HEDIIP) and the extensive engagement and dialogue conducted through the HESA training seminars to set out an analysis of future data capabilities at a system level, an organisational level and an individual level. It sets out an analysis of current and desired future states of the information landscape and considers some of the opportunities and challenges associated with delivering this level of change and the impact on the roles and skills of strategic planners.

Background

It is very easy to get blasé about the power of modern information technology. Moore's (1965) observation about the rate at which the number of transistors on a silicon chip increases (approximately doubling every eighteen months) has become the shorthand description by which this development is described. Although Moore's law (as it subsequently became known) is a single measure of this rate of development, analysis shows that this rate of increase applies to a whole basket of IT metrics. Measurements of the volume of data on the planet also suggest doubling at a similar rate, and we are all faced with an increase in the volume, velocity and variability of data that shows no sign of abating.

This rapid evolution in technology capability impacts almost every aspect of our lives – the ways in which we live, communicate and work have all undergone upheaval over the past couple of decades. But this upheaval has created and exposed weaknesses in some of our most fundamental structures and processes that inhibit, sometimes absolutely, the benefits that could be realised from this technological revolution.

The question of how we best respond to, and drive value from, these changes is one that exercises governments and organisations across the globe. In 2013 the UK government published a data capability strategy (BIS, 2013) as one of the seven pillars of UK industrial strategy. This explored the possibilities offered through increasing our analytical capabilities to improve existing, and create new, products and services. It set out a vision for an economy that is more open and agile, and it recognised the importance of developing human capital in order to deliver this vision. As a high-level strategy it, understandably, focuses on outcomes and benefits and places value-add activities to the fore. Its weakness was a failure to emphasise the foundations that need to be in place in order to deliver this new world.

In 2011 the Department for Business Innovation and Skills (BIS) published an HE white paper (BIS, 2011) that contained a call to redesign the information landscape to create a system that reduces duplication in the system and delivers more value through improved timeliness and accessibility. The HEDIIP programme was established, and initial work identified the true extent of data collections across the sector and investigated the scope for standardisation and rationalisation of this landscape. In 2015 HEDIIP published an architecture for the information landscape[1] based on a system-wide leadership and oversight capability, driving standardisation and rationalisation of data flows, combined with an improvement in data management and governance capabilities within HE providers.

System-level capabilities: leadership and oversight

The massive explosion in the capabilities of information technology has led to data collections like the blooming of a thousand flowers across the landscape. The first attempt to understand the true extent of data collections across the landscape – undertaken by the HE Better Regulation Group in 2011 – identified over 500 data collections across the sector each year. The system was clearly lacking control and coherence.

Early discussions around this topic quickly landed on the lack of governance across this landscape as being a significant problem. Traditional concepts of governance – providing oversight and assurance to an organisation – quickly floundered due to the absence of an authoritative national body that could steer the behaviours of the many independent, autonomous data processing regulatory or statutory organisations, each with their own strategies, goals and constraints.

In the absence of a traditional governance model, the HEDIIP New Landscape project[2] defined consensual and collective leadership as the best model to deliver the rationalisation and standardisation of data flows. But this model needs to overcome the tension that exists between working for the greater good and the pursuit of each regulatory organisation's own objectives and priorities.

The HE Data Landscape Steering Group has been established as the body to provide the national leadership and oversight required to make the information landscape more coherent, less burdensome and more effective. The group will promote greater cooperation and collaboration between data collectors and HE institutions, including the standardisation and rationalisation of data flows. It will work to change mindsets and behaviours around data collections from institutions, including the adoption of data and process standards, the promotion of data sharing and the better alignment of data issues with broader strategic and policy issues. A common understanding of good practice is sought – including the appropriate governance of data collections and adherence to data standards.

The key capabilities to deliver success at the national information landscape level are:

- Aligning data leadership with other power and influence structures across the national system;
- Aligning the data processes with sector-wide policies, strategies and trends;
- Balancing tactical and strategic development and being able to exploit system-level opportunities;
- Creating an environment where the standardisation of data specifications and processes is the norm;
- Creating an environment where data sharing and the repurposing of data is the norm.

Organisation-level capabilities: data management and governance

National data collecting and processing organisations are constantly looking for ways in which they can improve their efficiency and effectiveness and to develop new products and services for their stakeholders. HE institutions have undergone massive changes over the past couple of decades as core processes have become increasingly computer-based and, where appropriate, automated. Technology has been adopted at a rapid pace, and while significant benefits have been delivered, the pace and extent of change has caused problems. The implementation of new systems and processes often knock-on to roles and structures, and issues like this, although often difficult, are usually resolved as a part of any system implementation project. Where organisations have been slower to respond is in the establishment of an enterprise-wide data architecture, management and governance structure. As IT systems increase in complexity and number, and as the expectations of value-added activities like business intelligence (BI) increase, this lack of data oversight and leadership could become a more critical hindrance.

Data is now a critical asset for HE institutions. In many ways data is no different from other key assets such as people, money and buildings. However, unlike these other asset types, the management and governance of data assets have yet to reach maturity.

The national HEDIIP programme in the UK launched a major strand of work around data management and governance capabilities. This work set out to help HE institutions understand what data management capabilities they needed in order to support their broader strategic goals and then establish a plan to develop those capabilities. The project developed a toolkit[3] which included an online self-assessment tool that allowed organisations to analyse and understand their existing capabilities against a 5-level capability maturity scale. This assessment showed that data in many institutions tended to be held and managed in functional silos, with individual data structures not aligned to broader business processes and a general lack of integrated data governance.

The institutional and national challenges in this space are significant since they require not only changes to processes and structures, but in many cases a whole mindset change to truly recognise data as an asset at the organisational level. Organisational structures and processes can be slow and difficult to change, but culture and mindset can be even slower.

A community of practice and a number of common issues have emerged: the importance (and challenge) of finding senior colleagues to champion the data agenda; the extent to which development of data governance aligns with broader organisational objectives; and broader challenges around driving change in complex and dynamic organisations.

Some HE institutions are addressing these issues by plugging into existing organisational governance systems and processes and by enlisting support from the internal audit function. Others are taking a more opportunist approach by building data governance issues into existing transformation activities. Strategic planners are often the primary end users of data for analysis from the range of local systems. IT departments are often responsible for the system architecture which holds the data which supports the various corporate systems. The relationship between strategic planning and IT functions is a key one in defining solutions. What is clear from these early developments is that there is no one solution that is appropriate for all HE institutions.

Individual capabilities: skills and knowledge

If institutions and sector bodies can better understand that the volume, velocity and variability of data that they interact with is increasing at a rate similar to that described by Moore's law, then logically they might also think about the impact that this rate of development has on the types of skills, knowledge and experience needed by those interacting with it. The extent and pace of change (both in terms of policy and marketplace) experienced by the higher education sector since the turn of the century has meant that data-centric roles, and the skill set they demand, have changed fundamentally. In 2000 the strategic planning department (if it even existed) in many institutions principally existed to count – be it students, courses, activity, performance or money. In 2016 the role of the strategic planning department, and those strategic planners working within it, is to forecast, model, scenario plan, and guide strategic decision-making at the highest level.

The fundamental shift in the role of strategic planning departments and planners has inevitably had an impact on the types of skills and knowledge required in order to be successful, and to some extent has led to a skills and labour shortage in this area. Indeed, the latter point is not confined to strategic planning roles in the HE sector; moreover, it is a shared concern across all UK industries – a point alluded to in the 2015 Universities UK report 'Making the Most of Data'. Ostensibly you could argue that the role of a strategic planner and the skill set required are the same today as they were a decade ago. Planners are still to some extent expected to be data scientists utilising analytical skills across a range of platforms and disciplines, with a primary purpose to understand data (both in terms of its origins and uses) and communicate it as an evidence base for decision-making. However, where the change and development becomes apparent is in the types of soft skills that the role now demands.

The way in which audiences consume data has changed, and born out of this is the need for strategic planners to tell the story in a more inspiring, visionary and accessible manner – often to large audiences of differing levels of understanding and need. The tendency is to think of such communication skills as being typically associated with more creative roles in domains such as marketing or design, as opposed to the code-writing, number-crunching analyst hunched over a computer screen. The 2014 Nesta report 'Model Workers: How Leading Companies Are Recruiting and Managing Their Data Talent' argues to the contrary, suggesting that creativity is a prerequisite competency for 'generating unexpected solutions to problems, and exploring data from different angles'. Strategic planners in HE are now required to be a hybrid of individuals with technical/analytical competency and creative communicators engaging and working with a broad mix of people from across the academy.

Expert domain knowledge is another important aspect of an individual's capability to fulfil a strategic planning role, and one that has become more challenging in today's diverging and ever more complicated HE marketplace. The idiosyncratic, fluid and transient nature of the HE regulatory framework presents a range of challenges to planners around knowledge acquisition and preservation. In addition, with the marketisation of the HE sector the domain knowledge required is growing, with a need for a wider understanding of national and international government economic and immigration policy and the likely impact this will have on the institution and on its strategic goals.

Much of the change in the skills and knowledge of data-centric roles has been driven by the speed of change around technology and the impact this has had on business intelligence capability. As the platforms and systems used for analytics develop, offering unprecedented advancements in capability and speed, there is a need for the skills and knowledge of planners to develop at a similar rate to ensure they can derive as much value from new technology as possible. Given the rapid rate of change around the technology we all use, this places significant pressure on both the organisation and the individual to ensure skill sets remain relevant and current. It also places further emphasis on the need for the organisation to recognise data scientists and the continuing development of their skill set as a key staff development need. The development of data roles within the HE institutions should be of the highest priority in order to develop and implement meaningful strategy. The problem organisations face in this space is the absence of professional qualifications in this area, alongside a clearly defined career path. As a consequence, the development of data skills is often approached in an incoherent training strategy with multiple training providers commissioned across the broad range of soft and technical skills required to be developed.

The development of technology not only poses questions around how we ensure skill sets remain valid, but it also presents a challenge around how strategic planners can manage the proliferation of data and information. Key developments in business intelligence systems over the last decade have often centred around the user experience resulting in improved accessibility – Heidi Plus from HESA is a good example of this. Access to data and information is no longer confined to the strategic planning community (if it ever was) but instead is freely available for anyone with a keen interest, an Internet connection and even the most rudimental of systems. In some senses this democratisation of information is a positive development – it helps to place data and information at the heart of the organisation – however, it does have further implications for the types of skills strategic planners are required to possess. As an increased number of people interact with a greater number of data sources, there is a need to assess the validity of the analysis and quality of the sources and manage the outward flow of that information and its interpretation. This issue is only likely to deepen with the commitment of organisations like HESA to the open data agenda and the inevitable further development of technology, and therefore thought should be given to moderation and governance. It might reasonably be suggested that strategic planners, with their domain knowledge and analytical skills, have an important role to play as curator.

The importance and utilisation of the range of soft and technical skills described can be demonstrated through most types of analysis a strategic planner would routinely undertake. As an example, a planner undertaking a benchmarking exercise around projected student numbers in subject areas would require the wide range of skills and competencies shown in Table 10.1.

Given the changing nature of the skills and knowledge required within data-centric roles, it is vital to understand where gaps exist and attempt to close them. It is therefore incumbent upon both the individual and the HE institution to assess current capability and identify where development is needed. In order to address this requirement, an embedded, coherent and flexible staff development strategy is needed that addresses the range of technical and soft skills that those working with data need.

Sustainability of this skill set is also fundamental to continuing success, and as such an awareness and review of the technological and political environment staff are operating in today and tomorrow is important in understanding the types of skills and knowledge that will be needed. There is also a role within the staff development strategy for senior and experienced planners who should be incentivised to share domain knowledge and develop the technical and analytical skills of those new to the profession. Experienced staff should undoubtedly also be encouraged to be the 'crow's nest' in terms of identifying development needs

Table 10.1 Data skills required by strategic planners

Domain knowledge	**Data and information gathering** • Source data on population trends by UK region, EU and non-EU countries • Source economic forecast for relevant regions/countries • Source relevant HE data sources • Verify validity and relevance of data sources • Understand the data sources
Technical/ analytical skills	**Analysis** • Blend data sources in business intelligence system • Establish population and scope of analysis • Identify benchmark and comparator group • Execute analysis using appropriate system(s)
Soft skills	**Communication and dissemination** • Identify audience • Establish method of communication • Communicate results

and encouraging advocacy. A successful development strategy will likely include an agile internal process for identifying change and its impact on skill sets; however, it will also involve third-party training providers to address both the technical and soft skill requirements. In the UK, organisations such as HESPA, HESA and Jisc offer a range of staff development services that can enhance capability around data.

Why is it important that we consider fully the skills and knowledge required by those in data-centric roles? If we accept that data will play a central and fundamental role in supporting the insight and decision-making needed for achieving organisational success in the current and future higher education sector, then good analysts are central to that capability. Without highly skilled staff, whom the organisation is committed to developing further, then business intelligence and data capability will always be undermined, irrespective of the advancement of technology.

Notes

1 www.hediip.ac.uk/new-landscape/
2 www.hediip.ac.uk/new-landscape/
3 www.hediip.ac.uk/data-capability/

References

Department for Business, Innovation & Skills (June 2011), 'Students at the heart of the system' from www.gov.uk/government/uploads/system/uploads/attachment_data/file/31384/11-944-higher-education-students-at-heart-of-system.pdf

Department for Business, Innovation & Skills (October 2013), 'Seizing the data opportunity: A strategy for UK data capability' from www.gov.uk/government/publications/uk-data-capability-strategy

Moore, G. (1965), Cramming More Components onto Integrated Circuits. *Electronics Magazine*. 38(8), pp. 114–117.

Nesta (2014), 'Model workers: How leading companies are recruiting and managing their data talent' from www.nesta.org.uk/publications/model-workers-how-leading-companies-are-recruiting-and-managing-data-talent

Universities UK (2015), 'Making the most of data: Data skills training in English universities' from www.universitiesuk.ac.uk/policy-and-analysis/reports/Pages/data-skills-training-in-english-universities.aspx

Chapter 11

Business intelligence and analytics

Thomas Loya and Giles Carden

Introduction

Business intelligence (BI) and analytics is a term which refers to how higher education institutions (HEIs) exploit available data resources – both internal and external – for operational excellence and decision support, where the ultimate purpose is achieving and often shaping strategic priorities and contributing to an HEI's operational effectiveness, achievement or surpassing of quality objectives, efficiency and competitive advantage.

Robust BI and analytics gives an HEI the capability to measure and monitor activities, outputs, position and performance, using metrics aligned with its strategy (see Chapter 3). Beyond this, the targeted exploitation of data, and the development of forecasting and predictive analytics, promises to enable HEIs the capability to better understand themselves and their context, and to anticipate and even to change their own future and, when applied to students' data, their futures as well.

This type and calibre of decision support and the associated benefits require more than a set of merely technical capabilities in a central or in multiple BI and analytics teams; it describes a state of organisational and management maturity that is essential to being a successful HEI in an increasingly competitive environment.

This chapter covers the characteristics, benefits and underlying capabilities of BI and analytics provision. Impactful BI and analytics entails the timely mustering of the right data, of known quality, blended from multiple sources (internal and external) and domains (student, staff, finance, research etc.), to which appropriate statistical analyses are applied in order to address the most pressing organisational problems or opportunities. But to achieve the intended purposes, strategic planners in HE providing decision support must go further, and make intrinsically complex and multi-dimensional analyses readily understandable to senior decision makers and academic leaders who have little time and often limited exposure to BI and analytics. Sometimes no number of tables or charts can fully convey the key interrelations or trends or draw to the foreground the most important implications of an analysis. Innovative visualisations and companion narratives may be needed to bring the data to life and contribute to insights and confident decisions about what to change and potentially how to do so. These decisions may be about students and their experiences, the subject mix, improved research productivity or philanthropy or any other areas of activity. Equally important for achieving the intended benefits is the ability of BI 'consumers' and decision makers to develop proficiency in interpreting analytics.

This chapter does not cover specific tools, vendors and platforms. Tools, technologies, platforms and vendors have changed more in the last three years than in the preceding ten, and there is little to suggest that pace will slow. Underlying capabilities and the purposes they support are of more enduring importance, but even some of those may be rendered unnecessary by technological change. When assessing tools and technologies, and approaching solution partners and vendors, HEIs are best served by being clear on their purposes and the capabilities they want to develop, and why. Lacking that clarity, vendors and partners will likely focus on the capabilities their products and services support, rather than those the HEI most needs.

BI and analytics with the potential to transform an HEI needs to be for everyone involved in leadership and decision making – not for everyone else. This is true whether talking about operational excellence – meaning the highest standard of sustainable, effective and efficient day-to-day activity which drives the HEI towards its overarching goals – or competitive advantage, meaning substantively (rather than incrementally) improving quality of provision, outcomes, market share, reputation, sustainability and/or relative position. In a globalised and competitive HE sector, the purposes, capabilities, and benefits sought are best provided and used right across an HEI, at most if not all levels, rather than restricted to certain management strata or confined to core activities (teaching, research). To achieve its purposes and realise its benefits, using BI and analytics needs to become the normal way of working and of making informed decisions.

Types and purposes of BI and analytics

This section sets out some distinctions between the types of BI and analytics, concentrating on their primary purposes and benefits.

Operational reporting (OR)

OR draws on real-time data taken directly from core functional systems to enable smooth and effective operation and management of routine but essential processes and functions, for example admissions, graduation, income attribution or staff costs. There is usually some kind of 'list of records' type of reporting provided by most core transactional systems (student records, finance, human resources). However important, this type is nonetheless outside the scope of BI and analytics. The boundary is imperfect: it is often useful for the other types of reporting, covered below, to provide 'drill-down' to underlying granular data (e.g. lists of individual students, cost centres, staff, research projects) that appears little different from operational reporting, but their purpose is not to manage a transactional process but to aid diagnostics, expose source data to build confidence in the higher-level information and analyses provided, and to identify data quality issues so they can be remedied in source systems.

Management information (MI) reporting

MI reporting enables those responsible for the HEI or for an academic or business unit or function to make regular assessments about the outputs, outcomes or performance of that unit or function so that they can monitor and manage it and ensure purposes and targets are met, or else intervene in good time. MI reporting is distinct from operational reporting in that it is less focused on discrete processes or individual data items and may need to provide coherent reporting across several processes or data domains and systems and may draw on long-run or external data to put performance into the context of institutional or sector trends. Its primary purpose is to provide decision makers with information about 'what is' within the organisation and to maintain smooth operations. This is a necessary capability as well as a foundation for more advanced types of decision support, and may help drive management maturity, but its strategic and competitive benefit is limited. To support decision makers in finding root causes of performance issues and non-obvious solutions and opportunities requires different capabilities.

Business intelligence (BI)

BI is the purposeful exploitation for strategic purposes of MI, especially about competitor characteristics and provision in the HEI's broader context. Where MI reporting at most HEIs for example provides summary analyses of student outcomes at subject or course level or research outputs, citations, income and margin, BI would provide that for all key competitors as well, to identify strengths, gaps and opportunities. The volumes and complexity of data are many orders of magnitude greater than that required for MI reporting against an HEI's own activities, requiring a step change in underlying capabilities for data acquisition, management and analysis. A key challenge, which requires substantial investment of time, effort and understanding, is aligning data from multiple external sources gathered for different purposes to an HEI's own structures, activities and analytic purposes. As a result, the proportion of the production time that must be allocated to data preparation is much greater for BI.

These large data sets are used to identify or solve non-obvious performance problems and opportunities, with the overarching purpose of informing or achieving specific strategic priorities. BI is distinct in its closer alignment to strategy development than to operational efficiency. It also requires an outlook that accepts the immediacy of peer institution competition and the need to take and be accountable for decisions with immediate and far-reaching impacts, despite uncertainty.

The distinction can be better appreciated by considering the analogous definition of military intelligence from the US Department of Defense (2013), being 'the product resulting from the collection, processing, integration, evaluation, analysis, and interpretation of available information concerning foreign nations, hostile or potentially hostile forces or elements, or areas of actual or potential operations'. Like military intelligence, the focus in BI is on data and analysis about the larger competitive context to inform tactics and strategy. Extensive analysis and insight about competitors is intrinsic to BI's purpose.

Advanced business analytics

Advanced business analytics builds on the types of reporting above, and may include data mining, predictive analytics, machine learning, and quantitative modelling and forecasting to support scenario evaluation. These types of analytics are intended to address particularly complex challenges or enable deep diagnostics and insight, to facilitate step changes in performance and competitive position or to inform decisions about fundamental changes to an HEI's business model.

While MI and BI pertain to 'what is', whether in terms of an HEI's performance or that of its peers and competitors or trends in the market that have effectively already taken place, advanced business analytics concerns itself with discovery of relationships, problems and opportunities that are not obvious or are even hidden, and what is likely or what could be. It requires purposeful structured statistical exploration of a wide array of integrated data resources, and its results are often or largely probabilistic. For example, in the case of data mining and predictive analytics to drive student success (whether operationalised in terms of progression, completion or differential attainment), analytics teams identify statistical relationships among tens of millions of data points that allow high-confidence predictions (ideally) in real time, for example of the individual students at highest risk of an outcome of concern. HEIs can then apply interventions statistically likely to positively alter that risk. These programmes can improve the outcomes of individual students and contribute to higher student income and better performance, for example against league table measures (see Chapter 13) or helping to realise the HEI's mission and purposes. Looking at just two of the leading vendors of predictive analytics services enabling improved student retention and completion, they have over five hundred North American universities as clients, which already have or are implementing this capability, generating substantial additional student income and equally importantly altering the life chances of students.

Data mining and predictive analytics has been used for other purposes, including creating individually customised financial assistance packages to influence an offer-holder's decision about whether to accept. In this case, the HEI gathers data about individual students in numerous successive cohorts, their personal characteristics, and their decision (to accept or decline) the package offered. That data is mined and predictive analytics used to create algorithms that generate personalised financial assistance packages, for example the lowest net cost package with the highest probability of generating a positive decision from a student with a certain set of characteristics, optimising the yield of high-capability students while controlling costs.

This capability also has high value in the area of philanthropy: a North American Ivy League university used analogous techniques to correctly predict both the propensity and the capability of individual alumni to contribute to a campaign, in effect shifting fundraising efforts from 'shooting in the dark' to 'shooting in a barrel' and in the process added over a billion dollars to its endowment.

All three of the examples given – student success, financial assistance targeting and fundraising – contributed simultaneously to operational excellence and to achieving strategic objectives. Rising national and transnational competition, financial pressures on institutions, and rising expectations of students, funders and employers suggest that these types of analytics will be critical for future success and also require analytical expertise and the ability to understand and use statistical techniques.

Whatever the benefits of predictive analytics for optimising outcomes or reducing uncertainty and supporting decision making, it has limitations which if unrecognised can undermine good decision making. Predictive analytics are powerful assets for complicated systems and activities (as in the examples above), about which data can be acquired then used to model outcomes over several successive future cycles (whether entering cohorts, budget years, or any elapsing time unit). Things that are complicated have many aspects or dimensions, but the interrelationships among them are understandable. Complexity is different, reflecting conditions when the number of elements and their interactions and interrelationships are of a higher magnitude and intrinsically unknowable, whether due to the phenomenon itself or because it is being modelled over too extended a time period. One of the hallmarks of true complexity is unpredictability, and the complex is unlikely to yield to analytics techniques developed for the merely complicated. Applying predictive analytics to complex systems risks giving management false comfort that it understands the probabilities of certain outcomes when it takes important decisions. Recognising when the problem or opportunity and the corresponding decisions are not going to be better supported by predictive analytics is as important as knowing when they are.

The other forms of advanced business analytics mentioned above – quantitative modelling, forecasting and scenario evaluation – are similar to predictive analytics in that the reported outputs are more often potential and dependent for their accuracy on a set of explicit assumptions and conditions as well as the data, methodology and tools used. Quantitative modelling is a way to assess the impact or outcomes of 'what if' situations. Examples include modelling the consequences of a change in course pricing on applications, market share and net revenue – which might take into consideration enrolments sector wide, the costs of offering the courses, competitor pricing, the effects of prior price changes and broader economic and employment conditions. Forecasting is a tool using an array of data about the past and present combined with assumptions based on knowledge and experience about how any domain of activity works (e.g. undergraduate recruitment, student progression) to estimate a future state, to reduce uncertainty and to support decision making. When supporting decisions with large costs, benefits or risks, it is arguably better to undertake such forecasting and modelling than to not.

Commentary

MI reporting and BI are both important but increasingly something HEIs just have to do to maintain their efficiency and standards relative to other providers. They are unlikely to be the means of organisational transformation or powerful advancement in a competitive context.

Advanced business analytics are a potential differentiator in a competitive environment, and a powerful support and complement to robust strategy development and planning. The differentiator is the technical capability to acquire and manage voluminous data and generate business analytics and insights barely imagined five years ago as much as the HEI's leadership teams that learn to think and work and make decisions differently – faster, smarter and based on more accurate predictions – which gives a source of sustainable advantage. These capabilities also help shift the leadership from a 'rearview mirror' approach to performance to one that is future-focused.

Those now turning their attention to developing analytics capability compared to say five years ago have advantages, as the tools and technologies have advanced dramatically in recent years, and the availability of data has mushroomed, along with the tools to support and increasingly drive its exploitation.

Advanced business analytics do require a broader set of capabilities and additional investment and management support. But the increasing competition – for students, staff, research funding and a strong position in global rankings – means higher-risk and innovative and disruptive strategies are at times necessary. These are exactly the circumstances where advanced business analytics have the most value, in terms of supporting difficult decisions and the insights needed for achieving them. Given that an increasing number of leading global HEIs have or are developing and so are benefitting from these capabilities, the question should not be 'why start?' but rather 'why wait?'.

Underlying capabilities

Readiness

Prior to developing and supporting any specific BI or analytic capabilities, there are aspects of readiness which should greatly ease the journey. If they are not in place, or at least being cultivated, a more arduous path should be expected.

A first aspect of readiness is a motivation to create and embed a new set of capabilities that challenge but also help the organisation mature and advance on its chosen path. Building any type of new capability is difficult, and embedding it – that is changing how an organisation sees itself, how it works and how it makes decisions – is more so. One aspect of that commitment is for senior decision makers to be prepared and willing to learn things about the HEI they haven't been aware of or consider issues and options they have not thought of, as a good BI and analytics programme should challenge received views and provide new ones based on evidence. If BI and analytics capability were easy to achieve then every HEI would already be doing it. The fact is that it is not easy, and a significant level of commitment, funding, innovation, creativity, endurance and motivation among a number of key stakeholders is essential.

Second, the availability of trusted data from core internal business systems is important. Are those core business systems sound? Are they well supported? Is the quality of the data in the student records, staff and finance systems known, and is it trusted? Are there data dictionaries across the core data domains, documenting where and how key data items are held, what they mean and how they are calculated? A positive answer to these questions for core business systems is probably rare, but the questions indicate what a hypothetical state of readiness might look like. Negative answers suggest there will be diversionary challenges, but this is not an intrinsic impediment: a BI and analytics programme, open about the need for data quality improvement, can drive up the quality of core data by highlighting its value and exposing it to scrutiny.

Third is capacity, meaning not to develop, deliver and support an expanded business intelligence capability, but in terms of preparing to do so, which, depending on the start point, can be a significant undertaking. HEIs that do not perceive themselves to be under any particular pressure or competitive challenge have the luxury of working within their extant capacity. For those impelled by some form of urgency, whether from a vice-chancellor/principal or president's ambition, a governing body's encouragement, or the recognition of competitive pressures, rapidly creating the capacity to prepare to develop the key capabilities needed is an essential element of readiness. That capacity will likely be first applied to identifying a suitable solution partner (an organisation with experience of facilitating and supporting BI and analytics capability development) and for that partner to conduct a situational assessment. This includes identifying which prerequisites are, or are not, in place; assessing business system support and data quality and governance; judging the level and location of investment in technology and skills; developing a gap analysis and road map; and clarifying the benefits the HEI most needs to develop and defining what success looks like.

What is important in terms of readiness is to reach an informed judgement on what level of priority developing the necessary capabilities will be given, knowing that it will take time and resources, and having sponsors appreciate that while there can be 'quick wins' to justify the investment and build momentum, the transformative benefits of a BI and analytics capability are not easily or quickly acquired.

Data governance and data quality management

Apart from the statutory data reporting obligations common to many strategy and planning teams, prior to setting out on a BI and analytics programme there are likely to have been few internal imperatives for a sustained, focused enterprise programme of data governance, management and quality standards. It is also not the sort of initiative that members of an HEI's executive (except perhaps a chief information officer where one exists) are likely to get excited about, except on a reactive basis (e.g. following major data quality or security lapses), and is likely to be viewed as primarily an operational and technical issue.

Yet shared accounts of historic low trust in the quality of internally reported data will be familiar to many. Anecdotally, academic decision makers will report regular cases where the central HEI functions (e.g. HR, resource allocation, student records) report to them figures (whether on staff-student ratios, income generated, student progression etc.) which academic unit heads believe to be discrepant with their own local calculations. An HEI that experiences recurring internal challenges to its own reported metrics about position, progress and performance is one that is seeing its energy diverted away from determining the causes of performance issues and identifying and assessing the options for addressing them that would be most likely to improve the outcomes being contested.

The significance of governance and data quality for enabling a BI and analytics capability can also be evidenced by the experience of leading practitioners in higher education. In the Higher Education Data Warehousing Forum's most recent survey of member concerns (HEDW, 2016), of fifty options encompassing substantive core activities (student retention, net revenue, differential attainment etc.) and technical capabilities (big data, data modelling etc.), data governance was the top concern, followed by data quality. (The HEDW, founded in 2005, is a network of higher education DW and BI practitioners from more than seven hundred institutions and is dedicated to sharing best practice about knowledge management, data warehousing, institutional reporting, analytics and decision support.)

Data governance should arguably be considered as an element of governance more broadly (see Chapter 7). Also, if data is considered a key asset, it ought to attract the oversight and level of protection and exploitation of any physical, monetary or intellectual asset.

Regardless of where ownership and oversight of data governance sits, or what prompts attention to it, a programme minimally entails the following functions:

- Comprehensive inventory. It is difficult to govern anything unless you know where it is. A necessary first step is an inventory to identify what data is held, and at a minimum determine the volume, location, duration, condition and initial value (either the cost of acquisition or for decision making).
- Ownership and accountability. For each data domain (e.g. student, research, staff etc.) there will be set out clear responsibility for decision making about

who determines the relevant data quality standard and how it is measured, the purposes for which the data should be used, who should have access to data and restrictions or requirements (e.g. privacy) and its management.

- Management. Established policy and practice about such matters as acquisition, storage, usage, longevity, archiving, destruction, and some form of regular oversight to ensure policy and practice are followed.
- Enterprise data model. A data model is like any map: a graphical representation of where things are and the paths or relationships between them. An enterprise data model typically covers all data produced by the HEI (i.e. representations of activity as generated by transactional business systems) as well as information about how it is consumed, for example when it is represented in various kinds of reporting and analyses. It indicates repositories and types, directionality of data flows, and the processes the data is subjected to. It represents at any point in time both an inventory of all data resources and how they relate to each other.
- Data quality standards – continuous review and management. For any data asset there needs to be agreed standards and metrics for data quality, which may pertain for example to completeness, correctness, format, fitness for use, or elapsed time since its content was confirmed. The data quality management can refer to practices at the point of entry as well as regular scans and quality testing, either in operational business systems or against the stored data. Reporting of data quality standards attainment – or shortcomings – should be part of standard reporting to the senior management, up to and including the executive board, and arguably part of the HEI's KPI set.
- Data dictionary. An authoritative enterprise 'data dictionary' is a universal reference for all creators, administrators, managers and end users of data and analytics. It is distinct from the narrowly technical data dictionaries associated with databases and business systems. The data dictionary should provide for any data item, who 'owns' it and is responsible for its quality and use, what it means (in plain English), where it is stored, how it is calculated, where it is used and so forth. An enterprise data dictionary is best understood as a special case of knowledge management.

This outline of a data governance and quality management programme, particularly if extended to the tools used to carry out the necessary work, is also referred to as master data management (MDM). In practice, there is a strong interdependence between the advancement of a BI and analytics programme and the maturation of an MDM or data governance framework, and the two are best seen as mutually reinforcing. At its outset, any BI and analytics programme will unavoidably shine a spotlight on the absence or shortcomings of the data governance framework, as for any HEI lacking the functions set out above, almost every attempt to acquire and use data will be impeded: finding the right source, assessing its quality, agreeing on the data's meaning, gaining permission for the intended use and so forth will be a tedious process which may take weeks and months for each data item, rather than the minutes or hours if there were a single point of reference as a result of a MDM programme. HEIs that grapple with the significant challenges of MDM can greatly increase efficiency, speed and the strategic benefit of their analytics programme.

Data warehousing

Chief among the specialist and technical capabilities that underlay a BI and analytics programme is data warehousing. It is almost certain to be among the programme elements that is the most challenging and costly, especially at the outset, but like data governance will yield a wide range of broader benefits and is critical to progress and good practice. Whole books have been written on data warehousing (Corr and Stagnitto, 2011; Inmon, 2005; Kimball and Caserta, 2004; Kimball and Ross, 2013) and it is too substantial a field of expert practice to cover in depth or detail here. It is however worth outlining, in a non-technical manner, what a data warehouse is, what it does, and why it matters for developing a BI and analytics capability.

A data warehouse is a practical solution to the typically anarchic data environment which most leaders confront and which is almost entirely unsuitable for supporting a BI and analytics programme. Across the array of core business systems – finance, student records, research management, relationship management, HR, workload planning etc. – data will be captured by the owners of the processes and separately stored against a range of system and function-specific organisational structures, calendars (academic years, financial years etc.), operational definitions of key concepts (students, staff, course, programme) and so forth. Data in these separate systems will be structured to optimise the operational and transactional purposes of each system's transactional processes rather than for inter-system data analyses, and the individual systems will usually have limited capability to provide much beyond a 'snapshot' of the current status represented by the data. These narrow-purpose business systems themselves typically also have limited, inflexible and often basic functionality for extracting, analysing and presenting data. These typical conditions provide a limited, costly and volatile basis for BI and analytics and without a data warehouse will likely lead to contested or misleading reporting.

A data warehouse is not so much a 'thing', that is a piece of software or a database, as a broad term for a set of related technologies, processes and practices. First among these is that the data needed to support a BI and analytics programme is extracted via automated routines from each core transactional system on a recurring basis (whether nightly, weekly etc., depending on the business purposes and the data volatility). It is then restructured and stored centrally in a way that is optimised for queries, analyses and reporting based on strategic priorities and challenges, all of which are presumed to change over time, as are the systems themselves. The presupposition of change in source systems is important, because it means the warehouse is designed to both insulate analytics production from source system changes, allowing continuity of a standard of decision support, as well as to be able to accommodate changing analytical needs of the organisation without impacting core systems. This is accomplished by capturing and storing the business logic needed for analysis and reporting in a 'metadata' layer (meaning simply information about the data), rather than in operational systems or in reports themselves. The business logic refers to the tacit or formal rules by which the organisation works, what is assigned value and why, and the organisation's purposes and priorities, all of which are the central references for any analytics work. This approach to optimised data structure and storage also means queries and analyses can be designed and run in a fraction of the time that would be required if working directly with individual source systems. An additional benefit of the practice of recurring data extractions is the ability to build stable, federated repositories of long-run and cross-system data to support change and trend analyses, a capability that source systems usually intrinsically lack.

Second, the extracted data will typically be placed in a 'staging' area – a sort of way station – where it can be validated, cleaned and pre-processed before being loaded into one of the subject or purpose-specific data marts (e.g. repositories of data for specific purposes or encompassing certain domains such as students, staff, curriculum, research, finance etc.) comprising the warehouse. A key purpose of this practice is to protect the warehouse itself – a high-cost and high-value repository – from the consequence of contamination by poor-quality data, functionality faults and data structure changes which are a fact of life for any suite of individual enterprise systems from which data is sourced.

Another activity that takes place in the staging area is to conform the data from different sources, to reconcile and standardise the range of representations of the organisational structures, calendars, definitions and metrics, so data from disparate sources can be used together as needed. As an example of the potential benefits, this would allow production of a metric that allowed an HEI to know how much it cost to admit, teach and graduate a student of a certain quality (e.g. academic calibre, satisfaction with their experience, or employment outcome). Insights from such an analysis of the metric could lead to operational improvements. In this example, data would minimally be needed about students (personal characteristics, elements of the degree programme etc.), staff (and the associated costs of those involved in delivering the specific programme), finance (pulling in data about other costs including financial support) and student outcomes. Constructing a meaningful and reliable metric of this type without the benefit of warehoused data from the range of source systems would be highly problematic. Finally, the transformed data is loaded into the relevant data marts. Collectively this series of operations is referred to as the ETL (extract, transform and load) process.

After loading, data needs to be exposed in a managed way for use by analysts and report authors, via some form of data hub or presentation layer. It may be that those report authors are part of a BI and analytics team in a strategy and planning department, or they may be embedded subject area specialists (e.g. student support, research, HR, finance etc.), or even both, but the ideal is that they have the benefit of and access to a single controlled location where they obtain access to authoritative, high-quality, harmonised and integrated data to use for a range of ever-changing reporting and analytical purposes.

The tools and technologies used for data warehousing (e.g. extraction, optimised restructuring and integration) are distinct from the technologies for analysis, visualisation and distribution of data. Though some vendors may attempt to persuade clients of the benefits of a single platform, end-to-end solution, with increasingly open standards there is no intrinsic need or benefit to be gained from all elements being provided by a single vendor. Such arrangements can leave HEIs dependent and over-invested in a potentially inflexible platform and less able to take advantage of emerging technologies. An increasingly common approach is to use the mix of platforms and products that best meets organisational needs.

The elements of a data warehousing capability outlined are not merely technical, nor are the practices and processes outlined generic or obvious. They are necessarily designed on a case by case basis, and require expert translation of the HEI's strategy, priorities, and business problems; an understanding of the intended approach to analytics production and distribution; and knowledge about the full range of available enterprise data assets and the operational systems and their associated databases. This should result in a set of requirements against which the data warehouse, data marts, and extract and reporting routines are designed and built. Despite the up-front costs, challenges and complexity, data warehousing should ultimately be a cost-saving and performance-improving investment.

HEIs may seek to sidestep developing a data warehousing capability by overlaying existing separate transactional systems and data sources with an analytics and visualisation platform. This can offer a shorter and faster route to exposing existing data for analyses and monitoring, reporting and resolving strategic challenges. However, the underlying data sources driving the analytics outputs will remain un-harmonised and provide data about a single point in time, limiting the scope for robust cross-system and trend analysis and metrics. Also, while faster delivery of initial outputs can build support and engagement and produce quick returns, it may still over time prove beneficial to put in place a more robust and stable structure of underlying data – which may require redesign of the analytics resting upon it.

Data virtualisation

Data virtualisation technologies emerged and have matured over about the last ten years which can greatly augment the value of data warehousing as well as enable other data resources to be used more effectively. Data virtualisation addresses the need for HEIs in competitive and dynamic environments to have a more flexible and responsive BI and analytics capability.

Data virtualisation gathers together all the data needed to undertake analysis and reporting by creating an 'in-memory' environment (which is faster and more flexible than storage on physical media) where source system data, warehoused and historic data, unstructured data and organisational business logic can be flexibly interwoven and presented for use to business analysts including strategic planners – without requiring the physical extraction or movement of data from the core system where it physically resides. This means all types of outputs – management information, business intelligence, predictive analytics and even operational reporting – can be drawn from a single environment. Virtual data management tools also support data profiling and discovery, data quality analysis and advanced caching to greatly boost reporting system performance. Data virtualisation is not an alternative as much as an augmentation of data warehousing and ETL processes, as it presupposes a mature understanding of available data assets, a BI and analytics capability, a data governance framework, some form of capture and structured storage of historic data and a robust approach to change management.

For HEIs with the capabilities listed above, data virtualisation allows for a dramatic step change in data integration and near real-time data and analytics delivery, encompassing all of the purposes of the types of BI and analytics set out earlier. Analysts across the organisation no longer need be concerned with linking to transactional systems, operational data stores, warehoused data or external and unstructured data, as the virtual logical data warehouse presents pre-processed ready-to-use data from every source. This description no doubt sounds like a strategic planner's utopia. For those with a more advanced capability already in place, it remedies a range of routine impediments to help achieve the original vision for data-driven and evidence-based decision making and enables a genuine step change in impact and strategic benefit – all using technology and software that is available today. Implementation of data virtualisation entails a significant resource commitment and reorganisation of the relevant data utilisation architecture as well as policy, practice and governance.

Leading data virtualisation technology vendors have already established themselves across most major commercial sectors (pharmaceuticals, aerospace, energy, finance etc.). Data virtualisation technology provision is being used or explored by only a handful of HEIs worldwide, mainly those with mature data warehousing and BI and analytics capability. In 2016 data virtualisation made its first appearance among the topics at the annual conference of the Higher Education Data Warehousing Forum (HEDW) in North America. Given that HE embraced the technologies of data warehousing, BI, forecasting and predictive analytics only a few years after the commercial sector, and that virtualisation holds promise for HEIs in competitive markets and is already beginning to be used in the sector, we should expect its use to expand in the coming years in the HE sector.

Identity and access control

Identity and access management systems and processes are particularly important. Although, as argued, BI and analytics should be seen as for everyone, not all those with access to reporting and analytics outputs as 'consumers' will have the same level of access to data (for reasons of data security and confidentiality) or the same experience. Some staff will have rights or requirements for expansive or even unrestricted access, while some forms of information may be restricted, whether to certain parts of the management strata, to the individual concerned (for example in the cases of individual performance reporting) or to certain domains of activity (teaching, research, philanthropy). It may also be beneficial for BI and analytics consumers to have a personalised experience, for example for their default reports to initially be for the academic or functional unit that they lead. Both of these examples require that up-to-date data is held about each individual's position in the organisation structure and his or her role, responsibilities and access rights, and that these are made available to the systems delivering the outputs of the BI and analytics. IT departments often have identity and access control processes focused on access and rights to transactional systems (student records, finance, HR etc.) rather than on the outputs of an analytics programme, which may need more granular (table and row) level security information.

A high level of control of access to BI and analytics outputs is, at some level, an overhead on the programme, that is an activity that has to be managed and supported. Given this, there are advantages in opting for openness of access as a starting point, except when there is an overriding imperative that one not (for example research activity whose funders require confidentiality). Such an approach has additional benefits of enabling more staff to gain a broader perspective on organisational performance.

Recommended practices

This section describes recommended practices based on engagement across numerous HEIs, which have had value for a BI and analytics programme.

Engage decision makers and analytics consumers from the outset

User-centred design has long been standard practice in manufacturing, from cars to software to phones to aircraft, because it is more efficient (and profitable) to involve and listen to consumers to 'get it right the first time' than to redesign the product. This is true in analytics production: to be sure the outputs of any analytics programme achieve their purpose, involve the people who use them from the very outset. A structured framework for capturing business requirements from decision makers and developing the design of specific analytics solutions can engage and educate end users, introduce a measure of discipline in the process and improve effectiveness. The example design framework (see Figure 11.1) starts with identifying the activity to be investigated, followed by key stakeholders engaging in a process of brainstorming to establish the key questions that are to be answered using the proposed analytics. When considering who the report is for (step 3), it is important to go beyond the stated needs of the individual report

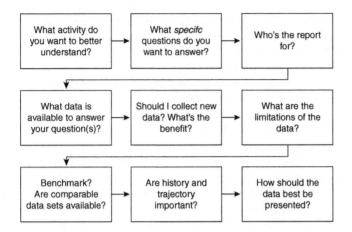

Figure 11.1 A structured framework for capturing business requirements

requester and deeply interrogate the needs of all those in such a role, and all who would use the report, and to understand the problem they are trying to solve or the decisions they will take, as well as the knowledge, skills and capabilities they can be expected to have to interpret and use the report. The next step involves identifying the data sources that can be used to answer the question. If existing data is not available, a cost-benefit assessment is needed to establish whether new data should be source or collected. At each step, end users' needs, decision times-cales and the value they place on the outputs will help decide how to proceed. The sixth step in the framework involves an explicit assessment of the limitations of the data, which again will be educative for decision makers to be involved with and help them use the analytics in a more informed manner. The seventh step requires establishing if benchmarking is necessary and if so whether data sets are available to enable this. The eighth step in the framework asks whether historical data and understanding performance trajectory are important. The final step involves careful thought regarding how the data should be visualised and presented. This particular framework can usefully structure a half-day workshop.

The process shown in Figure 11.1 reflects the questions that experienced analytics practitioners ask themselves throughout the development process, but it is more important to engage decision makers in answering these questions with them rather than to do so for them.

Expand the analytics visualisation repertoire

Having the capability to muster data and undertake the right analyses is not enough in itself: how analytics are presented and how they are embedded in decision making is crucial for generating impact and benefit. In principle, the data should largely speak for itself, but the responsibility and challenge for the strategic planner is to give the data its voice, and the production and design of such visualisations has to be discovered or learned, ideally both from experts of the practice (Few, 2006, 2012) and in the context of a specific organisation.

Regardless of where visualisation skills are learnt, like other forms of communication, they converge on a common truth that presentation should be clear, simple and unambiguous. But making something that feels simple or is easy to understand is not easy to do, and except for the truly inspired involves multiple iterations, close engagement with end users and decision makers and attending to their experience and refining the visualisation until people achieve the sought-after insight as close to instantly as is possible. If well presented, any narrative relating to analytics should spend as little time as possible explaining the data or the visualisation, and as much as possible prompting discussion about what the data does or does not show, what it means, and what can be done about it or what the next question is that gets at the root issue or the most transformative opportunity. Yet it is also important to leave analytics consumers and decision makers room to make the intuitive or inductive leap, and feel the sense of discovery and ownership of insight, which they are far more likely to act on than being effectively told or shown the performance problem or opportunity.

So what does effective presentation comprise? First and most important is knowing the audience. Is it a data savvy audience or a community that rarely looks at data and analyses? Can they genuinely understand the data, the measures, the meaning and the larger issue or purpose, or should the visualisation break down the information into smaller pieces? The next step is to acknowledge that each chart should endeavour to answer one or more questions. One should then choose the best and most appropriate type of chart to illustrate the data, for example, bar chart, scatter plot, chord diagram, heat map etc. In choosing the best form of graphical communication, it is also important to consider whether to contextualise, benchmark or normalise the data or show how it changes with time, and to think about using the appropriate scales and to ensure the visualisation is clearly labelled and titled. Finally, but of no less importance, is the choice of colour palette. As a broad principle, fewer and readily distinguished colours is better, highly consistent use of colours with clearly established meanings across many reports is ideal, and subjective preference for certain hues should be avoided in favour some form of standard usage. This is because with very few exceptions (e.g. red and green – but even those connotations of danger/stop and safe/go are culturally specific), colour has little intrinsic meaning and is not a particularly effective or efficient way to communicate. Relevant choices are shown to inform visualisation design in Figure 11.2.

Finally, analytics and impactful, innovative visualisations can play a role not only in answering questions that support decision making and improving performance, but by proactively provoking questions, displacing myths, challenging perceptions and prompting a fresh perspective on taken-for-granted aspects of an HEI's operations. Infographics can be particularly useful for these purposes. Infographics do not rely as much as other forms of visualisations on values and

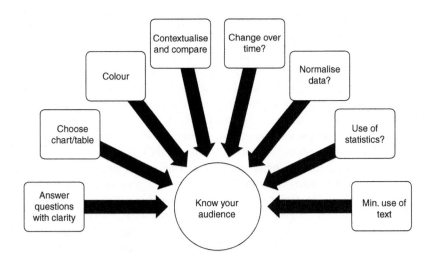

Figure 11.2 Visualisation design

labels and typically have minimal text. When well designed, they can convey very complex information quickly, with immediate and even emotional impact, and can generate a high level of curiosity-driven engagement with the subject matter.

Monitor usage

Well-designed visualisations are a key to impact and business benefit, but ensuring the outputs of any analytics capability are used in decision making is more important. Glossy dashboards and reports can languish in a corner of strategic planning or institutional reporting (IR) offices and play little part in supporting decision making. It is the responsibility of the strategic planner to rapidly recognise such situations, and to improve or cull those analytic outputs. Monitoring usage in real time is revealing: aim to know exactly who is looking at or downloading which analyses – and who is not. And for those who are not, the question is 'why not?' Is it a certain academic or functional unit, or a certain leadership stratum? Are they using other, local and potentially discrepant reports and analyses – or none at all? Are the incentives to use the most authoritative analyses too weak? In retail enterprises, analysts and decision makers know which products are the 'best sellers' and give them more shelf space. Action is taken about products with weak sales: they are improved, relocated or replaced. It is no different with business analytics: analytic outputs that are not used should be improved or else dropped.

Develop a BI and analytics competency centre or network

A common development across many sectors and which can also be found in higher education is a growing number of small, local pockets of BI and analytics capability, for example in the areas of research and citations analyses, philanthropy or any number of key university functions. These often arise in response to limited capability or capacity of central BI, strategic planning and/or IT teams to effectively support what are expert areas of practice and fast-moving analysis and reporting requirements. This can lead to variation in quality and alignment of analyses provided, failure to fully catalogue or exploit data resources acquired by such teams, uncoordinated provision, and a lack of clarity for decision makers about what is available and whom to ask for what.

Many strategy and planning departments have reporting and insight teams or resources. A BI and analytics competency centre (BICC) creates a practical working network of embedded subject area or functional expert analytics practitioners, with a central team providing coordination, expert support and thought leadership. A BICC is an alternative to a single, central team provision, which typically suffers from bottlenecks and requires more time to develop sufficient understanding of each business problem. Networked practitioner teams share data, expertise, problems, good practice and even capacity and coordinate development and delivery. The BICC also binds devolved teams to central data management, integration and quality audit capabilities. End users and decision makers are better served and provision more efficient and effective.

Build support for BI and analytics usage into staff development

The leadership team in an HEI may not have an innate ability to use the range of outputs of a BI and analytics programme. While it may be reasonable to expect that statistical representations of performance in a competitive context would be understandable to most in a management or leadership role, it would be unwise to assume that all those with decision-making responsibilities do in fact understand all core metrics, how they are composed, what they mean, what the implications are, or what their options for action are and how their choices may impact other performance measures. There will also be variation in how quickly and thoroughly staff new to leadership roles can take on board a continually evolving array of metrics and analyses which they may not have previously encountered.

When we consider the different skills needed to use advanced analytics (e.g. forecasting and probabilistic analyses), the gaps in ability will be even larger. Support for leadership in interpreting data about their academic unit across an HEI may not be efficiently delivered on an individual or team basis, especially given turnover rates in roles like head of department. An approach that is more efficient, and can ensure an analytics capability achieves maximum impact, is to provide a professional development programme which prepares new and/or future managers and leaders for this dimension of their role. Such a programme would ensure a better understanding of the range or metrics, how to understand their meaning and implications and limitations, how to apply them to business problems and how to engage the analytics capabilities for new challenges.

Recognise the limitations of BI and analytics

A strong BI and analytics programme can provide a means to answer a great many important questions about position, performance, operational excellence and opportunities. In the process, it will unavoidably give rise to further and deeper questions, some of which may also be answerable. However, there will come times when the analytics will take the enquirer no further to the root cause or solution, or acquiring the necessary data becomes too time-consuming or expensive. It is important to know when the limits of analytics have been reached and different approaches are needed, for example to look to lived experience.

As an example, a leading US university was using analytics to understand the causes of differential attainment. They had found that very high capability students from certain ethnic groups had longer average time to completion, which was not explained by differences in family backgrounds and prior academic achievement and other commonly cited explanatory factors. The data seemed to indicate a causal effect related to specific modules and even individual lecturers – though the data shed no light on what the underlying cause might be. In the end, they had to step away from the data and closely observe what was happening in the classroom, which highlighted unconscious bias in the behaviours of some academics, which entailed a much more person-focused programme of interventions, education, consciousness-raising and cultural change. It is therefore important not to become unjustifiably committed to finding answers via analytics alone.

Identify enabling and blocking aspects of organisation culture

There are many characteristics of an HEI's culture which can enable better progress and benefit realisation from a BI and analytics programme. Below we set out the three that are perhaps most fundamental.

- Openness. Openness, transparency and a high-level internal communication provide a strong cultural platform for an impactful BI and analytics capability, in two ways. First, wide visibility of performance reporting – at institutional, department and individual levels – can harness esteem as a source of intrinsic motivation to improve. Second, in an open culture, where there will be a constant stream of information, analytics that shed light on poor performance or outcomes are less likely to stand out and be stigmatised as 'bad news'. By way of contrast, an environment where institutional, department or individual performance is not well known or treated as 'private' or only shared on a need-to-know basis will greatly impede motivation to draw on and use BI and analytics outputs.
- A problem-solving culture. A problem-solving culture entails questioning and learning and a pragmatic, evidence-based non-ideological approach to identifying issues and finding solutions without being defensive about what the data finds or shows. Ironically, despite these behaviours being intrinsic to

academic practice, they are not necessarily always applied to managing HE operations, particularly where BI and analytics outputs are discrepant with an existing received or desired view of performance and position or relative contribution of certain academic or functional areas. The converse of a problem-solving culture might be a 'no bad news' culture, in which analytics outputs can be regarded as threatening rather than supporting.

- Genuine accountability. Where there are real material or reputational consequences, both positive and negative, for achievement (or the lack of it) by identifiable teams and key people, there will be more incentive to make use of the insights that can be provided by a BI and analytics programme.

Looking ahead

Looking ahead, perhaps the only prediction that can be made with any degree of confidence is that the pace of technological change and capability in the area of BI and analytics will increase. It is therefore difficult to address this topic in a way that will not quickly become obsolete, as what is described here as 'advanced analytics' (machine learning, AI, predictive analytics etc.) will within ten years almost certainly be commonplace or superseded. But there will be a need for strategic planners to present findings, judge meaning and weigh up options for which the many consequences cannot be quantified, and for academic leaders to take personal responsibility for key decisions, despite uncertainty, but with a desire to be well informed by the best available evidence.

The core competencies needed in ten years to achieve benefits for strategic planning from a BI and analytics capability will be, as they are today, sound knowledge about the institution and its environment, experience in using analytics intelligently, and discernment, judgement and leadership.

References

Corr, Lawrence and Stagnitto, Jim. 2011. Agile Data Warehouse Design: Collaborative Dimensional Modeling, from Whiteboard to Star Schema, Leeds, UK: DecisionOne Press.

Few, Stephen. 2006. Information Dashboard Design: The Effective Visual Communication of Data, Oakland, CA: Analytics Press.

Few, Stephen. 2012. *Show Me the Numbers*, Oakland, CA: Analytics Press.

HEDW 2016. 2015 HEDW Member Survey – Top 10 Issues. Retrieved 03/11/2016 from https://hedw.org/hedwpresentation/2015-hedw-member-survey-top-10-issues/

Inmon, William H. 2005. *Building the Data Warehouse*, Indianapolis, IN: Wiley.

Kimball, Ralph and Caserta, Joe. 2004. *The Data Warehouse ETL Toolkit: Practical Techniques for Extracting, Cleaning, Conforming, and Delivering Data*, Indianapolis, IN: John Wiley & Sons.

Kimball, Ralph and Ross, Margy. 2013. *The Data Warehouse Toolkit: The Definitive Guide to Dimensional Modeling*, Indianapolis, IN: John Wiley & Sons.

United States Department of Defense. 2013. *Joint Publication 1–02: Dictionary of Military and Associated Terms*, Military Studies Press.

Part 5

Insight and information

Chapter 12

Indicators for measuring and managing performance

Mike Kennerley

Introduction

The increased competition and regulation in higher education in the UK and globally have brought with them greater emphasis on performance and assurance. As well as using data for external reporting and assurance, HEIs are increasingly using performance management mechanisms to support delivery of their goals (Franco-Santos et al., 2014). To succeed in rapidly changing environments, HEIs need to make accurate informed decisions quickly, and there is a growing demand to leverage the data they have at their disposal.

Most academic leaders have enormous amounts of data, and a plethora of tools and techniques exist to analyse and interpret data (see Chapter 11). There is research evidence suggesting that better use of information can improve decision making (Ittner and Larker, 2006; Davenport and Harris, 2007). The use of information to improve decision making and organisational outcomes is a topic that is receiving considerable attention with academics and consultants attempting to provide insights into how information can better be used. Ittner and Larker (2006) report the growing evidence that greater use of effective analysis tools delivers better organisational performance.

By far the most well-known and adopted approach to organisational performance measurement and management is the Balanced Scorecard (Kaplan and Norton, 1992). Whilst many other approaches, models and frameworks exist, considering the evolution of the Balanced Scorecard concept is useful in highlighting important attributes of the systems and processes needed to measure and manage performance within HEIs. Since its inception the Balanced Scorecard has evolved from a framework for defining what to measure, through various iterations into a model for managing strategic organisational change, via the Strategy-Focused Organisation (Kaplan and Norton, 2000), characterised by:

- translating strategy into operational terms,
- aligning the organisation to strategy,
- making strategy everyone's job,
- making strategy a continual process and
- mobilising strategy through executive leadership.

These elements cover a wide range strategic planning and management activities and processes that fall within the remit of HE strategic planners. Indeed, Kaplan and Norton (2005) proposed the establishment of an office of strategy management, the functions of which align with, or are similar to, many strategic planning offices in higher education institutions (see Chapter 2). The strategy-focused organisation has emerged from the development of a performance measurement framework with origins in the fields of management accounting and operations management and is indicative of the crosscutting nature of the use and impact of performance measurement and management. Building on practice in other sectors, this chapter focuses on the design and use of performance indicators in higher education, recognising that their implementation and use will need to be integral to wider planning activities covered elsewhere in this book. Building on the definition of Neely et al. (1995), the development performance of indicators discussed in this chapter should include the interrelated elements of:

- individual indicators that quantify the efficiency and effectiveness of actions;
- a set of indicators that combine to assess the performance of an HEI as a whole;
- a supporting infrastructure that enables data to be acquired, collated, sorted, analysed, interpreted and disseminated; and
- management systems and processes for using performance indicators.

Why measure performance

In their review of the field, Franco-Santos et al. (2007) identified 17 different roles or purposes of performance measurement. They summarised these into five main categories:

- "measure performance": this category encompasses the role of monitoring progress and measuring performance/evaluating performance;
- "strategy management": this category comprises the roles of planning, strategy formulation, strategy implementation/execution and focusing attention/providing alignment;
- "communication": this category comprises the roles of internal and external communication, benchmarking and compliance with regulations;
- "influence behaviour": this category encompasses the roles of rewarding or compensating behaviour, managing relationships and control; and
- "learning and improvement": this category comprises the roles of feedback, double-loop learning and performance improvement.

Understanding why performance indicators are being developed and used is a critical starting point. Historically, HEIs and strategic planners have placed attention on the requirements of performance indicators in the context of statutory reporting as well as performance in league tables and benchmarking where indicators and data requirements are externally defined (see Chapter 13). There continues to be increased focus on performance indicators to support development and implementation of institutional strategy (Strike and Labbe, 2016) where there is a greater level of freedom to determine which indicators to use and how to define them.

What to measure – defining a set of indicators

A wide range of frameworks has been proposed to help organisations identify which performance indicators they should use to measure organisational performance. As previously mentioned, the Balanced Scorecard is the most widely known and adopted of these. When first introduced, the Balanced Scorecard was promoted as a tool to identify the measures that organisations should use to manage performance, prompting users to identify an equal number of measures in each of four perspectives: financial, customer, internal, and innovation and learning. This demonstrated the need to balance financial and non-financial measures, internal and external measures, leading and lagging measures, and short- and long-term measures. The approach encouraged managers to overcome the shortcomings of traditional financial measurement and ensure that managers didn't take a narrow view of performance based on too few measures.

However, since its introduction the concept has evolved, with less emphasis placed on the exact balance of measures and more on the need to explicitly link desired performance outcomes to the drivers that enable achievement of those outcomes. This change in emphasis is reflected by Cobbold and Lawrie (2002) and Speckbacher et al. (2003), who identify three different types of Balanced Scorecard. This can cause some confusion, particularly as this evolution has also seen the emphasis of the Balanced Scorecard change from performance measurement to strategy development and strategic control (a broader performance management view).

Having a strict balance in the number of measures is no longer considered necessary. In fact, Schneiderman (2001), who developed the first scorecard, which Kaplan and Norton found in his company Analog Devices, argues that balance is harmful and that "good scorecards will be unbalanced; containing mostly non-financial, internal, leading, short-term measures".

Kaplan and Norton (1996) propose the use of strategy maps to understand how the drivers of performance affect the top-level objectives. Strategy maps are just one example of a range of tools that can be used to identify cause-and-effect relationships that explicitly link performance outcomes to the drivers of those outcomes. The development of such maps provides a performance framework for the organisation which tells the story of the organisation's strategy that can be presented on a single piece of paper. When Schneiderman talks about a "good scorecard" he is referring to a performance framework with cause-and-effect relationships linking specific actions to ultimate organisational outcomes regardless of whether the Balanced Scorecard or any other measurement framework has been used as the basis of its development.

Designing performance measurement systems is all about deciding which measures to select and, just as importantly, which measures to ignore. The number of measures should be limited to give clarity to what the organisation is trying to achieve. Therefore, developing the right performance measures is all about selecting the key objectives that the HEI needs to improve and designing appropriate measures to track this improvement.

When management teams do this together it clarifies their thinking on what is important. Having a debate refines their views and makes explicit the mental models they hold in their heads about how they believe the HEI, faculty or department works and what it is trying to achieve. Experience shows that this process in itself is highly beneficial. It can help the management team to clarify and agree upon strategy even if the measurement process doesn't progress further.

An HEI's performance framework should show all the key objectives it is trying to achieve over the coming period, linked showing the main cause-and-effect relationships between the objectives. Further measures, aligned via cascade of the performance framework or map, can be added at different levels of the institution to ensure there is the appropriate level of focus and granularity without reporting all indicators at all levels. A succinct performance framework is an extremely good communication tool both within the management team and for communicating the objectives by demonstrating how the actions of colleagues throughout the organisation contribute to its overall objectives. Such performance frameworks explicitly show a vertically and horizontally integrated picture of the objectives of the organisation, making clear what should be managed to achieve the HEI's performance objectives.

Reviewing the array of performance measurement frameworks, including the evolving Balanced Scorecard, Neely et al. (2007) defined the criteria for developing a performance framework to ensure that the set of indicators:

- is "balanced", including financial and non-financial measures, internal and external measures, leading and lagging measures, and short- and long-term measures;
- provides a succinct overview of the organisation's performance;
- is multi-dimensional, reflecting all the areas of performance that are important to the organisation's success;
- is comprehensive;
- is integrated both across the organisation's functions and through its hierarchy, encouraging alignment of goals and actions; and
- explains how results are a function of determinates, demonstrating cause and effect.

There have been numerous examples of HEIs across the world that have taken a Balanced Scorecard approach to managing strategy and performance. Many have developed a strategy map to summarise the objectives, although this has tended to use a stakeholder perspective, such as approaches proposed by Atkinson et al.

(1997) and Neely et al. (2002), as the starting point of development. This can overcome the commercial focus of frameworks such as the Balanced Scorecard and include consideration of an organisation's requirements of its stakeholders as well as stakeholders' needs and demands. The satisfaction of the above criteria for a performance framework is more important than adhering to the rules of the particular framework used.

Kaplan and Norton (2008) report the development of a strategy map at the University of Leeds defining its vision, purpose and values, and stakeholders and partners in order to identify strategic objectives with performance indicators and targets to evaluate performance. With students identified as a key stakeholder, student satisfaction, staff-student ratio, average A-level score, applications per place, and percentage of students from lower socioeconomic groups are identified as strategic KPIs used to evaluate performance of the student theme. These strategic KPIs are then further disaggregated to establish operational indicators that can inform local actions.

How to measure – defining indicators

Much of the focus in the field of performance measurement is on the question of what to measure. However, of equal importance is the question of how we as strategic planners seek to measure performance, particularly concerning the collection of data. HEIs, and their strategic planners in particular, are well used to collecting large amounts of data.

When using data for performance measures or key performance indicators (KPIs) there are often issues with the data sources, how the data was collected, data collection points and timing, and generally how much trust can we put in the data and so forth. It is not unusual to observe two people heatedly arguing over some dimension of performance and later find that the root cause of their disagreement was the imprecise definition of a measure. As a result, organisations must ensure that they follow a systemic and structured data collection approach. The need for a clear approach to data governance and data management is covered in Chapters 10 and 11 of this book and is fundamental to the development and use of performance indicators.

Fundamentally, this process is concerned with translating the conceptual definition of information defined in the performance framework or model into an operational definition for each performance indicator. In his managerial and statistical writings, W. Edwards Deming placed great importance on the value of using operational definitions. As he said:

> An operational definition is a procedure agreed upon for translation of a concept into measurement of some kind.
>
> Deming (1993, p. 105)

The operational definition provides a common definition of a piece of data that everyone can understand. Without such a definition that is commonly understood, the only person who fully understands the meaning of that data is the person who defined it. Deming added:

> There is no true value of any characteristic, state, or condition that is defined in terms of measurement or observation. Change of procedure for measurement (change of operational definition) or observation produces a new number.
>
> Deming (1993, p. 104)

This statement emphasises the importance of the operational definition and lies at the heart of many misunderstandings and misinterpretations of data which led to the popular adage "lies, damn lies and statistics". It is easy to talk about changes or trends in a particular piece of data such as a performance measure, but unless we understand the precise formula used to calculate it and how the data was collected, we cannot be sure that everyone has the same understanding of what that change or trend actually means.

Whilst much of the data collected by HEIs is well defined, particularly when reporting for statutory purposes, when applying to performance indicators there is more information that must be defined to ensure that we fully understand the indicator. It is necessary to define more than just the title and value to fully define and understand an indicator. Neely et al. (2002) propose the information that needs to be defined and communicated to fully understand a performance indicator and develop an operational definition. This information includes the title of the indicator; the purpose of its use; the objectives or strategies it relates to; the formula for its calculation; the target level of performance aspired to; the frequency of measurement; the source of data; who is responsible for collecting, analysing and reporting the data; and who is responsible for acting on the indicator and what does he or she do.

KPIs in relation to student education provide examples of the need to have clear definitions of the performance indicators being used with in HEIs. Measures such as student satisfaction, graduate prospects and student non-continuation can be defined in different ways for purposes such as league tables, the Teaching Excellence Framework or internal use. Different purposes may use different sources of data (internal or external), include different cohorts of students, be analysed using different subject coding frames or organisational structures or cover different time frames. Similarly, comparisons and benchmark statistics can be based on different calculations. Each of these different definition characteristics will bring a different value for what on the face of it would appear to be the same performance indicator.

The more established principles and techniques of measurement science which have developed in the physical sciences and engineering can teach us a number of lessons about data which we collect and measurements that we make (Micheli and Mari, 2014). This field argues that data and information are attributed to entities by people and hence should not be considered to be fact or truth. A number of scholars have remarked that the "concept of objectivity in accounting is largely a myth" Morgan (1988, p. 477), although performance measurement, accounting and auditing are still seen as objective evaluations of reality by most academics and practitioners (Power, 1997).

It is also important to note that the context of, and purpose for which, data is collected can significantly affect data and its interpretation. A number of subject areas support Goodhart's law (Goodhart, 1975), which states that once a social or economic indicator or other surrogate measure is used as a target it becomes useless for its original purpose of measurement/assessment. Considerable care should be taken when using data in a context or for a purpose other than that for which it was originally intended.

These insights from the measurement field demonstrate that metrics rarely fully measure an entity, distinguishing indicators of an entity's attributes from comprehensive measurement of it. Indeed, Gray et al. (2015) support the argument that "it is not possible to define the perfect performance measure, but if you understand the weaknesses in the measures you utilise you can foresee some of the pitfalls". Rather than fully describing the performance of the institution, a performance framework populated with indicators provides data to which further information, including qualitative information, can be added to inform our understanding and provide context.

This inability to rely solely on metrics or indicators to evaluate performance was recognised by the Stern Review of the Research Excellence Framework (Stern, 2016), which emphasises the need to supplement metrics with further information including qualitative assessment. Further, Wilsdon et al. (2015), in *The Metric Tide* review of the role of metrics in research assessment and management, highlighted the limitations of using metrics and proposed a set of criteria for the responsible use of metrics, requiring:

- robustness – basing metrics on the best possible data in terms of accuracy and scope;
- humility – recognising that quantitative evaluation should support, but not supplant, qualitative, expert assessment;
- transparency – keeping data collection and analytical processes open and transparent, so that those being evaluated can test and verify the results;
- diversity – accounting for variation by field, and using a range of indicators to reflect and support a plurality of research and researcher career paths across the system; and
- reflexivity – recognising and anticipating the systemic and potential effects of indicators, and updating them in response.

These criteria highlight many of the criticisms of using metrics and KPIs that have accompanied the use of performance measurement and indicators in HEIs.

Gray et al. (2015) discuss many of these issues and actions to avoid common pitfalls, such as:

- failing to clarify the purpose of measurement;
- assuming that measurement is an instant fix for performance issues;
- gaming and cheating in the use of indicators;
- comparing sets of data that have nothing in common and hoping to learn something;
- overemphasising the use of targets; and
- using targets and rewards to promote certain behaviours, and achieving exactly the opposite ones.

These pitfalls in the use of performance indicators highlight the need to constantly review the design, use and impact of performance indicators to ensure they are delivering the desired result. Neely et al. (2002) provide ten tests of performance indicators that can help assess potential robustness of new or existing performance indicators:

- Truth Test – Are we really measuring what we set out to measure?
- Focus Test – Are we only measuring what we set out to measure?
- Relevancy Test – Is it the right measure of the performance factor we want to track?
- Consistency Test – Will the data always be collected in the same way?
- Access Test – Is it easy to locate and capture the data needed to make the measurement?
- Clarity Test – Is any ambiguity possible in interpreting the results?
- So-What Test – Can and will the reported data be acted upon?
- Timeliness Test – Can the data be accessed rapidly and frequently?
- Cost Test – Are the costs of measurement worth it?
- Gaming Test – Is the measure likely to encourage undesirable or inappropriate behaviours?

Supporting infrastructure

The Metric Tide review (Wilsdon et al., 2015) highlights the importance of having an appropriate data infrastructure, and examines their characteristics in the context of research assessment and management. Davenport and Harris (2007) argue that there is competitive advantage to be gained by using sophisticated qualitative and statistical analysis using information technology to improve the information available to managers and that leading organisations are "competing on analytics". They identify organisational, human and technological capabilities required to improve the use of information and propose a five-stage maturity framework to assess an organisation's analytic capabilities.

Through the evidence-based management movement, Pfeffer and Sutton (2006) promote the application of principles originating in medicine and education so that managerial decisions and organisational practices are informed by the best available scientific evidence.

The basis of these approaches is the conversion of data into information and information into knowledge to enable decisions to be made. Thus the assumption is that if we have better data this will enable us to have better information leading to better knowledge and hence better decisions. This is a rational view of decision making which is implicit in much of the management research in the field. Many tools, techniques and technologies have been developed to support the conversion of data into information to inform decision making.

The collection and manipulation of this data consumes considerable time, effort and resources. As a result, the way in which this information can be used to increase the value extracted from it, improve decision making and ultimately improve the outcome or performance of the HEI is the subject of intense interest. Davenport et al. (2000, p. 3) observed that "One of the most enduring traits of the information age is that we have focused too much on mastering transaction data and not enough on turning it into information and knowledge that can lead to business results". They conclude that identifying the right data to use for the right purpose and the right tools from those already available are significant issues in extracting value from data.

The conversion of data into information is based on analysis and interpretation. Analysis involves processing, manipulating and organising data in a way which enables insights to be extracted. Interpretation is the translation of analysed data into intelligible or familiar terms; it is at this point that data becomes information, having been given context. Spence (2001) refers to interpretation of information as achieving the A-ha moment – that is, arriving at the moment at which the messages in the data become clear. Information visualisation can be key to interpreting data and seeing trends or linkages that can inform decisions. There is a wide array of tools available, from simple Excel tables and charts to far more complex visualisation approaches, as drawn together by Kirk (2016) amongst others. As well as generating insights, visualisations are important in communicating insights to others whether through reporting or other communications. Helping others to achieve the A-ha moment provided by the analysis and interpretation of data is an important role of a data analyst, requiring an understanding of the audience and how best to communicate to them.

There are a wide range of systems and tools to support the analysis and interpretation of data to provide information. This includes production of static reports as well as analytics tools that allow bespoke analysis and interpretation. Increasingly, business intelligence (BI) tools are being developed that put the ability to analyse and interpret large data sets into the hands of decision makers. Chapter 11 discusses the use of BI tools for decision support and improving organisational outcomes.

Extracting value from information

In order to extract the maximum value out of the data that is available, a structured approach to working with data should be used to inform decision making. Tools and techniques can be applied to improve the execution of each stage of this structured approach.

In the field of quality management, the PDCA cycle is a well-established improvement methodology which incorporates four stages: Plan, Do, Check, Act. Popularised by W. Edwards Deming (Deming, 1993), it is based on Walter Shewhart's application of the "scientific method" of research ("hypothesis" – "experiment" – "evaluation") to factory production. Primarily, the PDCA cycle is applied to individual processes; however, its constituent phases lie at the heart of performance management as they integrate planning, action and monitoring of performance to ensure continuous improvement and the achievement of objectives. Furthermore, the PDCA cycle is all about learning – learning in a systematic way what works and what does not. This approach lies at the heart of improvement approaches such as Lean and Six Sigma evidence-based performance improvement approaches.

An HEI may want to improve assessment and feedback on coursework to students and creates a plan to achieve this. A baseline measure will be required, or may even have prompted the plan. Various strategies may be employed such as online marking and feedback, a personal tutor system etc. The indicator, if well founded and working, should show whether the strategies employed are having any effect. If not, then review and fresh action is required, or if yes, then success is evidenced. Without this approach, the inputs or actions can be mistaken for progress rather than the outputs.

If the skills and knowledge of academic leaders are to be fully exploited, then the performance review processes employed should focus their attention on the issues raised by the performance measures and the actions necessary to meet the HEI, faculty or departmental objectives, rather than merely trying to interpret what the measures actually say. To address this, authors such as Newman (1995), Rasiel and Friga (2001) and Neely et al. (2002) propose approaches which extend concepts in the Deming/PDCA cycle process to integrate performance measurement into the broader performance management activities by ensuring there is a systematic approach to identifying objectives; collecting, analysing and interpreting data; communicating insights; making decisions; and monitoring performance to ensure that objectives are achieved. In HEIs this cycle is often captured by a planning round, as described in Chapter 4. The effectiveness of these processes will be enhanced by development and exploitation of performance analyst skills and focus of review processes and meetings on the key performance outcomes represented in the organisation's strategy.

Following these steps moves the focus of performance management from review of past performance to the discussion of how strategy is executed to deliver future performance objectives. This focuses attention on the issues facing the HEI in the future and the achievement of strategic objectives. Micheli and Pavlov (2008) highlight that establishing a "culture of performance management" (as opposed to a culture of performance measurement) can help organisations improve their performance. Gray et al. (2015) focus extensively on the way in which performance indicators impact on behaviour within organisations and the need to ensure well-designed performance indicators are aligned to organisational objectives and management processes. Clearly this is linked to HR and people management, a field in which research and practice continues to extensively debate the use of performance reviews of individual staff, including the use of rewards, performance targets and performance-related pay. Kairuz et al. (2016) warn against detailed use of performance management and measures (including KPIs) in managing academic staff, as they argue that they add to the demands of academic work and undermine creative, reflective and critical thinking. Franco-Santos et al. (2014) argue that a "stewardship" approach based on aligned long-term outcomes and values is a more appropriate approach to managing academic staff than monitoring and control of short-term outcomes. It is possible to align decision making and actions to the HEI's objectives without prescriptive monitoring and control of individuals by aligning the institution's performance framework to the individuals' mental models that influence their decision making and actions.

As well as enabling monitoring of current performance and identification of improvement actions, Neely and Al Najjar (2006) highlight opportunities to use performance indicators and measurement systems to contribute to wider organisational learning. In the organisational learning field this distinction is often referred to as single- versus double-loop learning (Argyris, 1976; Argyris and Schon, 1996). In single-loop learning, corrective action is taken to bring performance back on track when it deviates. In double-loop learning, questions are asked about whether the track was right in the first place.

In the recruitment of students, an HEI or one of its departments might employ a strategy of increasing entry qualifications for students to increase intake quality, with the expectation that non-continuation rates will fall and student satisfaction will rise, as will the graduate outcomes and graduate employability. Similarly, the HEI might expect the strategy to lead to a reduction in applications but an increase in applicant conversion rate. Measuring the offer grades and intake quality along with each of the expected outcomes allows not only monitoring of progress to take corrective action where necessary (single-loop learning), but also analysis to understand whether the assumed outcomes materialise or the actions result in unexpected or unintended outcomes requiring the strategy to be changed.

Decision making

Evidence-based decision making, using KPIs and other data to improve insight, is based on a rational approach. However, people don't necessarily take a rational approach to making decisions. The field of psychology contains extensive research on decision making, describing different approaches. A wide range of authors has highlighted the errors people make in using data to make decisions. In order to improve decision making we need to understand how individuals make decisions and what role data and information play in that process. Nobel laureate Daniel Kahneman with Tversky and others established a cognitive basis for common human errors that arise from heuristics and biases (brought together in Kahneman, 2011). Meanwhile, Klein et al. (1993) have worked on the use of expert intuition in executive decision making using the naturalistic decision-making approach which argues that the brain is able to cope with making complex decisions in short time frames, with vague goals and changing conditions.

Intuitive approaches to decision making can be flexible and deal with complexity and uncertainty quickly. With cognitive approaches the need remains to align the mental model of the decision maker with the entity and decision being made, such as the performance framework in the case of the HEI's desired outcomes. Kahneman and Klein (2009, 2010) discuss the circumstances in which intuition would yield good decision making.

The vast majority of decisions are based on a combination of rational (evidence-based) and judgemental/intuitive elements. The balance of these will be influenced by the type of decision being made, the experience and personality of the decision maker, the reliability of data available, the certainty of outcomes and the cognitive biases that influence the decisions in a given situation. By understanding these factors in different contexts and for different decision makers, it is possible to better understand how decisions are made and provide the appropriate information in a manner that is most likely to influence the decision in question.

Conclusions

HEIs are increasingly using performance indicators and performance management not only in the context of external reporting and league table performance, but also to support delivery of their institutional objectives. In the field of performance management there is evidence that use of KPIs and supporting data can improve decision making and institutional outcomes. For this improvement to be delivered, the right KPIs need to be identified using an appropriate performance framework establishing objectives and drivers of performance. Evidence-based decision making requires the collection of data that is fit for the purpose using agreed and communicated operational definitions to ensure the indicators and their meaning are fully understood, whilst care should be taken when using data for a purpose other than that for which it was originally collected.

As important as the performance indicators are the subsequent analysis and interpretation to convert the data into information. Many tools and techniques are available to support the analysis and interpretation of data, with significant investments being made in management information and business intelligence solutions.

However, it is rarely, if ever, possible to fully evaluate performance on the basis of metrics or KPIs alone. Judgement or intuition will always need to be applied. However, establishing a comprehensive performance framework can guide decision making even where there are no robust KPIs or other data to ensure evidence-based decisions. People don't necessarily take a rational approach to making decisions. There is a need to understand how individuals make decisions and what role data and information play in that process.

References

Argryis, C. (1976). Single-Loop and Double-Loop Models in Research on Decision Making. *Administrative Science Quarterly.* 21(3), pp. 363–375.

Argyris, C. and Schon, D.A., (1996). *Organisational Learning II: Theory, Method, and Practice.* Reading, MA: Addison-Wesley Publishing.

Atkinson, A.A., Waterhouse, J.H. and Wells, R.B. (1997). A Stakeholder Approach to Strategic Performance Measurement. *Sloan Management Review.* 38(3), pp. 25–37.

Cobbold, I. and Lawrie, G. (2002). 'The Development of the Balanced Scorecard as a Strategic Management Tool' Proceedings of the PMA International Conference on Performance Measurement and Management, Boston, MA, 17–19, July.

Davenport, T., Harris, J., De Long, D. and Jacobson, A. (2000). *Data to Knowledge to Results – Building an Analytic Capability.* Institute for Strategic Change, Andersen Consulting, Cambridge, MA.

Davenport, T.H. and Harris, J.G. (2007). *Competing on Analytics: The New Science of Winning.* Boston, MA: Harvard Business School Press.

Deming, W.E. (1993). *The New Economics for Industry, Government, and Education.* Boston, MA: MIT Press.

Franco-Santos, M., Kennerley, M., Micheli, P., Martinez, V., Mason, S., Marr, B., Gray, D. and Neely, A. (2007). Towards a Definition of a Business Performance Measurement System. *International Journal of Operations and Production Management.* 27(8), pp. 784–801.

Franco-Santos, M., Rivera, P. and Bourne, M. (2014). *Performance Management in UK Higher Educations Institutions: The Need for a Hybrid Approach.* London: Leadership Foundation for Higher Education.

Goodhart, C.A.E. (1975). *Monetary Relationships: A View from Threadneedle Street, in Papers in Monetary Economics Volume I.* Sydney: Reserve Bank of Australia.

Gray, D., Micheli, P. and Pavlov, A. (2015). *Measurement Madness: Recognizing and Avoiding the Pitfalls of Performance Management.* Chichester: Wiley.

Ittner, C.D. and Larker, D.F. (2006). Moving from Strategic Measurement to Strategic Data Analysis, in Chapman, C.S. (Ed.), *Controlling Strategy.* Oxford: Oxford University Press, pp. 86–105.

Kairuz, T., Andriés, L., Nickloes, T. and Truter, I. (2016). Consequences of KPIs and Performance Management in Higher Education. *The International Journal of Educational Management.* 30(6), pp. 881–893.

Kaplan, R.S. and Norton, D.P. (1992). The Balanced Scorecard – Measures That Drive Performance. *Harvard Business Review.* 70(1), pp. 71–79.

Kaplan, R.S. and Norton, D.P. (1996). *The Balanced Scorecard: Translating Strategy into Action.* Boston, MA: Harvard Business School Press.

Kaplan, R.S. and Norton, D.P. (2000). *The Strategy Focused Organization: How Balanced Scorecard Companies Thrive in the New Business Environment.* Boston, MA: Harvard Business School Press.

Kaplan, R.S. and Norton, D.P. (2005). The Office of Strategy Management. *Harvard Business Review.* 83(10), pp. 72–80.

Kaplan, R.S. and Norton, D.P. (2008). *The Execution Premium: Linking Strategy to Operations for Competitive Advantage.* Boston, MA: Harvard Business School Press.

Kirk, A. (2016). *Data Visualisation: A Handbook for Data Driven Design.* London: Sage Publications.

Kahneman, D. (2011). *Thinking, Fast and Slow.* New York: Farrar, Straus and Giroux.

Kahneman, D. and Klein, G. (2009). Conditions for Intuitive Expertise. *American Psychologist.* 60(6), pp. 515–526.

Kahneman, D. and Klein, G. (2010). Strategic Decisions: When Can You Trust Your Gut? *McKinsey Quarterly.* 2, pp. 58–67.

Klein, G., Orasanu, J., Calderwood, R. and Zsambok, C.E. (1993). *Decision Making in Action: Models and Methods.* Norwood, NJ: Ablex Publishing Co.

Micheli, P. and Mari, L. (2014). The Theory and Practice of Performance Measurement. *Management Accounting Research.* 25(2), pp. 147–156.

Micheli, P. and Pavlov, A. (2008). Promoting a Culture of Performance Management in Public Sector Organisations. *Public Governance – Journal for Public Management* (Winter). pp. 22–24.

Morgan, G. (1988). Accounting as Reality Construction: Towards a New Epistemology for Accounting Practice. *Accounting, Organizations and Society.* 13, pp. 477–485.

Neely, A., Adams, C. and Kennerley, M. (2002). *The Performance Prism: The Scorecard for Measuring and Managing Business Success.* London: Pearson Education.

Neely, A. and Al Najjar, M. (2006). Management Learning Not Management Control: The True Role of Performance Measurement? *California Management Review.* 48(3), pp. 101–114.

Neely, A.D., Gregory, M.J. and Platts, K. (1995). Performance Measurement System Design: A Literature Review and Research Agenda. *International Journal of Operations & Production Management.* 15(4), pp. 80–116.

Neely, A.D., Kennerley, M.P. and Adams, C. (2007). Performance Measurement Frameworks: A Review, in A.D. Neely (Ed.) *Business Performance Measurement: Unifying Theory and Integrating Practice.* Cambridge: Cambridge University Press, pp. 143–162.

Newman, V. (1995). *Problem Solving for Results.* Aldershot: Gower Publishing.

Pfeffer, J. and Sutton, R.I. (2006). Evidence-Based Management. *Harvard Business Review.* 84(1), pp. 62–74.

Power, M. (1997). *The Audit Society – Rituals of Verification.* Oxford: Oxford University Press.

Rasiel, E.M. and Friga, P.M. (2001). *The McKinsey Mind: Understanding and Implementing the Problem-Solving Tools and Management Techniques of the World's Top Strategy Consulting Firm.* New York: McGraw Hill.

Schneiderman, A.M. (2001). Time to Unbalance Your Scorecard. *Business + Strategy.* 24, pp. 3–4.

Speckbacher, G., Bischof, J. and Pfeiffer, T. (2003). A Descriptive Analysis on the Implementation of Balanced Scorecards in German-Speaking Countries. *Management Accounting Research.* 14 (4), pp. 361–389.

Spence, R. (2001). *Information Visualisation.* New York: Addison Wesley.

Stern, N. (2016). *Research Excellence Framework (REF) Review: Building on Success and Learning from Experience*. London: Department for Business, Energy & Industrial Strategy.

Strike, T., & Labbe, J. (2016). Exploding the Myth: Literary Analysis of Universities' Strategic Plans, in R. Pritchard, A. Pausits, & J. Williams (Eds.), *Positioning Higher Education Institutions*. Rotterdam: Sense Publishers, pp. 125–140.

Wilsdon, J., et al. (2015). The Metric Tide: Report of the Independent Review of the Role of Metrics in Research Assessment and Management, HEFCE. doi: 10.13140/RG.2.1.4929.1363.

Chapter 13

Benchmarking and rankings

Nicki Horseman

Background

The higher education environment has been undergoing continual change in recent times with increasing pressures arising from growing student numbers and students' increased expectations. Combined with limitations of funding, this has demanded higher-quality and efficient operations within HE institutions. One tool that can help with identifying areas for performance improvement and the steps to take is benchmarking.

Benchmarking grew out of the development of strategic planning in the private sector and started becoming prevalent in the 1980s in that sector but has become standard practice in some form for UK HE institutions since the 1990s. It is often undertaken by strategic planning teams within institutions due to the use of data but would appear to be most useful when undertaken in its fullest sense with a cross-functional approach.

The relationship between strategic planning and benchmarking is strong, but as Boxwell (1994) notes, "Benchmarking itself is not necessarily a strategic planning tool, but it fits into the strategic planning process at the juncture of planning and execution . . . Benchmarking does not replace strategic planning but supports it."

Benchmarking definitions

There is no single consistent definition of benchmarking, and there are many varied but similar interpretations. From HEFCE's Glossary website,[1] benchmarking is:

> A process through which practices are analysed to provide a standard measurement ('benchmark') of effective performance within an organisation (such as a university). Benchmarks are also used to compare performance with other organisations and other sectors.

Andersen and Pettersen (1996, p. 4) suggest benchmarking is:

> The process of continuously measuring and comparing one's business processes against comparable processes in leading organisations to obtain information which will help the organisation identify and implement improvements.

It is instructive to return to some early discussions of benchmarking which emphasise the breadth of analysis that benchmarking implies. Again, as Boxwell (1994) notes:

> Benchmarking is two things: setting goals by using objective, external standards and learning from others – learning how much and, perhaps more important, learning how. . . . Setting quantative goals, often called metrics, through benchmarking is arguably the best way to set goals, but keep in mind that setting goals comparable to or beyond those of the best-in-class without understanding the underlying processes that enable the best-in-class to achieve their results can be useless or worse. Understanding how the companies you study achieve their results is usually more important and valuable than obtaining some precisely defined metrics.

In 2010 HESA undertook a project ("Realising Business Benefits through the Use of Benchmarking") aiming to build capability and capacity within the UK HE to carry out benchmarking and to gain the business benefits from such activities. The project resulted in the providing of a benchmarking tool kit from HESA/JISC (2012).

From one of the constituent reports commissioned as part of the development of the project by HESA (2010), the aim of benchmarking is described:

> The overarching aim of a benchmarking process is to place performance in perspective against the sector or a more specific group of institutions. A key element of benchmarking is the identification of institutions that achieve high levels of performance which can act as examples of good practice. By analysing, assessing and implementing actions based on examples of good practice, institutions can achieve more efficient processes and ultimately higher levels of performance. Sensible benchmarking can lead to realistic target setting processes in relation to a broad spectrum of performance indicators, which encourages a more efficient environment.

This was reported as being provided by a respondent from the planning community to a survey.

Types of benchmarking comparisons

Each HE institution will choose its own approach to benchmarking appropriate to its own needs and circumstances, but there are some main types of benchmarking that have been identified.

- Internal benchmarking – comparison in performance relative to other parts of the institution. Only applicable if an institution is sufficiently large with some commonality in components so that comparison is appropriate.

- Competitive benchmarking – comparisons with direct competitor(s).
- Sector benchmarking – comparisons more broadly and not necessarily with direct competitors but of a group within the same sector.
- Generic/strategic benchmarking – outside the sector.

The interpretation of these four comparisons for HEIs might be:

- Internal – comparing different subject areas and departments with each other where a comparison is valid.
- Competitive – investigating and comparing the performance against a selected group of competitor or peer universities.
- Sector – comparison with all universities in the same country or perhaps a mission group.
- Generic – comparison with overseas universities and other types of organisations outside the higher education sector.

In addition to this there are the types of benchmarking:

- Performance or metric benchmarking – comparison of key data and other performance measures which will indicate what might be a reasonable level of aspirational performance but not how to achieve it.
- Diagnostic benchmarking – looking beyond performance measures, but adding another dimension; comparing processes and practices that deliver that performance.
- Process benchmarking – selecting a specific process within an institution and comparing that process with other institutions, learning and implementing lessons.

Smith, Armstrong and Brown (2013) provide more detail on these three variations, but in summary, the first is more likely to appear as a continuous process, akin to monitoring key performance indicators (KPIs), which can be useful as a starting point highlighting areas for improvement. Diagnostic benchmarking can pinpoint priorities for change, whilst process benchmarking requires the greatest investment of time and resources but has the greatest potential to deliver efficiency improvement as noted by Smith, Armstrong and Brown (2013).

For all comparisons except for internal benchmarking, the comparisons could be carried out at an institutional level although the topic in question could itself be subject-specific. If undertaking an institutional-level project, then ideally it should be possible to drill down to more detailed levels of granularity to departments, subjects and disciplines. This means that benchmarking can be carried out at an appropriate level for the measures to be effective at the level of operational delivery. Again, this is influenced by the topic in question and the governance and degree of autonomy existing within a university's structure, but consideration should be given to this in the design of a benchmarking approach.

Benefits and limitations of benchmarking

HESA/JISC (2012) suggest, based on the European higher education project, that benchmarking strengthens an institution's ability to:

- Self-assess its performance.
- Better understand the processes which support strategy formulation and implementation in increasingly competitive environments.
- Measure and compare with other institutions or organisations, and assess the reasons for any differences.
- Encourage discovery of new ideas through a strategic look (inside or outside the institution).
- Obtain data to support decision making.
- Set effective targets for improvement.
- Strengthen institutional identity, strategy formulation and implementation.
- Enhance reputation.
- Respond to national (or international) performance indicators and benchmarks.
- Set new standards for the institution and sector.

To this might be added demonstrating and encouraging the need for change and the improvement required and providing a framework for change. If nothing else, by undertaking a benchmarking exercise the HEI gets a sense of where it is performing well in relation to others and increases its knowledge about itself. The HESA (2010) report suggests that the key outcomes of benchmarking have been recognised as demonstrating accountability to stakeholders, improved networking, collaborative relationships, management information (text, numerical or graphical information about the area of study), a better understanding of practice, process or performance and insights into how improvements might be made.

But benchmarking is not without its critics. The main criticism being that it entrenches existing thinking and stifles innovation. As argued by Hammer and Champy (1993), benchmarking focusses on processes and approaches that are already being employed and also sets a cap on ambition as only being equal to some current perception of the best. This is less valid when generic benchmarking is undertaken outside of the sector. Other limitations are a potential resistance to change arising from a view that "we are different" if the comparisons are not accepted, and a view that benchmarking is looking at current practice and often historic data rather than looking forward to future challenges set in a specific and localised context.

The benchmarking process

Some basic steps in following a benchmarking process are set out in the HESA/
JISC (2012) guide, but in summary they can consist of:

- Selecting the topic, setting objectives and investigating the context – the
  topic and objectives will typically be aligned with strategic aims and seek
  to translate the strategic objectives into operational objectives. It involves a
  self-appraisal of the university's current position, the environmental factors
  and the future context.
- Setting up the benchmarking team – what areas should be involved and the
  skills needed on the team.
- Research – what to measure and what qualitative and quantitative data sources
  are required and what is available. The data should have relevance, accessibility, timeliness, coverage, stability over time, quality and comparability.
- Gathering data and information – including selecting a comparator group if
  not already defined and visits to comparator institutions if appropriate.
- Measuring and evaluating – comparison of metrics and processes, sense-checking
  information and producing insightful interpretation of results, determining
  gaps and differences, setting targets and presentation of results.
- Managing improvements – prioritising improvement initiatives, implementing action plans and monitoring against targets.
- Reviewing strategic objective – lesson learnt and achievements from benchmarking feedback into develop of strategic objectives.

There are a number of factors to consider when choosing institutions to include
in benchmarking comparisons as in step 4 above. The nature of process benchmarking and the related need to gather detail about others' business processes
results in more potential factors and so may affect choice, including acquiring the
consent of the chosen comparators to participate. For simple performance benchmarking, if only publicly available, centrally reported data is used without the
direct involvement of the comparison group, then the considerations are fewer.

Factors for comparator choice in performance benchmarking include:

- Performance and trajectory – Does the comparator institution have similar
  or better performance, and is that performance static, on an upwards or on
  a downwards trajectory? An institution would probably not want to benchmark against another whose performance is dwindling.
- Similarity – Does the comparison institution have similar subject mix, size, mission and culture? Is it active in the same subject areas? A small institution strong
  in humanities would not want to compare itself to a large science-based institution. Other considerations are the research/teaching balance and performance, the institution's access to resources and its type of estate. Participation
  in the same mission group may also be a factor.

For diagnostic and process benchmarking, where the active participation of the benchmarking group is needed, the considerations extend to include:

- Willingness and ability – the willingness of the institution to participate and share information and its ability to source and share the information needed.
- Location/geography – the ease and cost of visiting the other institutions and a common geography or environment.

UK benchmarking

Despite the HESA project there is still a diversity of approaches to benchmarking across UK universities, but the availability of benchmarking data has continued to improve, not least with the ongoing development of the Higher Education Information Database for Institutions (HEIDI) (see Chapter 10). The UK has a wealth of numerical information available through HESA and the funding councils. It is in a strong position in terms of the data available to be able to make comparisons, and also in the discipline applied to data governance. That has been instigated in part by the need to undertake the reporting required to government agencies, which in turn has helped engender a culture of evidence-based decision making.

International benchmarking

The international dimension of benchmarking was addressed in HESA's benchmarking project "International Benchmarking in UK Higher Education", through a dedicated report from PA Consulting Group (2011). The starting point was the key performance indicators (KPIs) that institutions use to support and measure internationalisation, and the report focussed on benchmarking activities with overseas institutions through metrics that measure internationalisation, such as the recruitment of international students. The report highlighted issues that had been identified by institutions as barriers to international benchmarking, which included difficulties in selecting overseas institutions for comparisons as the depth of contextual knowledge is far lower and the different socio-economic and political factors that exist. Other issues were the perceived reliability of comparative data and also the limits of universities' own contextual knowledge of overseas markets and systems within which they could form judgements based on comparative data.

In both of the reports associated with the HESA benchmarking project (HESA [2010] and PA Consulting Group [2011]), the case studies and descriptions of projects tended to have a data focus. The descriptive and narrative-based benchmarking required in diagnostic and process benchmarking is possible but much less straightforward to carry out. These activities can be delivered through associations and member organisations or independent third parties but are reliant on high levels of mutual trust. Some membership organisations exist, such as

SUMS (Southern Universities Management Services), but in an era of increasing competition it is possible that this sort of co-operation will become less rather than more prevalent. The various mission groups provide the opportunity for collaboration, but that is not their main function and there are competition issues to consider. For international benchmarking there are also various member organisations that could facilitate projects such as Universitas 21 and Association of Commonwealth Universities. The latter has a strategic management programme offering the opportunity to compare key management process on select topics such as branding and marketing or students as co-creators. More recent developments in data sources include the European Tertiary Education Register (ETER), a database of European higher education institutions' information promoted by the European Commission building out of the European MicroData (EUMIDA) project, which currently covers 32 countries. This provides access to data for comparative analysis and is producing briefing documents on areas which are relevant to national and European higher education policies. There are of course commercial consultancy organisations that also provide benchmarking services.

Part of the PA Consulting Group report's (2011) conclusion was that "Higher Education is, more than ever before, a truly global enterprise, and all universities are increasingly competing for internationally global business with international competitors" and that "There are real dangers for UK universities if they continue to frame and benchmark their international KPIs and their academic operations against their domestic peers."

As Boxwell (1994) concludes, "Benchmarking is a process but is also a way of thinking." Benchmarking is not an end in itself and is not a panacea but is an effective tool that with commitment and resources can translate into action and organisational improvements. Each university will have its own strategy, its own challenges and be at differing levels of maturity with respect to benchmarking. Different issues and challenges will require tailored approaches, but benchmarking can be an effective tool in an HEI's toolkit.

Rankings

As Professor Sir David Eastwood commented in his foreword to the HEFCE (2014, p. 4) report on league tables and their impact:

> League tables are part of the higher education landscape and in the newspaper calendar. They are one of the sources to which prospective students refer when making choices, and bring attention to important issues such as 'the student experience', employability and retention. The league tables also have much wider impact – for example on the behaviour of academics, businesses and potential benefactors. Governing bodies take an interest in them as a means of assessing institutional performance, sometimes seizing on them in default of other, more sensitive indicators of institutional performance.

These comments, although made in 2008, are not outdated, and perhaps the main change in more recent years has been the increasing use and development of international league tables, partly due to the rise in student mobility.

In the same way that benchmarking has grown within higher education since the 1990s, not least with the availability of comparative data, so has the use of that data by third parties to make comparisons between HEIs, typically by newspapers, aiming to provide guidance to prospective students and their advisors, and more recently through Information, Advice and Guidance (IAG) initiatives. The third-party league tables and rankings can be a source of competitor and sector benchmarking material. Perhaps monitoring a league table position on its own is not that informative, but it can be productive to monitor the elements that make up the various league tables as described by some institutions in the case studies in HEFCE (2014). League table compilers aim to include indicators that are readily available on a standardised basis and which they believe are measures of quality and aspects that a university would want to improve.

UK league tables

There are three main university league tables or guides published about universities in the UK (*Times/Sunday Times*, *Complete* and *Guardian*). They are undergraduate focussed and aimed at informing prospective student choice. As such they are published to coincide with key points in the undergraduate admission cycle, and the overall ranking is accompanied by numerous subject tables and advice and guidance about factors to consider when choosing a university and course of study. The indicators used cover available areas of undergraduate performance in terms of admission quality, satisfaction, continuation, achievement and resources available. The intention is to assess and provide information about the quality of the institutions to inform prospective student choice. Whilst compilers are cognisant of the HEI's views and some convene review groups which, on an annual basis, review the methodology and discuss potential changes or adaptions as data returns and processes change, universities are not the main target audience. The degree to which universities have themselves been following league tables has increased significantly over the past years as the drive to marketisation of student recruitment continues but without prospective students necessarily having the information readily available for making choices from sources other than the HEIs themselves. In this context third-party league tables maintain their public prominence.

Times/Sunday Times

Until 2012, the *Times* and *Sunday Times* published separate UK university rankings based on different methods and metrics. The *Times* typically published in May and the *Sunday Times* published in September annually. The *Times* combined their metrics using z-scores and *Sunday Times* used a points-based scoring system. The two tables were brought together in 2012, and now one table is published in September in both publications. An overall table is produced from nine metrics as listed in Table 13.1 below, together with 67 subject tables based on a reduced number of metrics – research, entry standards, NSS (teaching quality and student experience) and graduate prospects. In the overall table, the NSS and research indicators are weighted more highly than the other six metrics, but all four elements are equally weighted in the subject tables, with teaching quality making up 67% of NSS score and student experience the remaining 33%.

Some indicators in the overall table are subject weighted, namely entry standards, student-staff ratio, good honours and graduate prospects, as these vary significantly by subject. Medicine is a particular standout subject where the student-staff ratio is small, entry standards and graduate-level employment are high and the degrees are not necessarily given a classification. The subject adjustment is carried out by comparing an institution's performance in a particular subject against the average for that subject in the sector and accounts for the university's volume of activity in that subject. The nine indicators are combined by z-scoring each indicator and adding them together. The overall score is then scaled out of a maximum of 100. The relative scale of the scores makes comparison of scores between years tenuous, but a comparison of rank between years is valid both at an overall and indicator level. The university guide is published on the *Times/Sunday Times* subscription website (see www.thetimes.co.uk).

Complete University Guide (CUG)

The Complete University Guide is published on their own website in May. Although formerly published in the *Daily Telegraph*, the *Independent* and the *Daily Mail* and whilst reported in the press, at the time of writing it is no longer associated with one particular publication. The creator of the guide, Bernard Kingston, previously generated the *Times* rankings up until 2007. There is some commonality of approach between the two rankings, but they have been diverging over the years, with subtle differences in the indicator definitions, particularly with regard to student satisfaction, research and spend metrics as set out in Table 13.1. Subject mix adjustments are applied to entry standards, student satisfaction, student-staff ratio (SSR), good honours and graduate prospects. *The Complete University Guide* also publishes some 70 subject tables employing entry standards, student satisfaction, research assessment and graduate prospects (see www.thecomplete universityguide.co.uk).

Guardian

The *Guardian* has a different approach to the other two national league tables discussed above. First, it does not include a research measure and it has a valued-added measure as well as entry standards, graduate prospects and other metrics. The 54 subject tables, which include all the eight main measures, build up into

Table 13.1 Data sources employed by third-party league table compilers

Indicator	Times/Sunday Times	Complete	Guardian*	Data source
National Student Survey	1 (11.1%) Teaching Quality+ 0.5 (5.6%) Student Experience++	1.5 (16.7%)	5% Overall Satisfaction (Q22) 10% Teaching** 10% Assessment and Feedback***	National Student Survey
Research Excellence	1.5 (16.7%) score based on HEFCE funding weightings and modified by intensity	1 (11.1%) GPA 0.5 (5.6%) intensity		REF 2014
Entry Standards	1 (11.1%)	1 (11.1%)	16.25%	HESA Student Return
Spend per Student	1 (11.1%) [spend on student facilities and academic services averaged over two years]	0.5 (5.6%) academic services spend 0.5 (5.6%) facilities spend [both averaged over three years]	10% [spend per subject excluding cost of academic staff plus academic services spend]	HESA FSR/ HESA Student Return
Student-Staff Ratio	1 (11.1%)	1 (11.1%)	16.25%	HESA Student Return/HESA Staff Return
Value Added			16.25%	HESA Student Return
Completion	1 (11.1%)	1 (11.1%)		HESA Performance Indicators
Good Honours	1 (11.1%)	1 (11.1%)		HESA Student Return
Graduate Destinations	1 (11.1%)	1 (11.1%)	16.25%	HESA Destination of Leavers from Higher Education Return

+Teaching Quality includes the Teaching, Assessment and Feedback, Academic Support parts of the NSS.

++Student Experience includes the Organisation and Management, Learning Resources, Personal Development and Overall Satisfaction questions of the NSS.

*Weightings are for all subjects except Medicine, Dentistry and Veterinary where Graduate Destinations are not used and the weightings redistributed between the other indicators.

** Teaching includes questions 1–4 of the NSS.

***Assessment and feedback includes questions 5–9 of the NSS.

the overall table bottom up. An institution is only included in subject tables if it has scores in six out of the eight indicators or better and if there are at least 35 student FTE in the subject area and 25 FTE in the corresponding cost centre. To be included in the overall ranking, institutions need to appear in at least eight subjects. Uniquely among UK league tables, the *Guardian* uses an added value indicator based on entry standards and degree classification outcomes calculated at a student level, but the other indicators are more straightforward measures with some commonality with the other tables. The value-added measure tracks individual students from admission to graduation. Each full-time student is given a probability of achieving a 1st or 2:1 degree based on their entry qualifications. If graduates achieve a 1st or 2:1 degree then points are awarded that reflect the difficulty of that achievement. Integrated master's degrees are treated as a positive degree result. For medicine, dentistry and veterinary science, where degree classification does not apply, the definition is extended to include non-completions (see www.theguardian.com/education).

Table 13.1 gives an indication of the data sources employed and the relative weightings of the indicators (as a weight and/or a percentage) of these three league tables, although the specific definitions should be sourced from each ranking's own methodology documents.

Institutions have sight of their data when it is commissioned from HESA by the compilers. This follows the usual process of bespoke data purchasing from HESA, with the institution-specific data being previewed through the HESA DDS (Data Dissemination System) to named contacts within each institution, and the universities have the opportunity to correct or comment on the data. For the tables published in May (*Guardian* and *Complete*), these employ the National Student Survey (NSS) from August of the previous year, the current Research Excellence Framework results (2014 if included) and the student, staff and income data from HESA returns made for the previous but one academic year. For example a table published in May 2016 uses 2015 NSS, the HESA student and finance returns for the 2014/15 academic year and DLHE data from 2014/15 return and HESA PIs based on data for 2014–15. For the *Times/Sunday Times* published in September, the NSS of that year published in August, just before the league table, is used.

International league tables

Global league tables are a comparatively new phenomenon. Three of the rankings discussed here date back to the 2000s; namely the Academic Ranking of World Universities (ARWU) in 2003 and the then Times Higher Education – QS collaboration in 2004. International league tables have been gaining importance with the growth of the number of transnational students. Figures from the OECD (2015) have shown that in the past three decades the number of students enrolled in countries outside their citizenship has grown fourfold, and it is estimated that there are now 5 million transnational students studying in the world, as shown in Figure 13.1.

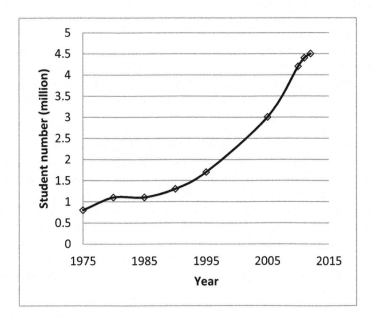

Figure 13.1 Long-term growth in students enrolled outside their country of citizenship
Source: OECD

The HEFCE (2014) league table report noted that "With increasing competition between institutions – not least on the world stage in the markets for student and academic recruitment, and research and consultancy funding – it is likely that rankings will continue to grow in importance." In her study of the impact and influence of rankings, Hazelkorn (2015) concludes that:

> Rankings are a manifestation of what has become known as the world wide 'battle for excellence' and are perceived and used to determine the status of individual institutions, assess the quality and performance of the higher education system and gauge global competitiveness. As internationalisation has become a priority for both government and higher education, the talent-catching and knowledge-producing capacity of higher education has become a vital sign of a country's capacity to participate in world science and the global economy. In the process, rankings are transforming universities and reshaping higher education.

The IAU World Higher Education Database (WHED) suggests that there are over 18,000 universities worldwide, and so a world ranking that covers 400 institutions is only including 2% of worldwide institutions.

The decision-making process through which students choose which university to apply to and what to study is complex and individual, but there is evidence that rankings play an important part. The Universities UK International Unit produced a report (2015), "International Undergraduate Students: The UK's Competitive Advantage", which includes data from i-graduate's International Student Barometer survey. The report found that the influence of rankings, whilst inconsistent by country, is one of the most significant factors in student choice along with agents, family, friends and institutional websites.

In the following pages, the main world rankings are summarised in terms of their factual content at the time of writing. The makeup of the different tables and the congruence with a university's mission will determine their applicability and relevance, for example the ARWU (Table 13.2) includes Nobel Prize/Fields Medal winners and the Leiden (Table 13.3) is entirely driven by bibliometrics and so both are likely to be less important to teaching-focussed institutions. Also included are the QS Top Universities (Table 13.4) and Times Higher Education World University Rankings (Table 13.5). Two of the rankings listed are more orientated to use as a tool with which to explore the data further; these are the Leiden rankings, which provide a variety of different bibliometric measures, and U-Multirank (Table 13.6), which covers performance in more breadth. Often the providers also offer a commercial benchmarking service in addition to the public ranking.

Table 13.2 Academic Ranking of World Universities (ARWU Shanghai Jiao Tong)

Organisation publishing	Published by ShanghaiRanking Consultancy since 2009 – an independent organisation dedicated to research on higher education information and not legally subordinated to any universities or government agencies. Conducted by researchers at the Center for World-Class Universities of the Shanghai Jiao Tong University.
History	From 2003
Aim and intention	Initially to find the global standing of Chinese universities, it now has more global presence and attracts attention from universities, governments and public media worldwide.
Release time frame (approx.)	August
Data sources	Public lists of Nobel Prize and Fields Medal winners, bibliometrics from Thomson Reuters, data on academic staff numbers from national agencies.
Inclusion criteria	Every university that has any Nobel laureates, Fields medallists, highly cited researchers or papers published in *Nature* or *Science*. Over 1000 institutions ranked, 500 published.
Indicators and weighting	Six indicators: Alumni (10%) – total number of alumni of an institution winning a Noble Prize or Fields Medal. Alumni may have obtained a bachelor's, master's or doctoral degree. Weighting applied to when the degree was obtained.

(Continued)

Table 13.2 (Continued)

	Award (20%) – Staff of institution winning Nobel Prize or Fields Medal. Staff were working at institution at the time of the award and a weighting is applied to when the award was obtained. HiCi (20%) – Highly cited researchers from Thomson Reuters N&S (20%) – Number of papers published in *Nature* and *Science*. This is not applied to specialist humanities and social sciences institutions. Attribution assigned to different authors: 100% corresponding author, 50% first author, 25% second, 10% for rest. PUB (20%) – Papers indexed in Science Citation Index Expanded and Social Science Index PCP (10%) – Per capita academic performance of an institution
Geographic coverage	HEIs from 44 countries are included in the top 500.
Subject breakdown	By field – natural sciences and mathematics, engineering/technology and computer sciences, life and agriculture sciences, clinical medicine and pharmacy, social sciences. By subject – mathematics, physics, chemistry, computer science and economics/business. Subjects employ similar indicators to the overall ranking.
Website	www.shanghairanking.com

Table 13.3 Leiden

Organisation publishing	CWTS B.V. undertakes independent contract research and evaluation studies. Leiden University's Centre for Science and Technology Studies forms the core of the company.
History	Since 2011/12
Aim and intention	"Offers key insights into the scientific performance of over 800 major universities worldwide. A sophisticated set of bibliometric indicators provide statistics on the scientific impact of universities and on universities' involvement in scientific collaboration."
Release time frame (approx.)	May
Data sources	Thomson Reuters Web of Science bibliometric database core publications (those written in English, not anonymous, not retracted, in core/international scientific journals), which form a subset of all publications in Web of Science.
Inclusion criteria	1000 (core) publications in a four-year time frame (for 2016: ranking 2011–2014, citations to 2015), resulting in 842 institutions.
Indicators and weighting	Field normalised on about 4000 fields Selection of measures – volume (P) or proportion (PP) P(top x%) – number of an institution's publications belonging to top x% most frequently cited compared with other publications in the same field and same year, i.e. size dependent PP(top x%) – proportion of an institution's publications belonging to top x% most frequently cited compared with other publications in the same field and same year, i.e. size independent

(Continued)

Table 13.3 (Continued)

	where x = 1, 10, 50 TCS/MCS – total and mean number of citations of institution's publication TNCS/MNCS – total and mean number of citations of publications normalized for field and publication year Also provides collaboration metrics
Geographic coverage	Inclusion criteria results in institutions from 53 countries.
Subject breakdown	Data available in five fields: biomedical and health sciences, life and earth sciences, mathematics and computer science, physical sciences and engineering, and social sciences and humanities.
Website	www.leidenranking.com

Table 13.4 QS Top Universities

Organisation publishing	Quacquarelli Symonds [QS]
History	Originally with Times Higher Education as THE-QS starting in 2004, but these separated in 2010 to develop own methodologies
Aim and intention	"To enable motivated people, around the world, to achieve their potential through fostering international mobility, education achievements and career development."
Release time frame (approx.)	Overall rankings September
Data sources and currency	Two surveys (academic and employers), Elsevier Scopus bibliometrics, students and staff data from institutions and other sources
Inclusion criteria	Teaching at undergraduate and postgraduate level and working in two out of the five faculty areas

Indicators and weightings	Academic reputation (40%) – global survey – academics identifying best institutions in their field. The 2016/17 rankings use 74,651 responses collected over five years; earlier years carry a lesser weight. Only most recent responses from an academic are used and cannot vote for own institution; regional weightings are applied.
	     Employer reputation (10%) – employers asked which institutions are producing the best graduates. The 2016/17 ranking uses 37,781 responses.
	     Student to faculty ratio (20%)
	     Citations per faculty (20%) – number of citations relative to the number of academic staff members. Methodology was changed for 2015/16 ranking to include subject weighting using five 'faculty' or subject areas, namely art and humanities, engineering and technology, life sciences and medicine, natural sciences, and social sciences and management. Bibliometrics exclude self-citations and exclude publications carrying more than ten institution affiliations in 2015 and with a variable affiliation cap by subject in 2016.

(Continued)

Table 13.4 (Continued)

	International faculty ratio (5%) International student ratio (5%)
Geographic coverage	Ranks 916 institutions from 81 countries
Subject breakdown	42 subjects within the five faculty areas, art and humanities, engineering and technology, life sciences and medicine, natural sciences, and social sciences and management based on survey and citation data.
Website(s)	www.topuniversities.com, www.iu.qs.com

Table 13.5 Times Higher Education World University Rankings

Organisation publishing	Times Higher Education – part of TES Global Limited
History	Originally ranking generated in collaboration with QS starting in 2004, but separated in 2010 to develop own methodology
Aim and intention	"Provide the definitive list of the world's best universities, evaluated across teaching, research, international outlook, reputation and more."
Release time frame (approx.)	September/October
Data sources and currency	Academic Reputation survey; Elsevier Scopus bibliometrics; student, staff and income data from institutions
Inclusion criteria	1000 total publications over a five-year period (for 2016–17 ranking: 2011–2015 timeframe) with a threshold applied per year (150 per year for ranking published in 2016)
Indicators and weightings	In five pillars or themes supported by 13 indicators
	Teaching Environment (30%)
	• Teaching Reputation (15%) – global academic invitation-only reputation survey asking academics to name best institutions for teaching in their field
	• Staff-Student Ratio (4.5%)
	• Doctorates Awarded/Academic Staff (6%) – adjusted for subject mix
	• Doctorates Awarded/Bachelor's Degrees Awarded (2.25%)
	• Income/Academic Staff (2.25%) – total institutional income divided by academic staff, adjusted for purchasing-power parity
	Research (30%)
	• Research Reputation (18%) – from reputation survey asking academics to name best institutions for research in their field
	• Research Income/Academic Staff (6%) – adjusted for subject mix, adjusted for purchasing-power parity
	• Publications/Academic Staff (6%) – adjusted for subject mix
	Citations (30%) – field-weighted citation impact – number of citations of publications relative to the expected number of citations for a publication of same type or subject
	Industry Income/Academic Staff (2.5%) – adjusted for purchasing-power parity

(Continued)

Table 13.5 (Continued)

	International Outlook (7.5%) • International-to-domestic faculty ratio (2.5%) • International-to-domestic student ratio (2.5%) • International co-authorship (2.5%) – adjusted for subject mix
Geographic coverage	Ranked 980 institutions from 79 countries in table published in 2016
Subject breakdown	Six subjects originally, expanded to eight in ranking published in 2016: arts and humanities, business and economics, clinical, pre-clinical medicine and health, computer science, engineering and technology, life science, physical sciences, social science. Subject tables use same 13 metrics as overall.
Website	www.timeshighereducation.com/world-university-rankings

Table 13.6 U-Multirank

Organisation publishing	Instigated by the European Commission, prepared by a European consortium overseen by Advisory Board. Partners include CWTS at Leiden University, INCENTIM at Leuven, academic publisher Elsevier, Bertelsmann Foundation and Folge 3 (software firm).
History	2014 first publication
Aim and intention	A new multi-dimensional, user-driven approach to international ranking of higher education institutions. Aims to provide a tool for the user to choose own personalised ranking. "Universities compared. Your way."
Release time frame (approx.)	May

Data sources and currency	Self-reported data from institutions through online questionnaire.
	    An online survey of 105,000 students asking for their opinions.
	    Bibliometric and patent data from Thomson Reuters Web of Science.

Inclusion criteria Indicators and weightings	Not overtly stated
	U-Multirank does produce a 'ready-made' ranking, but the emphasis is on providing flexibility to produce personalised ranking. Classifies institutions into different types to allow 'like-with-like' comparison.
	    Each indicator is ranked into five different performance groups (A 'very good' to E 'weak')
	
	Covers five broad areas:
	
	Teaching & Learning – bachelor graduation rate, master's graduation rate, graduating on time (bachelor and master's).
	    Research – citation rate, publications (absolute and size normalised), research income, art-related output, top cited publications, interdisciplinary publications, postdoc positions.
	    Knowledge Transfer – industry co-authorship, income from private sources, patents awarded (absolute and size normalised), industry co-patents, spin-offs, publications cited in patents, income from CPD.
	    International Orientation – e.g. foreign language bachelor and master's programmes, student mobility, international academic staff, international joint publications, international doctorate degrees.

(Continued)

Table 13.6 (Continued)

	Regional Engagement – graduates working in region (bachelor and master's), student internship in the region, regional joint publications, income from regional sources.
Geographic coverage	In 2016, 1300 institutions from 90 countries
Subject breakdown	13 subjects: biology, business studies, chemistry, computer science, electrical engineering, history, mathematics, mechanical engineering, medicine, physics, psychology, social work and sociology.
Website	www.umultirank.org

Influence of rankings and the future of data usage

As the HEFCE (2014) report concluded, the UK institutional responses to league tables varied, but one of the areas most influenced by the rankings was the institution's own choice of institutional key performance indicators. This could be as a rank target in a particular table or in terms of performance in the component indicators. The latter seems the more constructive approach, as it is at an individual indicator level that aspects for improvement can be identified, more investigation carried out, potentially as a benchmarking activity, and actions taken. Other impacts of the third-party ranking tables were an additional focus on data returns in terms of general quality but also in optimising the return in view of its subsequent use. Few institutions indicated that changes were made as a direct consequence of league tables, but they were seen as a catalyst for investment and changes and part of a wider set of comparisons.

Despite reservations that universities may have about them, third-party rankings will continue to be part of the higher education landscape, and if anything they are likely to further proliferate as public data improves and student choice increases. Universities desire and need to make comparisons for their institution's own benchmarking purposes, and learning from such benchmarking will endure. The use of comparative data is not diminishing, and the robustness and sophistication of data sources are being enhanced, for example by developments in HEIDI. The challenges of funding limitations and the need to deliver more with fewer resources will not abate. The dissemination of data within institutions is tending towards business intelligence systems (see Chapter 11) which are aimed at providing easier access to increasingly more extensive data. In this environment, making sense of that data and undertaking holistic benchmarking which adds value to that information, resulting in positive actions, will be increasingly valuable.

Note

1 HEFCE Glossary www.hefce.ac.uk/glossary/#letterB

References

Andersen, B. and Pettersen, P. (1996). *The Benchmarking Handbook: Step-By-Step Instructions.* Chapman and Hall, London Association of Commonwealth Universities www.acu.ac.uk.

Boxwell, R. J. Jnr. (1994). *Benchmarking for Competitive Advantage.* New York: McGraw-Hill Inc.

European Tertiary Education Register www.eter-project.com

Hammer, M. and Champy, J. (1993). *Reengineering the Corporation: A Manifesto for the Business Revolution.* New York: Harper Collins.

Hazelkorn, E. (2015). *Rankings and the Reshaping of Higher Education.* London: Palgrave Macmillan.

HEFCE (2014). Counting What is Measured or Measuring What Counts? League Tables and Their Impact on Higher Education Institutions in England, HEFCE 2008/1.

HESA (2010). Benchmarking to Improve Efficiency (Status Report November 2010). Retrieved on 29/12/2016 from www.jisc.ac.uk/guides/benchmarking/what-is-benchmarking

HESA/JISC (2012). Realising Business Benefits through the Use of Benchmarking. Retrieved from benchmarking.hesa.ac.uk

Higher Education Information Database for Institutions, https://heidi.hesa.ac.uk

International Association of Universities World Higher Education Database (WHED) www.whed.net

OECD (2015). OECD Education at a Glance 2015. Retrieved from www.oecd.org/edu/education-at-a-glance=2015.htm

PA Consulting Group (2011). International Benchmarking in UK Higher Education, PA Consulting Group, HESA. Retrieved from benchmarking.hesa.ac.uk

Smith, H., Armstrong, M., and Brown, S. (2013). *Benchmarking and Threshold Standards in Higher Education.* London: Routledge.

Southern Universities Management Services, www.sums.org.uk

Universitas 21, www.universitas21.com

Universities UK International Unit (2015). International Undergraduate Students: The UK's Competitive Advantage. Retrieved from www.universitiesuk.ac.uk/policy-and-analysis/reports/Documents/International/international-undergraduate-students-uk-competitve-advantage.pdf

Chapter 14

Responsible metrics

James Wilsdon

In the past decade, there has been an explosion in the range and reach of metrics and league tables to benchmark institutional performance, research qualities and impacts, teaching and learning outcomes. Yet some of the most precious qualities and contributions of higher education resist simple quantification. This chapter explores how to develop measurement and management systems that are both effective and supportive of responsibility, diversity and integrity. Building on *The Metric Tide* review, it also considers recent developments in the UK's approach to metrics for research and teaching, which are the focus of ongoing debate.

Between big data and quantophrenia

In his 2003 bestseller *Moneyball*, Michael Lewis describes how the fortunes of the Oakland Athletics baseball team were transformed by the rigorous use of predictive data and modelling to identify and invest in undervalued talent. These approaches soon spread through baseball and into other sports, and are now widely used in the financial sector, recruitment industry and elsewhere, to inform hiring and promotion decisions. A recent study by researchers at the MIT Sloan School of Management argues that universities are ripe for their own 'Moneyball' moment (Bertsimas et al., 2015; Brynjolfsson and Silberholz, 2016). As the authors note:

> Ironically, one of the places where predictive analytics hasn't yet made substantial inroads is in the place of its birth: the halls of academia. Tenure decisions for the scholars of computer science, economics, and statistics – the very pioneers of quantitative metrics and predictive analytics – are often insulated from these tools.
>
> (Brynjolfsson and Silberholz, 2016)

By analysing a set of metrics for publications, citations and co-authorship at an early stage in a researcher's career, and including these in hiring and promotion decisions, the MIT team suggests that it is possible to predict future performance with greater accuracy and reliability than through subjective judgements alone.

Given the role that citations, *h*-indices, journal impact factors, grant income and other conventional metrics already play in research management and decision-making (both explicitly and implicitly), some would no doubt welcome predictive analytics as a logical next step. Applications of 'big data' and 'broad data' within higher education institutions (HEIs) are still at a relatively early stage, given their longer-term possibilities (ICSU, 2016). Over the next decade, it is easy to envisage increasingly granular data on research qualities and impacts being combined with more sophisticated metrics for teaching and learning to give HEI managers, planners and policymakers access to an unprecedented wealth of real-time data and analytics on which to base a wide range of choices: from individual hires and course selection, through to funding priorities and faculty structures.

Yet hand in hand with the expanding possibilities of metrics, debates have intensified about the pitfalls of an over-reliance on such measures. Some see metrics as one element of a more managerial, audit-driven culture in universities (Graeber, 2015; Collini, 2016; Martin, 2016). More specific concerns tend to focus on three issues. First, a growing 'quantophrenia' in higher education: a narrowing of managerial attention onto things that can be measured, at the expense of those that cannot (Sorokin, 1956; Burnett, 2016). Second, a reduction in diversity, as an emphasis on particular metrics or league table performance (itself weighted towards a few key indicators) drives HEIs to adopt similar strategic priorities, and individual researchers to focus on lower-risk, incremental work aimed at higher-impact journals (Hicks et al., 2015). Third, a distortion of incentives, which is in turn exacerbating problems of research quality, integrity and reproducibility (Benedictus and Miedema, 2016; Sarewitz, 2016).

Experiments in responsible metrics

In response to such concerns, there have been a number of high-profile efforts to reform how metrics are used in higher education and research. These include:

- *The 2013 San Francisco Declaration on Research Assessment (DORA)*, which calls for research to be assessed on its own merits and for an end to the use of journal impact factors in funding, hiring and promotion decisions. As of January 2017, DORA has over 800 organisational and 12,500 individual signatories, including a handful of UK universities;
- *The Leiden Manifesto*, which was published in 2015 by a group of leading scientometricians, and sets out ten principles for the use of quantitative indicators in research evaluation (Hicks et al., 2015);
- *Science in Transition*, a movement established in 2013 by researchers in the Netherlands, with the aim of tackling systemic problems in research and university culture, which "has become a self-referential system where quality is measured mostly in bibliometric parameters and where societal relevance is undervalued" (Dijstelbloem et al., 2013);

- *The Meta-Research Innovation Center (METRICS)* at Stanford University, which was launched in 2014 with a focus on transforming research practices and tackling problems of research integrity and reproducibility (Ioannidis et al., 2015).

Each of these initiatives influenced the main UK contribution to these debates: the Independent Review of the Role of Metrics in Research Assessment and Management, which I chaired on behalf of the Higher Education Funding Council for England (HEFCE). After 15 months of evidence gathering, analysis and consultation, this published its findings as *The Metric Tide* in July 2015 (Wilsdon et al., 2015).

The main motivation behind *The Metric Tide* was a desire by government to look afresh at whether metrics could play a greater role in the next cycle of the Research Excellence Framework (REF). But the review group interpreted its role more broadly, and made a series of targeted recommendations to university leaders, funders, publishers and researchers designed to ensure that indicators and underlying data infrastructure would support the diverse qualities and impacts of higher education and research. Over and above these detailed points, we proposed a framework for *responsible metrics*, built on five principles:

- *Robustness:* basing metrics on the best possible data in terms of accuracy and scope;
- *Humility:* recognising that quantitative evaluation should support – but not supplant – qualitative, expert assessment;
- *Transparency:* keeping data collection and analytical processes open and transparent, so that those being evaluated can test and verify the results;
- *Diversity:* accounting for variation by field, and using a range of indicators to reflect and support a plurality of research and researcher career paths across the system;
- *Reflexivity:* recognising and anticipating the systemic and potential effects of indicators, and updating them in response.

Surfing on the metric tide

When *The Metric Tide* was published, it provoked a lively debate in the UK and further afield. Despite the spread of opinion encountered over the course of the review, members of the review group were encouraged by the degree of consensus in support of both our detailed recommendations and the broader idea of responsible metrics.

However, in the UK, these issues were far from settled. Following the May 2015 general election, the government announced ambitious plans to reform the higher education and research system. These were set out in a November 2015 green paper (BIS, 2015), a May 2016 white paper (BIS, 2016) and a bill, which at the time of writing is still making its passage through Parliament.

Proposed reforms include a reshaping of the regulatory architecture for HEIs and research funding, the replacement of HEFCE with a new Office for Students, and the introduction of a Teaching Excellence Framework (TEF) "to identify and incentivize the highest quality teaching" (BIS, 2015, p. 18). From the start, the government presented metrics as a non-negotiable element of the TEF, albeit with scope for peer review and expert judgement alongside. This has provoked intense arguments about the use and limitations of particular indicators for teaching and learning, mirroring established debates on the research side of the system. For its initial cycle, the TEF is set to proceed using flawed indicators. As one recent commentary describes the situation:

> It is now accepted sector wisdom that the Teaching Excellence Framework is neither a measure of teaching nor a measure of excellence. The designers know that and don't want to keep hearing it said.
>
> (Strike, 2016)

Debate is already shifting to which additional indicators can be introduced into the TEF cycles that follow, and whether these will address the sector's legitimate concerns. Work is ongoing, but the idea of responsible metrics remains a useful starting point from which to consider the place of metrics in the design of an evaluation system.

On the research side, the November 2015 green paper also reopened questions over metrics and the REF, and a comprehensive review of the REF, chaired by Lord Stern, was initiated in December 2015 and issued its findings in July 2016 (Stern, 2016). Despite pressure from some quarters to move to a metrics-based REF, the Stern Review concluded that peer review should remain the primary method of research assessment, supported by responsible uses of data. The approach that Stern outlines – maintaining the primacy of peer review, using carefully selected metrics in the environment section of the REF, and improving data infrastructure and interoperability – is fully in line with the findings of *The Metric Tide*. A further technical consultation by HEFCE is now looking in detail at the choices and challenges involved in implementing Stern's recommendations, and the framework for REF 2021 will be finalised by the summer of 2017.

UK Forum for Responsible Research Metrics

One of the conclusions of *The Metric Tide*, and of related initiatives like DORA and the Leiden Manifesto, is the need for ongoing effort to shift institutional cultures, practices and incentive frameworks that sustain damaging or irresponsible use of metrics. To this end, a UK Forum for Responsible Research Metrics has been established to bring together research funders, HEIs and their representative bodies, publishers, data providers and others. Chaired by

David Price, Vice-Provost of UCL, the Forum will carry forward activities on three fronts:

1   *Supporting the effective leadership, governance and management of research cultures within HEIs.* The Forum will encourage UK HEI leaders to develop a clear statement of principles on how research is managed and assessed, and the role of metrics within these processes. Particular attention will be paid to criteria and indicators used in academic appointments and promotions.
2   *Supporting the responsible use of metrics by key organisations in the funding system.* The Forum will work with funders to develop their own context-specific principles for the use of quantitative indicators in research assessment and management. There will be a particular focus in the first 12–18 months on specific technical issues around indicator definition, selection and use in the environment section of the REF, and on wider guidance to assessment panels for REF 2021.
3   *Improving the data infrastructure that supports research information management.* In light of ongoing reforms to the UK's research system – notably the establishment of UK Research and Innovation (UKRI) as a strategic umbrella body for public funding – there is scope to be ambitious about the design of a "next generation research data infrastructure", which can ensure greater efficiency and interoperability of data collection, and its intelligent and responsible use to inform HEI strategy, research assessment, funding prioritisation and national policy (e.g. around industrial strategy). Organisations like Jisc are heavily engaged in this agenda, and the Forum will add weight and build support for such efforts.

Outputs from the Forum's deliberations are likely to include good practice guidance on the use of metrics in HEI management and academic recruitment practices, recommendations for publishers on responsible uses of metrics in promotional materials, and recommendations on gaps and opportunities for technical infrastructure development.

Measuring progress

The Forum for Responsible Research Metrics is a step in the right direction. But despite all the initiatives outlined here, it too often remains the case that, in the words of Peter Lawrence, poorly designed evaluation criteria are "dominating minds, distorting behaviour and determining careers" (Lawrence, 2007, p. R583–R585). More work is needed to link debates across teaching and research, to develop better indicators, and to foster more sensitive management frameworks. Alliances can be forged beyond the higher education sector, by linking to wider streams of scholarship and advocacy around algorithmic accountability and the future of the workplace. And UK efforts need to be aligned and joined to parallel work across Europe, in the United States and further afield.

We now have the evidence we need to influence how the metric tide washes through higher education and research. Planners, strategists, managers and information professionals have a crucial role to play – alongside academics – in determining whether we sink or swim.

Bibliography

Benedictus, R. and Miedema, F. (2016), Fewer Numbers, Better Science. *Nature*, Vol. 538: 453–454, 27 October.

Bertsimas, D., Brynjolfsson, E., Reichman, S. and Silberholz, J. (2015), Tenure Analytics: Models for Predicting Research Impact. *Operations Research*, Vol. 63 No. 6: 1246–1261.

BIS (2015), Higher Education: Teaching Excellence, Social Mobility and Student Choice. London: BIS, November.

BIS (2016), Success as a Knowledge Economy: Teaching Excellence, Social Mobility and Student Choice. London: BIS, May.

Brynjolfsson, E. and Silberholz, J. (2016), 'Moneyball' for Professors? Frontiers blog. *MIT Sloan Management Review*, 14 December.

Burnett, K. (2016), Universities Are Becoming Like Mechanical Nightingales. *Times Higher Education*, 19 December.

Collini, S. (2016), Who Are the Spongers Now? *London Review of Books*, Vol. 38 No. 2, 21 January.

Dijstelbloem, H., Huisman, F., Miedema, F. and Mjinhardt, W. (2013), Why Science Does Not Work as It Should and What To Do about It. Science in Transition Position Paper, October 17.

Graeber, D. (2015), The Utopia of Rules: On Technology, Stupidity and the Secret Joys of Bureaucracy. London: Melville House.

Hicks, D., Wouters, P., Waltman, L., de Rijcke, S. and Rafols, I. (2015), The Leiden Manifesto for Research Metrics. *Nature*, Vol. 520: 429–431, 23 April.

ICSU (2016), *Open Data in a Big Data World*. Paris: ICSU/IAP/ISSC/TWAS.

Ioannidis, J. P. A., Fanelli, D., Dunne, D. D. and Goodman S. N. (2015), Meta-Research: Evaluation and Improvement of Research Methods and Practices. *PLoS Biol*, Vol. 13 No. 10: e1002264. doi:10.1371/journal.pbio.1002264

Lawrence, P. A. (2007), The Mismeasurement of Science. *Current Biology*, Vol. 17 No. 15: R583-R585.

Lewis, M. (2003), Moneyball: The Art of Winning an Unfair Game. WW Norton: New York.

Martin, B. (2016), *What is Happening to Our Universities?* SPRU Working Paper Series 2016–03. Brighton: SPRU.

Porter, T. M. (1995), Trust in Numbers: The Pursuit of Objectivity in Science and Public Life. New York: Princeton University Press.

Sarewitz, D. (2016), Saving Science. *The New Atlantis*, Spring/Summer, 49: 4–40.

Sorokin, P. (1956), Fads and Foibles in Modern Sociology and Related Sciences. Chicago: Regnery.

Stern, N. (2016), Research Excellence Framework Review: Building on Success and Learning from Experience. London: BIS, July.

Strike, T. (2016) The TEF Is a Statistical Wonderland. *Wonke.com*, 5 December. http://wonkhe.com/blogs/the-tef-is-a-statistical-wonderland/ (accessed 10 January 2017)

Wilsdon, J., et al. (2015), The Metric Tide: Report of the Independent Review of the Role of Metrics in Research Assessment and Management, HEFCE. doi:10.13140/RG.2.1.4929.1363

Index

Note: Page numbers in italic indicate a figure or table on the corresponding page.